Y0-CSH-471

Bound Beckman 6/29/64

ELIZABETHAN
PLAYS AND PLAYERS

ELIZABETHAN
PLAYS AND PLAYERS

G. B. Harrison

Ann Arbor Books
The University of Michigan Press

Reissued in 1956
All Rights Reserved

Manufactured in the United States of America

PR
651
.H2

CONTENTS

CHAPTER		PAGE
	PREFACE	vii
I.	THE BUILDING OF THE THEATRE	3
II.	JOHN LYLY	24
III.	STAGE AND UNIVERSITY	42
IV.	NEW DRAMATISTS	57
V.	GREENE TURNS PLAYWRIGHT	75
VI.	THE DEATH OF GREENE	94
VII.	THE DEATH OF MARLOWE	117
VIII.	EDWARD ALLEYN AND THE ADMIRAL'S MEN	130
IX.	THE CHAMBERLAIN'S MEN	145
X.	THE HUMOURS	154
XI.	BEN JONSON	168
XII.	THE GLOBE	191
XIII.	BOY PLAYERS	205
XIV.	ESSEX'S REBELLION	237
XV.	THE STAGE WAR	248
XVI.	THE END OF AN ERA	282
	INDEX	297

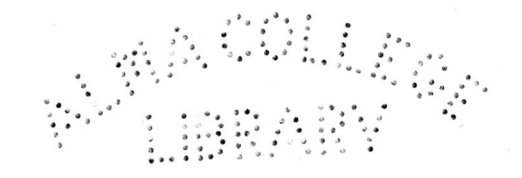

PREFACE

THIS book is intended for those interested in the English Theatre, to show something of the world in which Elizabethan players and dramatists worked. There have indeed been many books on the Elizabethan Theatre and the Elizabethan Drama, but scholars and critics tend to keep to themselves. Scholars are not always interested in the drama, nor critics in the facts. Yet, although one may fetch infinite enjoyment from a play regardless of its history, one cannot study drama apart from its environment. To the making of *Hamlet* went not only Saxo Grammaticus and François de Belleforest, but Burbage, the Chamberlain's Men, the Globe Theatre, the Stage War, the melancholy of the generation, and the whole turmoil of life seething around Shakespeare as he wrote. Moreover, though some critics tell me that I am wholly wrong on this matter, I hold impenitently that authors and players are not less interesting than the plays which they produce.

Years ago I first attempted a sketch of the conditions of Elizabethan drama in a little book called *Shakespeare's Fellows* (1923), long since out of print. It appeared before Sir Edmund Chambers's vast storehouses *The Elizabethan Stage* and *William Shakespeare : a study of facts and problems*. Since then I also have learnt something of the period in writing *The Elizabethan Journals*. In this book I have incorporated such parts of *Shakespeare's Fellows* as seemed worth keeping. *Elizabethan Plays and Players* covers the period from the building of the Theatre in 1576 to the death

PREFACE

of the Queen in 1603; and to some extent overlaps those parts of *Shakespeare at Work* which showed what was happening in the theatrical world when Shakespeare was writing, but the treatment is wholly new, and the intention of the book quite different.

There are naturally many quotations. These I have produced in modern spelling and punctuation, for I believe that the reader loses more than he gains by a continued shift from modern to ancient usage.

The times are difficult for abstract meditation and remote inquiry, and I have been unable to pursue certain matters as far as I had intended. But it seemed better to let the book go as it is than to wait for the indefinite day of peace.

I wish particularly to thank my two friends, Dr. S. H. Atkins and Dr. D. C. Collins, who read the proofs and made valuable suggestions. To Dr. Atkins I am doubly grateful, for he also compiled the Index.

G. B. H.

ELIZABETHAN
PLAYS AND PLAYERS

ELIZABETHAN PLAYS AND PLAYERS

Chapter I

THE BUILDING OF THE THEATRE

THE English as a race are partial to drama ; they prefer to symbolize and to dress the part. They set a real crown on the head of their king ; their mayors are still distinguished with gilt chains ; and their professors and schoolmasters teach in medieval gowns. Their greatest poetry is drama.

Nevertheless the remarkable crop of plays called by literary historians 'Elizabethan Drama' (which generally includes any play written between 1530 and 1640) was sudden and short-lived. *Tamburlaine* was written late in the 1580's, *Hamlet* at the turn of the century ; few plays written later than 1615 are still readable and fewer actable. Moreover, in spite of vast research and monumental erudition, the immediate beginnings and developments of this Elizabethan drama are quite obscure.

Much remains of the dramas of the fourteenth and fifteenth centuries. The whole story of the Christian Faith from Creation to Redemption was acted again and again on stages or carts ; and many of the books of these playlets still exist. Their authors are anonymous, but they had stage sense ; and they were hearty, good actors of drama, tragic, but especially comic. They had no narrow pedantic regard for sources. The Book of Genesis gave the story of Noah, his ark and its miscellaneous cargo; but the details are meagre. Some nameless wit, his imagination fired by the domestic inconveniences of the Noah family cooped up for the forty days of the Deluge, endowed Noah's wife with a personality; she became, and remained, the first of the arrant shrews of the English stage.[1]

Others took on character as roarers; Cain, for instance, and Herod. But at least these worthies had a name, and a place in the Bible, however brief their appearance. Other persons were invented from the pure fancy. Mack, the rascal who steals a sheep from the Shepherds of Bethlehem, and distracts them from their watch by night, had never a part in the Gospel story.

Drama was thus popular and very much alive before the literary minded had realized that it existed to be labelled, classified, criticized and examined.

Then at the end of the period of anarchy of the Wars of Lancaster and York, more erudite writers evolved the allegorical type of play called the Morality, which—to modern readers—is usually tedious. At rare intervals they produced a work of such real genius as *Everyman*, which is still fresh to see or to read. But allegory can flourish only in certain conditions. It needs readers bred in the tradition of parables and double meanings. It is not suited to a frank, outspoken generation.

By the beginning of the sixteenth century, the learned were becoming conscious of drama. Students at the University or the Inns of Court were producing plays. Zealous headmasters set their scholars to act the comedies of Terence

---

[1] Mr. Disney's film *Father Noah* is exactly in the tradition of the miracle plays, but I suspect that this is no accident and that Mr. Disney is a considerable student of early drama.

and Plautus ; and in no long time they began themselves to try to write comedies, of a sort, in English—such as *Ralph Roister Doister*, or *Gammer Gurton's Needle*.

There remains a fair-sized collection of dramatic pieces of all kinds written between 1450 and 1550. For the next thirty years there are specimens of plays written for genteel and private occasions, or as literary exercises, or translations ; but of the plays produced on the public stages there remain only the notorious *Cambises* and *The famous Victories of Henry V*, which was printed in 1594 but was written several years earlier.

Cambises was entered in the Stationers' Register in 1569, and was then probably not new. It was a popular play and worth examining as a rare specimen which illuminates the taste of playgoers in the 1560's : an amazing hybrid of the crudest tragic drama, farce and morality, as its full title implies—' A Lamentable Tragedy mixed full of pleasant mirth, containing the Life of Cambises, King of Persia, from the beginning of his kingdom unto his death, his one good deed of execution ; after that many wicked deeds and tyrannous murders, committed by and through him, and last of all, his odious death by God's justice appointed. Done in such order as followeth.' There are thirty-eight characters in the play, but it was intended for a company of nine persons, and the author conveniently indicated how the parts were to be distributed. The names themselves show the mixture of person and personification.

' Council
Huff
Praxaspes
Murder
Lob
The third Lord ⎬ For one man.

Lord
Ruff
Commons' Cry
Commons' Complaint
Lord Smirdis
Venus
} For one man.

Knight
Snuff
Small Hability
Proof
Execution
Attendance
Second Lord
} For one man.

Cambises
Epilogus
} For one man.

Prologue
Sisamnes
Diligence
Cruelty
Hob
Preparation
The first Lord
} For one man.

Ambidexter [the Vice]
Trial
} For one man.

Meretrix
Shame
Otian
Mother
Lady
Queen
} For one man.

Young Child
Cupid
} For one man.'

The dramatization was very elementary. After a lecture on Cambises of thirty-four lines by the Prologue, Cambises enters with his Council (i.e. Knight, Lord and Council) and appoints Sisamnes to be his judge. The group having departed, enter '*the Vice, with an old capcase on his head, an old pail about his hips for harness, a scummer and a potlid by his side, and a rake on his shoulder.*' He fools around, and is joined by three ruffians, Huff, Ruff and Snuff. They indulge in knockabout. Meretrix passes by. More knockabout follows. The stage being cleared, the Vice (Ambidexter) returns, meets Sisamnes, who is proving a dishonest judge, and they exchange confidences. Small Hability asks for justice, but having no adequate bribe, is kicked out.

Cambises is rapidly going to the dogs. To make this plain to the audience, Shame enters with a black trumpet sounds a blast, explains who she is, and relates Cambises' wicked deeds as prelude to an exhibition of the tyrant acting tyrannious. Commons' Complaint, Proof and Trial accuse Sisamnes, and the king condemns him to death. Enter Execution. Sisamnes is smitten in the neck '*with a sword to signify his death*' and afterwards flayed '*with a false skin.*' The king grows worse and worse. Being drunk, he takes it into his head to shoot an arrow at a living child, and the heart is produced as token of his accurate archery. Then he decides to murder his brother Smirdis. The episode was played thus :

Enter Lord Smirdis alone.

SMIRDIS. I am wandering alone, here and there to walk ;
The Court is so unquiet, in it I take no joy.
Solitary to myself now I may talk.
If I could rule, I wist what to say.

Enter Cruelty and Murder with bloody hands.

CRUELTY. My coequal partner, Murder, come away;
From me long thou may'st not stay.

MURDER. Yes, from thee I may stay, but not thou from me;
Therefore I have a prerogative above thee.

CRUELTY. But in this case we must together abide.
Come, come! Lord Smirdis I have spied.
Lay hands on him with all festination,
That on him we may work our indignation!

SMIRDIS. How now, my friends? What have you to do with me?

MURDER. King Cambises hath sent us unto thee,
Commanding us straightly, without mercy or favour,
Upon thee to bestow our behaviour,
With cruelty to murder you and make you away.

SMIRDIS. Yet, pardon me, I heartily you pray!
Consider, the king is a tyrant tyrannious,
And all his doings be damnable and pernicious:
Favour me therefore; I did him never offend.

CRUELTY. No favour at all! Your life is at an end!
Even now I strike, his body to wound.

Strikes him in divers places.

Behold, now his blood springs out on the ground!

A little bladder of vinegar pricked.

MURDER. Now he is dead, let us present him to the king.
CRUELTY. Lay to your hand, away him to bring.

Exeunt.

It is a curious mixture of realistic and symbolical action. Similarly, when the king is overcome with lawless lust, the episode begins with:

'*Enter Venus leading out her son, Cupid, blind. He must have a bow and two shafts, one headed with gold and the other headed with lead.*' And, inevitably, Cupid shoots.

At last Cambises has filled the cup of iniquity to overflowing and the time has come for him to die:

Enter the King, without a gown, a sword thrust up into his side, bleeding.

KING. Out! Alas! What shall I do? My life is finished.
Wounded I am by sudden chance; my blood is minished.
Gog's heart, what means might I make my life to preserve?
Is there nought to be my help? Nor is there nought to serve?
Out upon the Court, and lords that there remain!
To help my grief in this my case will none of them take pain?
Who but I, in such a wise, his death's wound could have got?
As I on horseback up did leap, my sword from scabbard shot,
And ran me thus into the side—as you right well may see.
A marvellous chance unfortunate, that in this wise should be!
I feel myself a-dying now; of life bereft am I;
And Death hath caught me with his dart, for want of blood I spy.
Thus, gasping, here on ground I lie; for nothing I do care.
A just reward for my misdeeds my death doth plain declare.

Here let him quake and stir.

AMBIDEXTER. How now, noble king? Pluck up your heart!
What! will you die, and from us depart?
Speak to me and ye be alive!
He cannot speak. But behold, how with Death he doth strive.
Alas, good king! Alas, he is gone!
The devil take me if for him I make any moan.
I did prognosticate of his end, by the mass!
Like as I did say, so is it come to pass.
I will be gone. If I should be found here,
That I should kill him it would appear.
For fear with his death they do me charge,
Farewell, my masters, I will go take barge;
I mean to be packing; now is the tide;
Farewell, my masters, I will no longer abide.

Exit Ambidexter.

Three lords conveniently appear to remove the carcase after which Cambises comes back, speaks the epilogue and calls on the audience to pray for the Queen.

It would thus appear that the taste of playgoers was as yet easily satisfied.

Nevertheless, although so few plays remain, formal records show that playing was becoming more and more popular at Court and in the towns. Court Accounts and local records mention payments which illustrate what was happening all over the country. My Lord of Leicester's Company were paid £6 13s. 4d. for acting at Court at Christmas 1560; and again in 1561, 1562 and at many other times. In 1573 they acted two plays, and were paid £13 6s. 8d., and ' by way of special reward for their charges, cunning and skill shewed therein—£6 13s. 4d.'[1]

Town clerks record their comings and goings in the country—to Norwich, Canterbury, Dover, Oxford, Bristol, Plymouth, Gloucester, Leicester, Ipswich, Stratford-upon-Avon, Barnstaple and elsewhere.[1]

Sometimes the clerk who made out the account had sufficient interest to note the name of the play, and very occasionally some illuminating detail. Seven plays were given at Court in the Christmas and Shrovetide holidays of 1567–8. They were *As plain as plain can be*, *The painful Pilgrimage*, *Jack and Jill*, *Six Fools*, *Wit and Will*, *Prodigality*, ' *Orestes* and a *Tragedy of the King of Scots* to which belonged divers houses as Stato's house, Gobbin's house, Orestes' house Rome, the Palace of Prosperity, Scotland, and a great castle on the other side.'[1]

These plays acted at Court are for the most part only names at best.

Occasionally a writer gives a hint of the matter of a play. Stephen Gosson, once playwright, now turned parson, in 1579 published *The School of Abuse*, his notorious attack on ' poets, pipers, players, jesters and suchlike caterpillars of the commonwealth.'

[1] *Elizabethan Stage*, iv, 142, 144, 146.

THE BUILDING OF THE THEATRE

Gosson attacked plays because they attracted undesirable spectators, encouraged 'goings-on' and—of course—debauched the public. But Gosson himself had once written plays, so there was some good to be said of them.

'And as some of the Players are far from abuse, so some of their Plays are without rebuke: which are as easily remembered as quickly reckoned. The two prose books played at the Bel Savage, where you shall find never a word without wit, never a line without pith, never a letter placed in vain. *The Jew* and *Ptolemy*, shown at the Bull, the one representing the greediness of worldly choosers, and bloody minds of usurers: the other very lively describing how seditious estates, with their own devices, false friends, with their own swords, and rebellious commons in their own snares are overthrown; neither with amorous gesture wounding the eye, nor with slovenly talk hurting the ears of the chaste hearers. *The Blacksmith's Daughter*, and *Catiline's Conspiracies* usually brought into the Theatre: the first containing the treachery of Turks, the honourable bounty of a noble mind, and the shining of virtue in distress; the last, because it is known to be a pig of mine own sow, I will speak the less of it, only giving you to understand, that the whole mark which I shot at in that work was to show the reward of traitors in *Catiline*, and the necessary government of learned men, in the person of Cicero, which foresees every danger that is likely to happen, and forestalls it continually ere it take effect.'[1]

Gosson's abuse evoked a reply from Sir Philip Sidney in the *Apology for Poetry*. He nobly defended poets and their mystery, but even he had little good to say of 'naughty play-makers and stage-keepers.' His objections were æsthetic: play-makers ignored the rules; they did not practise the proprieties.

[1] Edited by E. Arber, p. 40.

'Our tragedies and comedies (not without cause cried out against), observing rules neither of honest civility nor of skilful poetry, excepting *Gorboduc* (again, I say, of those that I have seen), which notwithstanding, as it is full of stately speeches and well-sounding phrases, climbing to the height of Seneca his style, and as full of notable morality, which it doth most delightfully teach, and so obtain the very end of Poesy, yet in troth it is very defectious in the circumstances, which grieveth me, because it might not remain as an exact model of all tragedies. For it is faulty both in place and time, the two necessary companions of all corporal actions. For where the stage should always represent but one place, and the uttermost time presupposed in it should be, both by Aristotle's precept and common reason, but one day, there is both many days, and many places, inartificially imagined. But if it be so in *Gorboduc*, how much more in all the rest, where you shall have Asia of the one side, and Africk of the other, and so many other under-kingdoms, that the player when he cometh in must ever begin with telling where he is, or else the tale will not be conceived? Now ye shall have three ladies walk to gather flowers, and then we must believe the stage to be a garden. By and by, we hear news of a shipwreck in the same place, and then we are to blame if we accept it not for a rock. Upon the back of that comes out a hideous monster, with fire and smoke, and then the miserable beholders are bound to take it for a cave. While the meantime two armies fly in, represented with four swords and bucklers, and then what hard heart will not receive it for a pitched field? Now of time they are much more liberal, for ordinary it is that two young princes fall in love. After many traverses, she is got with child, delivered of a fair boy; he is lost, groweth a man, falls in love, and is ready to get another child; and all this in two hours' space: which, how absurd it is in sense, even sense may imagine, and Art hath taught, and all the ancient examples justified, and, at this day, the ordinary players in Italy will not err in.'

As for comedy :

' But besides these gross absurdities, how all their plays be neither right tragedies, nor right comedies, mingling kings and clowns, not because the matter so carrieth it, but thrust in clowns by head and shoulders, to play a part in majestical matters, with neither decency nor discretion, so as neither the admiration and commiseration, nor the right sportfulness, is by their mongrel tragi-comedy obtained.' [1]

Nevertheless Sidney's criticisms, allowing for a little humorous exaggeration, would still apply thirty years later to several of Shakespeare's maturer plays. Sidney objected, not to crudities of characterization or dialogue, but to a freedom of plot and action, which, in his eyes, was licentious. There is little to show whether dramatists for the public stages had as yet learned how to create a character or write a dialogue. If *Cambises* is typical of stage plays of the 1560's and 1570's, then it is surprising that drama ever survived as a popular entertainment. It was all due to the Renaissance, say the critics !

In fact, however, the sudden flowering of Elizabethan drama was due primarily neither to the Renaissance (if indeed the word ' Renaissance ' now means anything) nor to any ebullition of spiritual or literary forces, but to certain sordid speculations in land, timber and plaster of one James Burbage, at one time a joiner, and later chief player to the Earl of Leicester, and John Brayne, grocer, his brother-in-law.

As playing had become more and more popular in the 1550's, many great households produced their company and acted their Christmas play. The players at first were

[1] *An Apology for Poetry*, edited by J. C. Collins, pp. 51, 54.

amateurs; Shakespeare has illustrated the process in *Love's Labour's Lost*. Great houses included many gentlemen serving-men—younger sons of good family and education—as well as artisans of all kinds who could ' gleek on occasion.' After a successful production the company (as records reveal) would sometimes ask their Lord for licence to repeat the show in the neighbourhood, and sometimes they even came to Court.

There was thus rivalry and some profit in play-making. As standards became higher, more and more time and rehearsal were necessary, until playing became a whole-time occupation.

By 1570 the players were so popular that the authorities of the City regarded them as a public and dangerous nuisance. Thereafter for some years there was war between the players and successive Lords Mayor. It was a complex affair, for there were various and sometimes conflicting vested interests.

As yet there were no regular playhouses. The players acted in certain inns by arrangement with the innkeeper, who was glad to collect a crowd to whom he sold drink. The authorities were in perpetual and very proper terror of the plague, which was easily spread in close-packed crowds. Various attempts were therefore made to control the players. On the 27th November 1571 the Court of Aldermen drastically ordered that henceforth no play or interlude should be allowed in any ward of the City upon Sundays, holy-days, or other days of the week, or else at night until such time as other order should be taken.

Unfortunately for themselves, the Aldermen were not entirely free agents even within their own City. Great lords, especially those who were members of the Privy Council, could always bring pressure which might not conveniently be resisted. A few days later—the 6th December—the Aldermen were obliged to yield and to grant a licence to my

Lord of Leicester's men to play within the City such matters as were allowed to be played at convenient hours and times so that it were not in time of divine service.[1]

In the following May there was another encounter. The Privy Council wrote to the Lord Mayor requesting that permission should be granted to certain persons for plays to be acted in their houses provided that they tended to repress vice and extol virtue. The plays—as the Council pointed out—would provide the people with recreation and draw them from worse exercises, and moreover the Lord Mayor should appoint a discreet person or persons to examine the plays and take bonds from the housekeeper for the proper fulfilment of the order.

Such a request was difficult to refuse, but the Aldermen countered it with the old argument that the weather was hot and therefore that it was very perilous to have such conventicles of people whereof the greatest number were of the meanest sort, and therefore they prayed that the matter might be forborne for the time.

During these weeks Parliament was sitting. The old, rigorous but ineffectual laws against rogues and vagabonds were debated in both Houses, and a revised statute passed into law on the 29th June 1572. It detailed the punishments for vagabondage from whipping and branding to death, and it defined rogues as ' all and every such person and persons, that be or utter themselves to be, proctors or procurators, going in or about any County or Counties within this Realm, without sufficient authority, derived from, or under our Sovereign Lady the Queen : and all other idle persons going about in any County of the said Realm, using subtle, crafty and unlawful games or plays, and some of them feigning themselves to have knowledge in phisnomy, palmistry, or other abused sciences, whereby they bear the people in hand

[1] *Elizabethan Stage*, iv, 268.

they can tell their destinies, deaths, and fortunes, and such other like fantastical imaginations ; and all and every person and persons, being whole and mighty in body, and able to labour, having not land or master, nor using any lawful merchandise, craft, or mystery, whereby he or she might get his or her living, and can give no reckoning how he or she doth lawfully get his or her living ; and all fencers, bearwards, common players in interludes, and minstrels, not belonging to any Baron of this Realm, or towards any other honourable personage of greater degree ; all jugglers, peddlers, tinkers, and petty chapmen, which said fencers, bearwards, common players in interludes, minstrels, jugglers, peddlers, tinkers, and petty chapmen, shall wander abroad, and have not licence of two Justices of the Peace at the least, whereof one to be of the Quorum, where and in what Shire they shall happen to wander ; and all common labourers, being persons able in body, using loitering and refusing to work, for such reasonable wages as is tasked and commonly given in such parts where such persons do or shall happen to dwell ; and all counterfeiters of licences, passports, and all users of the same, knowing the same to be counterfeit ; and all scholars of the Universities of Oxford or Cambridge, that go about begging, not being authorized under the seal of the said Universities, by the commissary, Chancellor, or Vice-Chancellor of the same : and all shipmen, pretending losses by sea, other than such as shall be hereafter provided for : and all persons delivered out of gaols, that beg for their fees, or do travel to their Counties or friends, not having licence from two Justices of Peace of the same County where he or she was delivered, shall be taken, adjudged and deemed rogues, vagabonds and sturdy beggars.' [1]

If it was intended by this Statute to attack the professional players generally, then the policy was shortsighted. It may

[1] Statutes of the Realm, 14 Elizabeth, cap. v.

THE BUILDING OF THE THEATRE

have deterred for a while some of the poor strolling players, but the natural effect was to make the licence given by a Lord to his own servants more valuable, and to make the Lord himself more jealous for the privileges of those who bore his badge.

There was further trouble in 1574. The Lord Chamberlain had proposed that one Holmes should be appointed to supervise plays to be acted in the City. This was a clear threat to the privileges of the City. On the 2nd March the Lord Mayor and Aldermen retorted with a full broadside :

' Our duty to your good Lordship humbly done. Whereas your Lordship hath made request in favour of one Holmes for our assent that he might have the appointment of places for plays and interludes within this City, it may please your Lordship to retain undoubted assurance of our readiness to gratify, in any thing that we reasonably may, any person whom your Lordship shall favour and recommend. Howbeit this case is such, and so near touching the governance of this City in one of the greatest matters thereof, namely the assemblies of multitudes of the Queen's people, and regard to be had to sundry inconveniences, whereof the peril is continually, upon every occasion, to be foreseen by the rulers of this City, that we cannot, with our duties, beside the precedent far extending to the heart of our liberties, well assent that the said appointment of places be committed to any private person. For which, and other reasonable considerations, it hath long since pleased your good Lordship, among the rest of her Majesty's most honourable Council, to rest satisfied with our not granting to such person as, by their most honourable letters, was heretofore in like case commended to us. Beside that, if it might with reasonable convenience be granted, great offers have been and be made for the same to the relief of the poor in the hospitals, which we hold as assured, that your Lordship will well allow that we prefer before the benefit of any private person. And so we commit your Lordship to the tuition of Almighty God. At London, this second of March, 1573.'[1]

It was signed by the Lord Mayor and sixteen of his brethren. The Lord Mayor followed this up by restraining all playing. On the 22nd March the Council thereupon asked for the reasons which had moved the Lord Mayor to restrain all playing. The reply, if sent, has been lost.

Six weeks later the Earl of Leicester again caused the decisions of the Common Council to be overruled, for he procured a Royal Patent from the Queen licensing his own players.

'Elizabeth by the Grace of God Queen of England, etc. To all Justices, Mayors, Sheriffs, Bailiffs, Head Constables, Under Constables, and all other our officers and ministers, greeting. Know ye that we of our especial grace, certain knowledge, and mere motion have licensed and authorized and by these presents do license and authorize our loving subjects, James Burbage, John Perkin, John Lanham, William Johnson and Robert Wilson, servants to our trusty and well-beloved cousin and Councillor, the Earl of Leicester, to use, exercise and occupy the art and faculty of playing comedies, tragedies, interludes, stage plays and such other, like as they have already used and studied, or hereafter shall use and study, as well for the recreation of our loving subjects, as for our solace and pleasure when we shall think good to see them. As also to use and occupy all such instruments as they have already practised, or hereafter shall practise, for and during our pleasure. And the said comedies, tragedies, interludes and stage plays, together with their music, to show, publish, exercise and occupy to their best commodity during all the term aforesaid, as well within our City of London and liberties of the same, as also within the liberties and freedoms

[1] *Elizabethan Stage*, iv, 271.

of any of our cities, towns, boroughs, etc., whatsoever, as without the same, throughout our Realm of England. Willing and commanding you and every of you as ye tender our pleasure, to permit and suffer them herein without any your lets, hindrance, or molestation during the term aforesaid, any act, statute, proclamation or commandment heretofore made or hereafter to be made, to the contrary notwithstanding. Provided that the said comedies, tragedies, interludes, and stage plays be by the Master of our Revels for the time being before seen and allowed, and that the same be not published or shown in the time of common prayer, or in the time of great and common plague in our said City of London.'[1]

There was plague in the autumn and so playing was restrained, but on the 6th December, the Common Council of the City, finding that they could not persist in utterly denying the players any longer, drew up a long Act to regulate playing. In the preamble they gave their reasons for objecting to players:

'Whereas heretofore sundry great disorders and inconveniences have been found to ensue to this City by the inordinate haunting of great multitudes of people, specially youth, to plays, interludes and shows, namely occasion of frays and quarrels, evil practices of incontinency in great inns, having chambers and secret places adjoining to their open stages and galleries, inveigling and alluring of maids, specially orphans and good citizens' children under age to privy and unmeet contracts, the publishing of unchaste, uncomely and unshamefaced speeches and doings, withdrawing of the Queen's Majesty's subjects from divine service on Sundays and holy-days, at which times such plays were chiefly used, unthrifty waste of money of the poor and fond persons, sundry robberies by picking and cutting of

[1] *Malone Society's Collections*, i, 262; and *Elizabethan Stage*, ii, 87-8.

purses, uttering of popular, busy and seditious matters, and many other corruptions of youth, and other enormities, besides that also sundry slaughters and maimings of the Queen's subjects have happened by ruins of scaffolds, frames and stages, and by engines, weapons and powder used in plays. And whereas in time of God's visitation by the plague such assemblies of the people in throng and press have been very dangerous for spreading of infection . . .'[1]

It was then enacted that:

(*a*) No play should be shown 'wherein shall be uttered any words, examples or doings of any unchastity, sedition or such unfit, uncomely matter.'

(*b*) Plays must first be perused and allowed by the deputy of the Lord Mayor; and no matter should thereafter be 'interlaced, added, mingled or uttered.'

(*c*) No one should allow plays to be acted in his house, court or other place without permission or unless he had first been bound with proper securities.

(*d*) Plays should not be performed when, because of the plague or other adequate reason, the Lord Mayor forbade them, nor in the usual time of divine service on Sundays or holy-days.

(*e*) Licensees should pay an agreed sum to the hospitals of the City or other charities or forfeit their licences. All fines levied for breach of the rules should likewise be paid to charity.

(*f*) These regulations (except as touching unchaste, seditious or unmeet matters) should not apply to private performances in the houses of noblemen, citizens and gentlemen where there was no public or common collection of money from the beholders.

These regulations were not in themselves unreasonable or harsh, but by this time there was considerable feeling on

[1] *Malone Society's Collections*, i, 175; and *Elizabethan Stage*, iv, 273-4.

THE BUILDING OF THE THEATRE

both sides, and the players were too powerful and too popular to be easily suppressed.

The Earl of Leicester's players were led by James Burbage. He was about forty-five years old. He had started life as a joiner, since turned player. Burbage had no money. He was truculent, violent and not over-honest, but he had ideas. He had also a wife as hearty as himself, and two sons, Cuthbert and Richard, who had genius. Burbage realized that if playing could be freed from the continual interference of the authorities and from the exactions of innkeepers, there might be vast profit. He therefore conceived the notion of building a house solely for plays, and in a place where the Lord Mayor and Aldermen could not touch him.

London had long since grown beyond its civic boundaries : but in the suburbs, to the north of the City and on the south bank of the Thames, the rule lay, not with the Lord Mayor, but with the magistrates of Middlesex and Surrey, who were far more complaisant. The City was bounded by its walls and gates. North of Bishop's Gate, Bishop's Gate Street ran into Shoreditch. Farther west the road through Moor Gate led to Finsbury Fields, a regular recreation ground for London citizens. In Shoreditch on the edge of Finsbury, Burbage found a suitable piece of ground. It was owned by Giles Alleyn, gentleman ; and the property included five tenements in bad repair, a large tumbledown stable, one end of which was used for a slaughter-house, and a horse-pond. Between the tenements and stable lay an empty space large enough for the erection of a theatre.[1]

On 13th April 1576 Burbage and Alleyn signed a lease whereby Burbage agreed to pay a rent of £14 per annum for twenty-one years. He agreed further that in the next ten years he would expend £200 on restoring the tenements.

[1] For fuller account of the history of the Theatre see *Shakespearian Playhouses*, by J. Q. Adams.

21

When this had been done, he was to have the option of taking out a new twenty years' lease, otherwise the lease was to run for twenty-one years, that was, until 1597. It was further agreed that any time before the expiry he might remove any building which he had erected on the void ground; buildings still standing when the lease lapsed passed to the landlord.

Burbage had no capital, but his brother-in-law, John Brayne, grocer, was eager to come into partnership. Brayne found most of the money. According to a witness in one of the many lawsuits which followed, he borrowed £600 to £700, sold his house and stock, and even pawned his wife's clothes. Unfortunately for Brayne he soon began to quarrel with Burbage and to suspect—not unreasonably—that his partner was not altogether to be trusted. In 1578 he went to law. Thereafter for the next twenty-five years there was continual litigation about the Theatre. Fortunately the papers survive, and from numerous judgments and depositions of witnesses the history of the Theatre can largely be reconstructed.

Nothing detailed is known about the building, but it was a success from the first. Players and owners benefited.

Within a few months another and rival house was put up in the near neighbourhood. This was the ' Curtain.' Not much is definitely known about its origin or its history; but some years later, in July 1592, in the course of a lawsuit, Henry Lanman, described as ' of London, gentleman, of the age of 54 years,' deposed: 'That true it is about 7 years now shall be this next winter, they, the said Burbage and Brayne, having the profits of plays made at the Theatre, and this deponent having the profits of the plays done at the house called the Curtain near to the same, the said Burbage and Brayne, taking the Curtain as an " esore " to their play-house, did of their own motion move this deponent that he would agree that the profits of the said two playhouses might for seven years space be in divident between them.'[1]

Both playhouses were flourishing in 1577—to the enormous indignation of the godly, especially the preachers who found good matter for sermons in these 'continual monuments of London's prodigality and folly.' They were denounced at the sermon at Paul's Cross on the 3rd November 1577, and again on the 24th August 1578, in the often-quoted sermon of John Stockwood:

'Will not a filthy play, with the blast of a trumpet, sooner call thither a thousand than an hour's tolling of a bell bring to the sermon a hundred? Nay, even here in the City, without it be at this place, and some other certain ordinary audience, where shall you find a reasonable company? Whereas, if you resort to the Theatre, the Curtain and other places of plays in the City, you shall on the Lord's Day have these places, with many other that I cannot reckon, so full as possibly they can throng.'[2]

Playing thus became 'big business.' Henceforward there was good money waiting for those who could give the public what it wanted. Its first need was good actors and competent dramatists.

[1] Wallace, *The First London Theatre*, pp. 109-52, quoted by J. Q. Adams, *Shakespearian Playhouses*, p. 78. Adams conjectured that 'esore' meant 'easer'; and Chambers even asserts (*Elizabethan Stage*, ii, 402) that 'from 1585 to 1592, indeed, it was used as an "easer" to the Theatre.' It is not explained how such an arrangement could possibly work. The word 'easer,' in this sense, is not to be found in the *Oxford English Dictionary*. Actually 'esore' is 'eyesore.' In other words, the owners of the Theatre and of the Curtain, finding that they were ruining each other by cut-throat competition, decided to pool profits: combines are not a twentieth-century invention.

[2] From *A Sermon Preached at Paules Crosse*. Quoted in *Elizabethan Stage*, iv, 199.

Chapter II

JOHN LYLY

In the 1570's there were two distinct and different publics interested in plays. The Theatre and the Curtain attracted large crowds, but mostly of apprentices. Courtiers and gentlemen were not vastly interested in such places. Burbage's successful speculation encouraged another adventurer to try his luck with the gentlemen spectators.

The choirs in the Queen's chapels—the Chapel Royal in London and at Windsor—each had their choir-master. William Hunnis was Master of the Children of the Chapel Royal, and his deputy, Richard Farrant, was Master of the Children of Windsor Chapel. They were responsible for training the boys to sing in chapel and also to present plays and entertainments when called upon before the Court at the chief holy-days. The choir-boys of St. Paul's were likewise trained both for sacred music and for entertainments, and they also often acted at Court. Such performances needed considerable rehearsal. Accordingly, Farrant thought that if he could acquire a suitable building as a rehearsal-room he might admit spectators to the rehearsals and charge them gate-money. In this way he, too, would make a profit from the growing enthusiasm for plays.

In the old days before the Reformation, the Black Friars had built a monastery within the City of London. Its precincts were privileged and free from the jurisdiction of the Lord Mayor. Since the dissolution of the monasteries some forty years before, the old Black Friars' building had been secularized, but the legal position of the precincts was still uncertain.[1] Most of the old buildings remained and were now used as dwellings or offices. Amongst them was the old refectory.[2] It was owned by Sir William More. Farrant became tenant of this part of the old buildings.

The playhouse was then opened for plays given by a company made up of boys from the two Royal Choirs. The venture lasted for four years, to the annoyance of Sir William More, who had been given to understand that Farrant intended the room for rehearsals only. Farrant, however, had broken a clause in his lease by subletting a small part of the property without the owner's consent. Sir William prepared to take action, but on 30th November 1580 Farrant died, leaving many debts, ten young children and a widow. She petitioned that she might deal with the lease, and apparently secured Sir William's reluctant permission, for she transferred Farrant's lease to William Hunnis, Master of the Children of the Chapel Royal, whose efforts were supported by the great Earl of Leicester himself. Formal transfer to Hunnis and one John Newman was made in December 1581.

The new tenants were as unsatisfactory as the old, and Sir William grew restive. Accordingly, in 1583, they in turn transferred their lease to Henry Evans, a Welsh scrivener. This was the second breach of the original lease, and Sir William now claimed its cancellation. But Evans knew how to work the law, and various actions followed : Mistress Farrant *versus* Hunnis and Newman ;

---

[1] In 1593, for instance, those who wished to avoid being pressed for military service were taking refuge in the Blackfriars and other privileged zones. I *Elizabethan Journal*, p. 192.

[2] *Elizabethan Stage*, ii, 496. Adams, however, says that it was the buttery.

and More *versus* Evans. Evans complicated matters still further by selling his lease to the Earl of Oxford, who in turn gave it to his secretary, John Lyly. It took Sir William some time to catch up on these transactions.

During these months Lyly, Hunnis and Evans combined to run a company of choir-boys. Early in 1584 they produced Lyly's play *Campaspe*.

John Lyly at this time was about thirty years old. He had gone up to Magdalen College, Oxford, and matriculated in 1571. He took his Bachelor's Degree in 1573, and his Master's in 1575. Then, being ambitious and hoping for promotion at Court, he came to London, where he had the reputation of a dapper wit. He entered the service of Lord Delawarr. He became famous with the novel *Euphues, the Anatomy of Wit*, which was entered in the Stationers' Register on the 2nd December 1578. The book was the success of its generation. It went into five editions in two years, and for a while Lyly had an immense influence on the arts of speech and writing. As Edward Blunt [1] put it more than fifty years later : ' Our nation are in his debt for a new English which he taught them. *Euphues* and his *England* began first that language : all our ladies were then his scholars : and that beauty in Court which could not parley Euphuism was as little regarded as she which now there speaks not French.'

Few modern readers can endure *Euphues* to the end, but no serious student may ignore it, for it perfectly reflects and explains the literary taste of the best of Lyly's own generation.

Lyly had luck. There was a zeal for experiments in the arts at the time, manifested in many places. Within three years were written *Euphues*, Sidney's *Arcadia* and his *Defence of Poetry* (the first attempt in England to study

[1] In the Epistle to the Reader to his edition of Lyly's *Six Court Comedies*, 1632.

critical principles), Spenser's *Shepherd's Calendar* and North's translation of Plutarch's *Lives*.

Lyly himself was a courtier, and he realized that there was a considerable public, many of them ladies, for a book which would reflect courtly manners and conversation, and set a style for others to copy.

But there was much more than style in *Euphues*. The story of how Euphues went to Naples, filched Lucilla from his friend Philautus, and was in turn cozened by Curio, was a pleasant change from the interminable adventures of the knightly heroes of chivalric romance. If not wholly fact, Euphues was certainly not all fiction. Moreover, Lyly was not merely concerned with incident. Behind the fine, fanciful phrasings in which Euphues, Lucilla and Philautus pour out their emotions, there was some attempt at psychology.

The germ of the introspective soliloquy which was so common, and often so skilful, in plays twenty years later is to be found in such a passage as Lucilla's musing when first she begins 'to fry in the flames of love' for Euphues: 'Ah, wretched wench, Lucilla, how art thou perplexed? What a doubtful fight dost thou feel betwixt faith and fancy? Hope and fear? Conscience and concupiscence? O my Euphues, little dost thou know the sudden sorrow that I sustain for thy sweet sake. Whose wit hath bewitched me, whose rare qualities have deprived me of mine old quality, whose courteous behaviour without curiosity, whose comely feature without fault, whose filed speech without fraud, hath wrapped me in this misfortune. And canst thou, Lucilla, be so light of love in forsaking Philautus to fly to Euphues? Canst thou prefer a stranger before thy countryman? A starter before thy companion? Why Euphues doth perhaps desire my love, but Philautus hath deserved it. Why Euphues' feature is worthy as good as I, but Philautus his faith is worthy a better. Ay, but the latter love is most fervent. Ay, but the first ought to be most faithful. Ay, but Euphues hath greater perfection. Ay, but Philautus hath deeper affection. . . .

'Let my father use what speeches he list, I will follow mine own lust. Lust, Lucilla, what sayst thou ? No, no, mine own love I should have said, for I am as far from lust as I am from reason, and as near to love as I am to folly. Then stick to thy determination, and show thyself what love can do, what love dares do, what love hath done. Albeit, I can no way quench the coals of desire with forgetfulness, yet will I rake them up in the ashes of modesty, seeing I dare not discover my love for maidenly shamefastness, I will dissemble it till time I have opportunity. And I hope so to behave myself as Euphues shall think me his own, and Philautus persuade himself I am none but his. But I would to God Euphues would repair hither that the sight of him might mitigate some part of my martyrdom.'[1]

Apart from the novel, Lyly added various essays and epistles on such matters as love, atheism and education, particularly at the University of Athens, which even a dull wit could recognize for Oxford.

Euphues, the Anatomy of Wit, was dedicated to ' My very good Lord and Master, Sir William West, knight, Lord Delawarr ' : the sequel *Euphues and his England* to My very good Lord and Master, Edward de Vere, Earl of Oxford and Lord Great Chamberlain of England. *Euphues and his England* was even more popular. Lyly used the device long since grown stale of bringing imaginary foreigners to England, with ample advice about the manners and customs of the islanders, and observations on the beauty and charm of the ladies.

---

[1] *Euphues, the Anatomy of Wit*, in the works of John Lyly, ed. R.W. Bond, i, 205–7.

JOHN LYLY

Nothing of Lyly's writing during the next two years is known; but on New Year's Day 1584, his play *Campaspe* was played before the Queen by a combined company of children from the Chapel and Paul's. It was afterwards repeated at Blackfriars.

Campaspe is not a good play. It lacks plot and the characters are hardly alive. Apparently it was staged in the old-fashioned manner in a series of ' houses '—little box scenes strung out across the stage, side by side. The disadvantage of this kind of staging is that it tends to split the play into a series of brief dialogues, for it discourages movement. In their own way, the dialogues were good; for those who liked euphuism this was a feast for gluttons. Lyly wrote in prose, whereby his dialogue gained speed, deftness and fluidity. At its best euphuism is a whetstone for the wits. It stimulates the mind to enjoy verbal cleverness.

The play was published during the year, and three editions are known, all dated 1584. It is an indication of its popularity, and shows that Lyly's audiences were ready to be pleased by a comedy that depended entirely on its verbal wit and lacked altogether the usual bawdy knockabout of popular comedy.

Lyly followed *Campaspe* with *Sapho and Phao*, which was played before the Queen on Shrove Tuesday ' by Her Majesty's Children and the boys of Paul's ' and entered for printing on the 6th April 1584.

As with most of Lyly's plays, the story of *Sapho and Phao* is slight and simple. Phao, the ferryman, is endowed with beauty by Venus so that Queen Sapho may fall in love with him; but the young man becomes so beautiful that Venus herself is caught. Ultimately Sapho's pangs of love for Phao and Phao's for Venus are relieved by special arrows made for Cupid, and the ferryman is left to lament his own luckless fate.

Sapho and Phao is not up to the standard of *Campaspe*. It is a slight little Elizabethan ditty in prose, all talk and no action, though there is at times an artificial delicacy about the piece. The euphuistic style is too often verbose. When once a speaker has started the movement of a sentence, it must needs swing back and forth for at least three clauses before it can come to rest : ' Ah, Phao, the more thou seekest to suppress these mounting affections, they soar the loftier, and the more thou wrestlest with them, the stronger they wax, not unlike unto a ball, which the harder it is thrown against the earth, the higher it boundeth into the air, or our Sicilian stone, which grows hardest by hammering.'

When Lyly kept his dialogue to short exchanges it was much livelier.

As with *Campaspe*, the printed version of *Sapho and Phao* gave the alternative prologues and epilogues spoken at Court and at Blackfriars.

Lyly's tenure of the Blackfriars soon came to an end. Sir William More won his case and regained possession of his property in the early summer of 1584. About the same time there was a change in the Mastership of the Paul's choir-boys. On the 22nd May Nathaniel Giles became their Master, and in years following Lyly wrote several plays for him. Giles took the boys to act at Court during Shrovetide 1587 : on the 1st January, the 2nd February, the 27th December in 1588 ; on the 1st and 12th January, and the 28th December 1589 : and on the 1st and 6th January 1590. Of these performances, three were of Lyly's plays—*Galathea* (published in 1592), ' as it was played before the Queen's Majesty at Greenwich on New Year's Day at night' : *Endimion* (published in 1591), played at Greenwich on Candlemas Day : and *Midas* (published in 1592), played before the Queen on Twelfth Night.

Galathea was an improvement. The story was still set in the land of classical-pastoral, but it moves and entertains. In a mythical Lincolnshire Neptune demands his five-yearly tribute of a young virgin, who is carried away by the Egar (that is, the bore of the river personified). Tyterus, the father of Galathea (who is likely to be the next victim), disguises her as a boy in the hope of saving her. Cupid, repulsed by one of Diana's nymphs, swears vengeance. Melebeus, the father of Phillida (who also is in danger of being sacrificed), in like manner disguises her as a boy. Raff, Robin and Dick are shipwrecked and set out to seek their fortune. There are four brief scenes introducing each set of characters and then the story begins. Galathea and Phillida, both disguised, meet and each supposing the other to be a boy falls in love. Cupid, disguised as a girl, gets among Diana's nymphs. Raff takes service with an alchemist. Cupid is soon at work and all the nymphs fall lovesick. Raff forsakes his alchemist for an astrologer. Diana arrests Cupid. At last the day comes for the sacrifice to Neptune. Hebe—failing a fairer—is chosen as Neptune's victim. She is pitiful and Neptune angry, but Venus and Diana appear and begin to wrangle. Neptune agrees to abandon his tribute if Diana will restore Cupid to Venus. Venus has now to settle the problem of Phillida and Galathea, who both dote on each other. She leads them away, promising that at the marriage, one will be changed into a man.

It needed considerable skill to make such a tale endurable, for it was fatally easy either to fall into sheer tedium or grossness. This is the first play which makes much of the situation where a boy player acts the part of a girl disguised as a boy that afterwards became so common in Elizabethan comedy. Lyly kept his little fantasy delicate and charming, though such entertainments, however successful, need a specialized taste. Yet it was a forecast of what was to come. It has something of the fuller delicacy of *Twelfth Night*.

It will be clear to anyone who studies Lyly's plays that he is not so much a dramatist as a deviser of entertainments. He was indeed the first of the masque writers and a master of Court compliment. In *Endimion* a special audience, which included the Queen, knew that the play had a particular and local significance, for Cynthia, wherever and whenever she appeared, personified the courtiers' divine, if ageing Mistress. The old myth of the love of the mortal Endimion for the immortal moon had its special chances for subtle flattery and fine phrasing.

Endimion dotes on Cynthia and confides in his friend Eumenides. Tellus dotes on Endimion and confides in her friend Floscula—it was natural that the arch-euphuist should have symmetry in his plots as in his phrases—but Tellus has more character than any of Lyly's previous creatures, and she is angry at neglect.

Then by way of contrast comes in Sir Tophas, accompanied by his own page, Epiton, and the two little pages of Endimion and Eumenides. Sir Tophas is one of the considerable company of stage *milites gloriosi*. He is not a serious character (even for comedy) but rather a poor halfwit who, like Don Quixote later, but without his idealism, romanticizes a schoolboy's love of blood and turns even fishing into an act of war and sheep-slaying into a furious encounter.

'There cometh no soft syllable within my lips,' he rants; 'custom hath made my words bloody, and my heart barbarous: that pelting word love, how waterish it is in my mouth, it carrieth no sound; hate, horror, death, are speeches that nourish my spirits. I like honey but I care not for the bees; I delight in music but I love not to play on the bagpipes; I can vouchsafe to hear the voice of women, but to touch their bodies I disdain it, as a thing childish, and fit for such men as can digest nothing but milk.'

Sir Tophas is one of those characters whose success depends partly on the mood of the reader, and greatly on the skill of the actor. Either he is very funny or very tedious and slightly disgusting; but again he too is a forecast of the 'irregular humorists,' such as Bobadil, of half a generation later.

Some of Lyly's editors have tried to trace out an elaborate political allegory in *Endimion*, providing a set of names for the *dramatis personæ*, but differing widely between each other. There was certainly some topicality in the play, but Court poets had to walk warily, and too saucy an allegory was dangerous, as Spenser found to his lasting regret.

There was probably topicality also in Lyly's next play, *Midas*. Again he dramatized a Greek myth, and perhaps with the suggestion that Midas and King Philip of Spain had much in common in their lust for gold; though except for a hint or two the parallels were not stressed.

Lyly gave the chief incidents of the old story. He began with Midas, King of Phrygia, invited by Bacchus to make his choice of the gifts of the gods, to which Midas answers: 'It is gold, Bacchus, that Midas desireth. Let everything that Midas toucheth be turned to gold; so shalt thou please thy guest and manifest thy godhead.' His rash wish is fulfilled to the letter, and immediately proves inconvenient. So Midas repents, and his awkward endowment is taken away. He goes hunting to recover from the shock. Apollo and Pan are indulging in a contest of singing. Midas is bidden to judge between them, and he prefers Pan. So Apollo in anger endows him with ass's ears. He is greatly embarrassed by this disgrace, but at last, by means of the oracle, he is cured and repents, and the play ends with a general pæan.

These episodes are separated by comic scenes of the usual kind—matches of repartee between witty girls who want love, and little pages who want smacking. There is a take-off of the jargon of huntin' folk, and a new character in Motto, the barber, who does well out of Midas's golden hairs, and is a very *Tully de oratore* in the barber's art:—
' " How, sir, will you be trimmed ? Will you have your beard like a spade, or a bodkin ? A penthouse on your upper lip, or an alley on your chin ? A low curl on your head like a bull, or dangling lock like a spaniel ? Your moustachios sharp at the ends, like shoemakers' awls, or hanging down to your mouth like goats' flakes ? Your love-locks wreathed with a silken twist, or shaggy to fall on your shoulders ? " '

It was all very much according to pattern, though Lyly's wit had become sharper ; and his euphuism had shed much of its fluffiness to become neatly epigrammatic : ' What is it that gold cannot command, or hath not conquered ? Justice herself, that sitteth wimpled about the eyes, doth it not because she will take no gold, but that she would not be seen blushing when she takes it : the balance she holdeth are not to weigh the right of the cause, but the weight of the bribe : she will put up her naked sword if thou offer her a golden scabbard.'

On the other hand, some of the speeches are inordinately long, even for Lyly. When Midas repents, he indulges in an uninterrupted harangue of seven hundred and forty words. It was certainly a tribute to the memory of the small boy player who had to learn this and a number of other long speeches, all in prose.

In *Mother Bomby* Lyly tried a kind of play that was new to him. It was a comedy on the Terence pattern, a gallimaufry of intrigue, all very symmetrically worked out. Four fathers with marriageable children : four witty boy servants: an old nurse with a boy and a girl whom she had changed at birth. The intentions of the parents and the desires of the children differ; and the two hours' entertainment is filled up by the intrigues of all parties, which result in the victory of age over youth, as disguised lovers are betrothed under the noses of their disapproving parents. Mother Bomby is a wise woman to whom all turn for advice, which she delivers in rhyming couplets. When at last the nurse has confessed her duplicity everyone is satisfied. This play also was apparently designed for performance in 'houses.' So staged it would, perhaps, have been amusing to watch.

Lyly also wrote *The Woman in the Moon*, which was likewise presented before the Queen and afterwards published in 1597. It was his single surviving attempt at a play in verse, and may have been produced some years after the others. In this play he returned to the old mythological kind, setting his scene in Utopia, where the shepherds pray Nature for a female to 'propagate the issue of our kind.' Pandora is therefore created, and plays the vixen with everything about her. The gods grow jealous of her, each according to his influence, so that havoc follows everywhere, until Pandora is sent off to the moon as the best place for such a fickle and disturbing wanton. *The Woman in the Moon* is not a play but a Court masque, and, as such, has a lively charm.

Lyly's connection with the Paul's boys came to an untimely end. They all became involved in the affair known as the Marprelate Controversy.

From the beginning of the reign Catholics and extreme Puritans had continuously opposed the ecclesiastical settlement of Queen Elizabeth. The motives of the many opponents of the Church of England as by law established were mixed, and the opposition took divers forms. The notion that a man's religion was his own private affair was as yet universally repugnant. The Church of England was an essential part of the organization of the State, and everyone, no matter what his religious creed, at least believed that Church and State were inseparable, and that intolerance of other beliefs was right and natural. The extreme Puritan parties, however, claimed that the Church of England and especially its bishops were anti-Christian.

In 1583, John Whitgift, then Bishop of Worcester, was appointed Archbishop of Canterbury, and he was charged by the Queen to restore order in the Church. Whitgift was a keen churchman and a firm disciplinarian, but, as soon as he began to coerce those who disagreed with the position of the Church of England, tension increased. For years there had been desultory pamphleteering. In 1584 Whitgift's opponents produced: *A brief and plain declaration concerning the desires of all those faithful Ministers that have and do seek for the discipline and reformation of the Church of England; which may serve for a just apology against the false accusations and slanders of their adversaries.*

An answer was prepared, but it was not ready till 1587. It was written by Dr. John Bridges, Dean of Sarum, and was an elaborate and enormous apologetic, called *A Defence of the Government established in the Church of England for ecclesiastical matters.* As the book contained fourteen hundred pages, it is not likely to have been popular reading, and, indeed, so far the controversies had been conducted in the higher atmosphere of theological disputations.

Suddenly a new series of attacks began to appear. The name of the writer or writers was unknown; they were printed secretly and distributed mysteriously.[1] The first,

---

[1] For the secret history of the Marprelate Tracts, see W. Pierce, *The Marprelate Tracts*, and *Historical Introduction to the Marprelate Tracts*; and R. B. McKerrow's edition of *Nashe's Works*, v, 34, 184.

known as the EPISTLE, was entitled: *Oh read over Dr. John Bridges, for it is a worthy work; Or an epitome of the first book of that right worshipful volume written against the Puritans in the defence of the noble clergy, by as worshipful a priest, John Bridges, Presbyter, Priest or elder Doctor of Divinity, and Dean of Sarum. Wherein the arguments of the Puritans are wisely prevented that when they come to answer Master Doctor, they must needs say something that hath been spoken. Compiled for the behoof and overthrow of the Parsons, Fickers, and Curates that have learnt their Catechisms and are past grace: By the reverend and worthy Martin Marprelate, gentleman, and dedicated to the Confocation House. The Epitome is not yet published, but it shall be when the Bishops are at convenient leisure to view the same. In the meantime let them be content with this learned Epistle. Printed oversea in Europe, within two furlongs of a bouncing priest at the cost and charges of M. Marprelate, gentleman.*

It was brightly, wittily and scurrilously written, and copies were snapped up eagerly. Whatever the rights or wrongs of the matter, the reading public always loved a spicy wit combat. The promised EPITOME soon followed. Hue and cry was made for authors and printers, but meanwhile an official apology was being prepared by Dr. Thomas Cooper, Bishop of Winchester, a learned cleric, who had compiled a Latin dictionary that is still of considerable use to scholars. The book appeared in 1589 and was entitled: *An Admonition to the People of England: Wherein are answered, not only the slanderous untruths, reproachfully uttered by Martin the Libeller, but also many other crimes by some of his brood, objected generally against all Bishops, and the chief of the Clergy, purposely to deface and discredit the present state of the Church.*

Martin at once hit back with a brilliantly irreverent

repartee entitled : *Ha y' any work for the Cooper :* [1] *Or a brief Pistle directed by way of an hublication to the reverend Bishops, counselling them, if they will needs be barrelled up for fear of smelling in the nostrils of her Majesty and the State, that they would use the advice of reverend Martin for the providing of their Cooper. Because the reverend T. C. (by which mystical letters is understood, either the bouncing parson of Eastmean, or Tom Cokes his Chaplain) to be an unskillful and deceitful tubtrimmer.*

Wherein worthy Martin quits himself like a man, I warrant you, in the modest defence of his self and his learned Pistles, and makes the Cooper's hoops to fly off, and the Bishops' tubs to leak out of all cry. Penned and compiled by Martin the Metropolitan.

Printed in Europe, not far from some of the bouncing priests.

The controversy was becoming more exciting as the secret press was harried from place to place, but yet succeeded in functioning in spite of the Archbishop and his eager searchers. It was clear that Dr. Cooper was not a suitable opponent for Martin, and at the suggestion of Richard Bancroft, at this time Canon of Westminster, the Archbishop decided to reply to Martin in his own kind. Wit must be countered with wit. Professional writers were therefore brought in ; amongst them Thomas Nashe, who had just attracted attention by his preface to Greene's *Menaphon*, and John Lyly, who was considered just the right person to take a lively part in the flyting. A number of counter-attacks appeared from the press with various fancy names, such as *Pap with a Hatchet, An Almond for a Parrot, A Whip for an Ape.* They are all anonymous and it is hardly possible to discover the authors. Jeremy

---

[1] This was one of the regular tradesmen's cries in the City at a time when barrels were much used, and the cooper's skill often needed.

Collier, indeed, in his *Ecclesiastical History*, assigned them to Nashe :

' " 'Twas thought therefore the best way to answer a fool according to his folly, and combat these pamphleteers at their own weapon. They were attached in this manner by one Tom Nashe, in his *Pasquil and Marforio*, his *Counter-Scuffle*, *Pap with a Hatchet*, etc. This Nashe had a genius for satire, a lively turn and spirit for the encounter. By these advantages, together with that of the cause, he broke the enemy at two or three charges, and drove them out of the field." '[1]

Lyly certainly wrote some of them ; but they do not add to his reputation.

Not only did the wits lend a hand in counter-cuffing Martin, the players were likewise encouraged, and particularly the Paul's boys. None of these plays have survived, but some of the incidents can be discovered from the pamphlets. Martin was brought on attired like an ape, whipped, made to wince, then wormed and lanced. He was shown wearing a cock's comb, an ape's face, a wolf's belly and cat's claws. At another time Divinity appeared as a character whom Martin tried to rape. Being prevented, he then scratched her cheeks with his nails and poisoned her with the vomit which he gave her to make her cast up her dignities and promotions.

Playwrights and players were entering into the contest with such zest that they quickly became a bigger nuisance even than Martin. Once a young man of Nashe's temperament was let loose with official sanction there was no end to his ribaldries. The authorities were soon tired of the yesty spirit of mischief which they had called up.

On the 12th November 1589, the Council directed that

[1] Quoted by R. B. McKerrow in his edition of *The Works of Thomas Nashe*, v, 48.

certain letters should be written. The first was to the Archbishop of Canterbury, informing him that 'whereas there hath grown some inconvenience by common plays and interludes in and about the City of London, in that the players take upon themselves to handle in their plays certain matters of Divinity and of State unfit to be suffered, for redress whereof their Lordships have thought good to appoint some persons of judgment and understanding to view and examine their plays before they be permitted to present them publicly. His Lordship is desired that some fit person, well learned in Divinity, be appointed by him to join with the Master of the Revels and one other to be nominated by the Lord Mayor, and they jointly with some speed to view and consider of such comedies and tragedies as are and shall be publicly played by the companies of players in and about the City of London, and they to give allowance of such as they shall think meet to be played, and to forbid the rest.'[1]

At the same time the Lord Mayor of London was instructed to appoint 'A sufficient person, learned and of judgment to join with the Master of the Revels.'

The third letter was sent to the Master of the Revels, authorizing him, in collaboration with the other two 'to call before them the several companies of players (whose servants soever they be) and to require them by authority hereof to deliver unto them their books, that they may consider of the matters of their comedies and tragedies, and thereupon to strike out or reform such parts and matters as they shall find unfit and undecent to be handled in plays, both for Divinity and State, commanding the said companies of players, in her Majesty's name, that they forbear to present and play publicly any comedy or tragedy other than

[1] *Acts of the Privy Council*, edited by J. R. Dasent, xviii, 214, reprinted in *Elizabethan Stage*, iv, 306.

such as they three shall have seen and allowed, which if they shall not observe, they shall then know from their Lordships that they shall be not only severely punished, but made incapable of the exercise of their profession for ever hereafter.'

The Paul's boys did not survive these events; and nothing more was heard of them for several years. During his time with the boys, Lyly had done much. His immediate influence on drama was small; his delicate trifles were neither suited nor intended for the hearty jostling crowds at the Theatre or the Curtain. Indeed, it was not until his plays were printed that dramatists for the public stage took much notice of them. Then it was realized that Lyly had certain qualities of ease, grace and wit which were conspicuously absent from most popular comedies.

Chapter III

STAGE AND UNIVERSITY

IN the twelve years since the building of the Theatre, the professional companies had flourished. In 1588 there were four or five regular London companies patronized by the Queen or the great lords. There were now three playhouses—the Theatre, the Curtain, and the Rose, newly built on the bank side of the south shore of the Thames by the disreputable suburb that clustered round the south end of London Bridge, as well as inns where performances were still regularly given—the Bull Inn in Bishopsgate, the Bel Savage on Ludgate Hill, and the Cross Keys in Gracechurch Street.

In the Theatre there had been continual trouble. James Burbage and his brother-in-law soon quarrelled. Brayne wanted the large sums which he had laid out on the playhouse to be regarded as a first charge on the takings, and he was suspecting that Burbage was dishonest. They took the dispute to an arbitrator and quarrelled so violently before him that they fell to blows, but when they had been separated, an agreement was made—and broken. Then a third party—one Edmund Peckam—claimed the land on which the playhouse was built and tried to gain possession by force. Burbage was obliged to pay for a guard. Peckam's assaults were bad for business, for the players, never knowing when a performance might not be interrupted by this squabble, left the Theatre. So Burbage refused to pay his full rent to Alleyn, and there was considerable trouble from that quarter too. In 1586 Brayne died, leaving his share to his widow. For a while Burbage paid her a half-share of the takings of the gallery, but then he refused on the grounds that the debts of the house had first to be paid. And the disputes continued.

Then the authorities looked askance on the Theatre. There was trouble in 1584 on Whit-Monday. It so happened that an apprentice lay sleeping on the grass in the fields between the Theatre and the Curtain. A sportive young gentleman danced on his belly, whereupon the apprentice started up, and after words, they fell to blows, encouraged by a crowd of at least five hundred. The gentleman called the apprentice a rascal and said that prentices were but the scum of the earth. Broken heads followed, and some of the apprentices were put in prison. Next day there was an attempt to fetch them out; on the Wednesday there was another fray at the Theatre door, caused by one Brown, a serving-man. The next Sunday Chief Justice Anderson, who had sat in judgment on the offenders for the most part of Wednesday, Thursday, Friday and Saturday, sent two Aldermen to court to request that the Theatre and the Curtain might be pulled down. The Council, except the Lord Chamberlain and the Vice-Chamberlain, agreed. So the Recorder of London sent for the Queen's players and the Earl of Arundel's players, who advised him to send also for Burbage. When the Recorder's message reached Burbage he sent back answer that he was my Lord of Hunsdon's man and that he would not come, but that in the morning he would write to his Lord. So the undersheriff was sent for Burbage, and brought him before the Recorder, who complained to Lord Burghley ' at his coming he stouted me out, very hasty, and in the end I showed him my Lord his master's hand, and then he was more quiet, but to die for it he would not be bound.'[1]

In spite of Burbage's troubles the actors themselves were prospering, and some were becoming famous. Of the elder generation, Richard Tarlton was the chief favourite and there are many references to him.[2] He was Queen Elizabeth's jester.

Bishop Fuller's brief biography at the end of *The Worthies of Staffordshire* reads as follows:

THOMAS TARLTON

' My intelligence of the certainty of his birth-place coming too late (*confessed* by the *marginal mark*), I fix him here, who indeed was born at *Condover* in the neighbouring County of Shropshire, where still some of his name and relations remain. Here he was in the field, keeping his father's swine, when a servant of Robert, Earl of Leicester, (passing this way to his Lord's lands in his Barony of Denbigh) was so highly pleased with his *happy unhappy* answers, that he brought him to Court, where he became the most famous *Jester* to Queen Elizabeth.

' Many condemn his (*vocation* I cannot term it, for it is a *coming* without a *calling*) *employment* as unwarrantable. Such maintain that it is better to be a *fool* of *God's making* born so into the world, or a *fool* of *man's making*, jeered into it by *general derision*, than a fool of one's *own making*, by his voluntary affecting thereof. Such say also, he had better continued in his trade of *swine-keeping*, which (though more painful and less profitable) his *conscience* changed to *loss*, for a *Jester's* place in the Court, who, of all men have *the hardest account to make* for every *idle word* that they abundantly utter.

[1] *Malone Society's Collections*, i, 163; and *Elizabethan Stage*, iv, 297.
[2] See *Dictionary of Actors*, by E. Nungezer, who reprints the most important.

' Other allege in excuse of their *practices* that Princes in all ages were allowed their ἀρητόλογοι, whose *virtue* consisted in speaking any thing *without control* : that *Jesters* often *heal* what *Flatterers hurt*, so that Princes by them arrive at the notice of their errors, seeing Jesters carry about with them an *Act of Indemnity* for whatsoever they say or do : that Princes, over-burdened with *state business*, must have their *diversions* : and that those words are not censurable for *absolutely idle*, which lead to *lawful delight*.

' Our Tarlton was master of his *Faculty*. When Queen Elizabeth was *serious* (I dare not say *sullen*) and out of *good humour*, he could *un-dumpish* her at his pleasure. Her highest *Favourites* would, in some cases, go to *Tarleton* before they would go to the *Queen*, and he was their *Usher* to prepare their advantageous access unto her. In a word, *he told the Queen more of her faults* than most of her *Chaplains*, and *cured her melancholy better* than all *of her physicians*.

' Much of his merriment lay in his very looks and actions, according to the Epitaph written upon him :

> Hic situs est cuius poterat vox, actio, vultus,
> Ex Heraclito reddere Democritum.

' Indeed, the self-same words, spoken by another, would hardly move a merry man to smile, which, uttered by him, would force a sad soul to laughter.

' This is to be reported to his praise, that his *Jests* never were *profane*, *scurrilous* nor *satyrical*, neither trespassing on *Piety*, *Modesty* or *Charity*, as in which *plurimum inerat salis, multum aceti, aliquid sinapis, nihil veneni*. His death may proportionably be assigned about the end of Queen Elizabeth.'

Fuller's information is sketchy. Tarlton's name was Richard, not Thomas, and his reputation for clean wit is hardly borne out by the tales foisted on him in contemporary jest books. Tarlton apparently began his professional career as a private jester, but in 1583, when a new company called the 'Queen's Men' was formed, he joined it. He wrote for them a play called *The Seven Deadly Sins*, which was very popular, but does not survive. He also wrote a number of ballads and ditties, including

The Crow sits upon the Wall,
Please one and please all

—which Malvolio, in relaxation, approved. Tarlton had a squint and a flat nose, and he wore an enormous pair of slops (or baggy breeches) as famous in their day as Mr. Chaplin's boots. He was buried in Shoreditch on the 3rd September 1588, leaving a son named Philip after his godfather, Sir Philip Sidney. After his death the Queen's Men languished and broke.

Three of Tarlton's contemporaries in the Queen's company—Robert Wilson, John Bentley and Knell—were also famous as serious actors, but no details of their style remain, only a letter of one of Edward Alleyn's admirers who had laid a wager that Alleyn would prove himself a better actor.

Edward Alleyn was the first of the younger actors to make a name. He was born on the 1st September 1566, and began playing young. In 1583, when he was only sixteen, he was a full member of the Earl of Worcester's company, but he transferred his services to the Lord Admiral and remained his man for the rest of his professional life. By 1592 Alleyn was regarded—at least by enthusiastic Englishmen—as the greatest actor who had ever lived. Nashe, who was always an accurate mirror of current opinion, says:

'Our players are not as the players beyond sea, a sort of

squirting bawdy comedians, that have whores and common courtesans to play women's parts, and forbear no immodest speech, or unchaste action that may procure laughter; but our scene is more statelily furnished than ever it was in the time of Roscius, our representations honourable and full of gallant resolution, not consisting, like theirs, of a pantalon, a whore and a zany, but of emperors, kings and princes, whose true tragedies (*Sophocleo cothurno*) they do vaunt.

'Not Roscius not Æsop, those admired tragedians that have lived ever since before Christ was born, could ever perform more in action than famous Ned Allen. I must accuse our poets of sloth and partiality that they will not boast in large impressions what worthy men (above all nations) England affords. Other countries cannot have a fiddler break a string but they will put it in print, and the old Romans in the writings they published, thought scorn to use any but domestic examples of their own home-bred actors, scholars and champions; and them they would extol to the third and fourth generation: cobblers, tinkers, fencers, none escaped them, but they mingled them all in one gallimaufry of glory.

'Here I have used a like method, not of tying myself to mine own country, but by insisting in the experience of our time: and if I ever write anything in Latin (as I hope one day I shall) not a man of any desert here amongst us, but I will have up. Tarlton, Ned Allen, Knell, Bentley, shall be made known to France, Spain and Italy; and not a part that they surmounted in, more than other, but I will there note and set down, with the manner of their habits and attire.'[1]

Alleyn's most famous parts were in Marlowe's three plays, *Tamburlaine*, *Dr. Faustus*, and *The Jew of Malta*;

[1] *Piers Penniless*, in *The Works of Thomas Nashe*, edited by R. B. McKerrow, i, 215.

and as Hieronimo in Kyd's *Spanish Tragedy*. His style was heavy and robustious. It was admired at first, but afterwards was considered ludicrous. Various references to *Tamburlaine* give a hint of his manner, thus 'E. S.,' the author of *The Discovery of the Knights of the Post*, wishing to describe a man in a furious temper, wrote: 'with that S. bent his brows and fetched his stations up and down the room with such furious gesture as if he had been playing Tamburlaine on a stage.'

But Alleyn was not only an impressive player; he was also a fine business man, and he realized that if he was to get the best results from his own magnificent presence and voice, he needed the finest plays that money could buy. As it happened, for a variety of causes, good writers were becoming available.

Bacon in his Essay *Of Seditions and Troubles* observed that three things bring a State to necessity: the multiplying nobility; an overgrown clergy who bring nothing to the stock; and 'in like manner when more are bred scholars than preferment can take off.' The problem of the scholar without preferment was one of the minor anxieties of statesmen throughout Bacon's lifetime, and out of this surplus of scholars came Elizabethan drama.

Then, as now, the best prizes went to the University man; and so to Oxford and Cambridge crowded the brilliant hopeful young men of all classes. At the best a tradesman's son might win high place in the State or Church; even the failures could hope for something better than serving behind the counter. All the same, there was not enough to go round. Every year the Universities discharged a large number of men who could not be satisfied, men who had become quite unfitted for manual labour, yet too ambitious to be contented with the miserable £10 a year which was the pay of an usher or clerk. The whole problem is most vividly illustrated in three college plays which were produced at St. John's College, Cambridge, in 1598, 1600 and 1601. The first of these plays, *The Pilgrimage to Parnassus*,[1] is an allegory of University life.

Philomusus and Studioso are two hopeful young students who approach the Muses' spring on Parnassus Hill to drink of learning. They can have few illusions if they listen to old Consiliodorus, who warns them, in a speech of some sixty-six lines, of the trials and disappointments before them. On the way the pilgrims meet various types of student still common in any University—Madido, the drinking man, who studies Horace with the aid of sack, and finds his Parnassus near at hand; Stupido, the puritan, who wishes to lead them off to a prayer meeting; and Amoretto, the wencher, who holds them for a while. Excess produces surfeit and the journey is resumed. They are nearing the top of the hill when Ingenioso, the disillusioned scholar, accosts them and tries to persuade them not to waste their time :

' I talked with a friend of mine that lately gave his horse a bottle of hay at the bottom of the hill, who told me that Apollo had sent to Pluto to borrow twenty nobles to pay his commons. He added further, that he met coming down from the hill a company of ragged vicars and forlorn schoolmasters, who as they walked scratched their unthrifty elbows and often put their hands into their unpeopled pockets, that had not been possessed with faces this many a day. There one stood digging for gold in a standish ; another looking for cockpence in the bottom of a pew ; the third tolling for silver in a belfry ; but they were never so happy as Æsop's cock to find a precious stone. Nay, they could scarce get enough to apparel their head in an unlined hat, their body in a frieze jerkin, and their feet in a clouted

[1] *Parnassus : Three Elizabethan Comedies,* edited by W. D. Macray.

pair of shoes. Come not there, seek for poverty no further; it's too far to go to Parnassus to fetch repentance.'

Two years later, the same author produced a sequel, *The Return from Parnassus* (Part 1). The first hopeful illusions were gone, and, incidentally, with experience the writer had immeasurably improved as a dramatist. The *Return* was not an allegory like its predecessor, but a piece of powerful satire on University life at Cambridge.

Their studies now completed, Studioso and Philomusus must leave Parnassus to earn a living. The first person to meet them is Ingenioso, now turned pamphlet writer, who is trying at the moment to persuade a 'great lump of drowsy earth' to be his Maecenas. With great pomposity this patron rewards him—with two groats. The party is joined by Luxurio, and all four set off quietly and speedily for London, 'lest *aes alienum* be knocking at our doors.'

A good scene follows when their flight is discovered by a Draper, a Tailor, and Simson, the Tapster. The Tailor has the greatest grievance:

'They came to me, and were as courteous as passeth. I do not like they should put off their hats so much to me. Well, they needs upon old acquaintance would borrow 40s. for three days: I (as I had always been a kind man to scholars) lent it them, and delivered them their breeches new turned and their stockings new footed, even as though I had been privy to their running away.'

Simson has more philosophy:

'O my frozen balderkin of strong ale!' he remarks; 'well might I have foretold by the burning of a pot of your liquor that some dry luck hung over my moist head! And is Luxurio gone? The answer is, he is gone! Ey, but one will say, Will not Luxurio return again? I answer, I know not. Ey, but some will object and say, Did not

Luxurio strike off the score before he went ? I answer, he did not.'

By this time Philomusus and Studioso have both obtained employment. Studioso is earning five marks a year as private tutor to a young gentleman, as well as making himself useful by waiting at meals and working in the fields at harvest-time. Philomusus has turned sexton and clerk, using ' the voice that was made to pronounce a poet or an orator . . . like a belman, in the inquisition of a strayed beast.'

Two scenes show the scholars at their uncongenial work. Ingenioso also has attached himself to another patron, Gullio, the vainglorious courtier who reads the less edifying parts of Shakespeare and makes sonnets to his mistress.

Everything goes wrong. Philomusus is dismissed because he is too proud to whip the dogs out of church ; Studioso offends his pupil ; Ingenioso forgets himself and speaks the truth to his patron. So all determine to try their luck at Rome or Rheims, where the seminaries founded for English Catholics attracted a mixed gathering of saints preparing for a martyr's crown, and worldlings who came to glean from the pious.[1]

In the second part of the *Return* (1601) the scholars fall still lower, and unsuccessfully try their luck at quack medicine, acting and fiddling. The play is full of allusions to the chief actors and writers of the time ; it shows that the undergraduate of 1600 was as familiar with theatre gossip as certain kinds of undergraduate to-day. In one scene, Judicio and Ingenioso sum up the merits of some dozen writers—Marlowe, Shakespeare and Jonson among them. In another, Burbage and Kemp, the great tragedian

[1] Anthony Munday, who appears in these pages, was one of the latter, and wrote a very vivid account of his adventures in *The English Roman Life*.

and comedian of the age, are brought on to give a lesson in acting.

Ingenioso and Luxurio are typical of many University students; they lived wild, vicious lives at the University, with the result that they soon became quite incapable of steady work and unwilling to try any ordinary occupation. Naturally enough such men made straight for London, where they could hope to live on their wits. It was a precarious life at the best: the competition was keen, the dangers innumerable. A few succeeded, but most of them simply disappeared.

On the other hand, there were good chances for the steady student. Colleges recommended their best men to the patronage of the great, and statesmen like Burghley, who was Chancellor of Cambridge University, were good judges of character, on the look-out for promising youths. The normal course for a bright young man was to bring himself into notice by some poem, or display of intellectual agility, which he dedicated to a likely patron. If he succeeded, he was taken into the great man's household. Thereafter his promotion depended on luck and his own ability. Writing was not yet a profession.

Lord Burghley himself was not very kindly disposed towards poets, as Spenser grumbled, but Leicester, Sir Philip Sidney and his sister Mary, Countess of Pembroke, were always ready to give practical encouragement to literature. When Spenser left Pembroke College, Cambridge, he was introduced, through the good offices of Gabriel Harvey, to both these patrons. When Sidney and Leicester died (in 1586 and 1588) there seemed no one to take their place, and many were the laments from poets that the golden age of encouragement had gone for ever.

Patrons at all time have more petitioners than they can ever hope to satisfy or even to acknowledge: many failed to attract notice. There were others who could never conform to the standard of behaviour which a great man might expect from his household, where there was no place for those Ingenios who could not learn to wait patiently in the ante-room. Not a few of the wilder Bohemians preferred the discomforts and dangers of liberty to the restraints of dependence on the great.

Complaints are many of disappointed students who looked back with bitterness on their University career as time wasted in the pursuit of barren sophistries that led neither to preferment nor to intellectual satisfaction.

An excellent picture of the odd life which many scholars led in London is to be found in the play of *The Puritan Widow*, obviously the work of an Oxford man.[1] George Pyeboard was a student sent down for stealing a cheese from Jesus College, and so pursued by a Welshman that he took his staff to London. There, as he says, ' was I turned to my wits to shift in the world, to tour among sons, and heirs, and fools, and gulls, and ladies' eldest sons, to work upon nothing, to feed out of flint, and ever since has my belly been much beholding to my brain.'[2]

One method of raising money was by means of the bogus dedication. Having collected the names of likely victims, the needy author had his book printed with the usual florid Dedicatory Epistle ; the different names were then inserted in separate copies, and the author, in the guise of a humble admirer, proceeded to call on his patrons, to offer them this slight token of his respect. Dekker describes the interview. Having obtained an interview, the author begins :

' " Sir, I am a poor scholar, and the report of your virtues hath drawn me hither, venturously bold to fix your worthy

[1] Possibly Marston.
[2] Printed in *Shakespeare Apocrypha*, ed. C. F. Tucker Brooke, I, ii, 54.

name as a patronage to a poor short discourse which here I dedicate (out of my love) to your noble and eternal memory."

' This speech he utters barely.

' The hawking pamphleteer is then bid to put on, whilst his Miscellane Maecenas, opens a book fairly apparelled in vellum, with gilt fillets and fourpenny silk ribbon at least, like little streamers on the top of a marchpane castle, hanging dandling by at the four corners. The title being superficially surveyed, in the next leaf he sees that the author he hath made him one of his gossips, for the book carries his worship's name, and under it stands an Epistle just the length of a henchman's grace before dinner, which is long enough for any book in conscience, unless the writer is unreasonable.

' The knight, being told beforehand that this little sunbeam of Phœbus (shining thus briskly in print) hath his mite or atomy waiting upon him in the outer court, thanks him for his love and labour, and considering with himself what cost he hath been at and how far he hath ridden to come to him, he knows that patrons and godfathers are to pay scot and lot alike, and therefore to cherish his young and tender Muse, he gives him four or six angels, inviting him either to stay breakfast, or if the sundial of the house points towards eleven, then to tarry to dinner.' [1]

The Elizabethan—like the Oriental—lived close. Privacy was unknown except to the great. Men slept in garrets where they could. They fed in public, at the ordinary if they could afford it, with ' Duke Humphrey ' when they were penniless. Class distinctions were more noticeable than to-day: courtier and actor, merchant and lawyer, kept each to his own centre, his inn or guild.

These conditions naturally had far-reaching effects. In such a society, gossip played a great part in men's lives.

[1] *Lanthorn and Candlelight* in *Non-dramatic Works by Thomas Dekker*, edited by A. B. Grosart, iii, 240.

New books, jokes and plays were eagerly discussed; the good lines repeated and the bad mimicked. To the modern Englishman, a visit to the theatre is an evening's entertainment; he leaves the drama behind as he gets into his taxi. But to the keen Elizabethan playgoer, the drama was part of his life. He never ceased to discuss, quote and criticize. Marston has drawn the type.

> Luscus, what's played to-day? Faith, now I know,
> I set thy lips abroach, from whence doth flow
> Naught but pure Juliet and Romeo.
> Say, who acts best? Drusus, or Roscio?
> Now I have him, that ne'er of ought did speak
> But when of plays or players he did treat.
> H'ath made a commonplace book out of plays,
> And speaks in print, at least whate'er he says
> Is warranted by Curtain plaudities;
> If e'er you heard him courting Lesbia's eyes,
> Say, courteous sir, speaks he not movingly
> From out some new pathetic tragedy?
> He writes, he rails, he jests, he courts, what not,
> And all from out his huge long scrap'd stock
> Of well penn'd plays.[1]

Another result of this public kind of life was that all prominent men in every profession were well known by sight, so that quarrels in Court and personalities of all sorts were really interesting. The letters of John Chamberlain or Manningham's diary are good examples of the unwearied inquisitiveness of the Elizabethan.

The conventions of behaviour were strict and intricate. Gentlemen with a literary turn might write for the amusement of themselves and their friends; but it was the sign of an ill-bred desire for notoriety to print any but the most learned works. The genteel method of publication was by

[1] *Scourge of Villainy*, in *Bodley Head Quartos*, xiii, 107.

means of a scrivener's manuscript copy. Even sixty years later (1643) Thomas Browne complained that he was only persuaded to print *Religio Medici* because the printer had pirated so faulty a copy.

As the interest in literature grew, booksellers found means of satisfying the public without unduly offending the gentleman author, who, being human, was not utterly reluctant to see his name in print. Sometimes a manuscript was borrowed, sometimes the zealous but injudicious friend gave his copy to the printer lest the author's fame should otherwise perish.

The hungry scholar cared for none of these subtleties. In the growing appetite of the age for every kind of literature he recognized that there was a chance for him to make a meal by his pen; and so by translation and plagiarism, less often than by originality, he kept the booksellers of Paul's supplied with their most profitable wares. By 1580 authorship was becoming a regular profession; and, of the early professional writers, the one outstanding figure was Robert Greene.

Chapter IV

NEW DRAMATISTS

POSTERITY has dealt hardly with the memory of Robert Greene. He had many faults; above all he committed the unpardonable sin of making an uncomplimentary (and possibly justifiable) remark about Shakespeare, then only in the promising stage. His life—chiefly on the dark side—is better known than that of most of his contemporaries. Just before he died, when the pains of hell rose very vividly before his eyes, he wrote two autobiographical pamphlets in which he spares nothing. He had, moreover, recently offended Gabriel Harvey, who completed the picture in his *Four Letters*.

Yet there was obviously another side to Greene's character. Many of his contemporaries regarded him with admiration and defended his memory against the calumnies of Harvey. His writings, too, are surprisingly pure for the age, and at times show an intense moral purpose; all of which suggests that, however low he sank, he was never quite happy in his wallowing, and had a soul far above the ' lewd wits his companions.'

Greene was born at Norwich in 1558 and baptized on the 11th July.[1] Nothing is known of his boyhood. On the 26th November 1575 he matriculated as a sizar (or poor

[1] The best accounts of Greene's life and work are in the introduction to *The Plays and Poems of Robert Greene*, edited by J. Churton Collins, and *Robert Greene et ses romans*, by René Pruvost.

student) at St. John's College, Cambridge, where he does not seem to have been a very accurate scholar, as several rather elementary errors in Latin appear in his works. Yet he cannot be said wholly to have wasted his time. Then, as now, a man was educated in the University not so much in the lecture-room as by the friends he made and the enthusiasms he pursued. He took his B.A. degree in 1578 and his M.A. in 1583.

These facts can be supplemented by what Greene says of himself in the *Repentance* :

'I need not make long discourse of my parents, who for their gravity and honest life is well known and esteemed amongst their neighbours, namely, in the City of Norwich, where I was bred and born. But as out of one self-same clod of clay there sprouts both stinking weeds and delightful flowers, so from honest parents often grow most dishonest children ; for my father had care to have me in my nonage brought up at school, that I might through the study of good letters grow to be a friend to myself, a profitable member to the commonwealth, and a comfort to him in his age. But as early pricks the tree that will prove a thorn, so even in my first years I began to follow the filthiness of mine own desires, and neither to listen to the wholesome advertisements of my parents, nor be ruled by the careful correction of my master. For being at the University of Cambridge, I light amongst wags as lewd as myself, with whom I consumed the flower of my youth, who drew me to travel into Italy and Spain, in which places I saw and practised such villainy as is abominable to declare. Thus by their counsel I sought to furnish myself with coin, which I procured by cunning sleights from my father and my friends, and my mother pampered me so long, and secretly helped me to the oil of angels, that I grew thereby prone to all mischief; so that being conversant with notable braggarts, boon companions and ordinary spendthrifts, that practised sundry superficial studies, I became as a scion grafted into the same stock, whereby I did absolutely participate of their nature and qualities. At my return into England, I ruffled out in my silks, in the habit of *Malcontent*, and seemed so discontent, that no place would please me to abide in, nor no vocation cause me to stay myself in; but after I had by degrees proceeded Master of Arts, I left the University and away to London, where (after I had continued some short time and driven myself out of credit with sundry of my friends) I became an author of plays and a penner of love pamphlets, so that I soon grew famous in that quality that who for that trade grown so ordinary about London as Robin Greene. Young yet in years, though old in wickedness, I began to resolve that there was nothing bad that was profitable: whereupon I grew so rooted in all mischief that I had as great a delight in wickedness as sundry hath in godliness, and as much felicity I took in villainy as others had in honesty.'[1]

Soon after his return from Italy—he proceeds—he was powerfully moved by a sermon preached at St. Andrew's Church in Norwich; but the effect was shortlived and he soon returned to his old life. 'Nevertheless soon after I married a gentleman's daughter of good account, with whom I lived for a while; but forasmuch as she would persuade me from my wilful wickedness, after I had a child by her, I cast her off, having spent up the marriage money which I obtained by her.

'Then left I her at six or seven, who went into Lincolnshire, and I to London, where in short space I fell into favour with such as were of honourable and good calling. But here note, that though I knew how to get a friend, yet I had not the gift or reason how to keep a friend, for he that

[1] *The Repentance of Robert Greene*, in *Bodley Head Quartos*, vi, 19.

was my dearest friend, I would be sure so to behave myself towards him that he should ever after profess to be my utter enemy, or else vow never after to come into my company.

'Thus my misdemeanours (too many to be recited) caused the most part of those so much to despise me, that in the end I became friendless, except it were in a few alehouses, who commonly for my inordinate expenses would make much of me until I were on the score far more than ever I meant to pay by twenty nobles thick.'[1]

Greene at once realized the significance of Lyly's success with *Euphues*. He could always copy a style and immediately he set about an imitation, in *Mamillia, a mirror or looking-glass for the Ladies of England*, printed in 1580. Apparently he travelled in the next three years. Then he came back to Cambridge and wrote a second part of *Mamillia*, which he dedicated 'from my study in Clare Hall, the 7 of July.'

He took his M.A. degree at this time. Then he came to London and *Mamillia, the Second Part of the Triumph of Pallas*, was entered on the 6th September 1583. In a short time he was well known. 'These vanities and other trifling pamphlets I penned of Love and vain fantasies, was my chiefest stay of living, and for those my vain discourses, I was beloved of the more vainer sort of people, who being my continual companions, came still to my lodging, and there would continue quaffing, carousing and surfeiting with me all the day long.'

Gabriel Harvey supplemented this picture: 'I was altogether unacquainted with the man, and never once saluted him by name; but who in London hath not heard of his dissolute and licentious living; his fond disguising of a Master of Art with ruffianly hair, unseemly apparel and more unseemly company; his vainglorious and thrasonical braving: his piperly extemporizing and tarltonizing [i.e. playing

[1] *The Repentance of Robert Greene*, in *Bodley Head Quartos*, vi, 24.

the clown] : his apish counterfeiting of every ridiculous and absurd toy : his fine cozening of jugglers, and finer juggling with cozeners : his villainous cogging and foisting : his monstrous swearing and horrible forswearing : his impious profaning of sacred texts : his other scandalous, and blasphemous raving : his riotous and outrageous surfeiting : his continual shifting of lodgings : his plausible mustering and banqueting of roysterly acquaintance at his first coming : his beggarly departing in every hostess's debt : his infamous resorting to the Bankside, Shoreditch, Southwark, and other filthy haunts : his obscure lurking in basest corners : his pawning of his sword, cloak and what not, when money came short : his impudent pamphletting, fantastical interluding, and desperate libelling, when other cozening shifts failed : his employing of Ball (surnamed Cutting Ball) till he was intercepted at Tyburn, to levy a crew of his trustiest companions to guard him in danger of arrests : his keeping of the aforesaid Ball's sister, a sorry ragged quean, of whom he had his base son, Infortunatus Greene : his forsaking of his own wife, too honest for such a husband : particulars are infinite : his contemning of superiors, deriding of other, and defying of all good order ? ' [1]

Greene thus became a legend. Chettle described him as ' a man of indifferent years, of face amiable, of body well proportioned, his attire after the habit of a scholarlike gentleman, only his hair was somewhat long.' [2]

Nashe, who knew him best, tells several tales :

' I saw him make an apparriter once in a tavern eat his citation, wax and all, very handsomely served twixt two dishes.'

' He inherited more virtues than vices : a jolly long red peak, like the spire of a steeple, he cherished continually

[1] Gabriel Harvey, *Four Letters*, in *Bodley Head Quartos*, ii, 19.
[2] *Kindheart's Dream*, in *Bodley Head Quartos*, iv, 13.

without cutting, whereat a man might hang a jewel, it was so sharp and pendant.'

'In a night and day would he have yerked up a pamphlet as well as in seven year, and glad was that printer that might be so blest to pay him dear for the very dregs of his wit.'[1]

By 1586 Greene was well established as a professional writer; but as yet he had not condescended to write for the stage. About this time Thomas Kyd sold the manuscript of *The Spanish Tragedy* to Edward Alleyn.[2]

Thomas Kyd remains an obscure person. He was baptized in the church of St. Mary Woolnoth, Lombard Street, in London, on the 6th November 1558, and was entered in the parish register as 'Thomas, son of Francis Kidd, citizen and writer of the Court Letter in London.' His father was a scrivener, a man of good local standing who served as churchwarden. Thomas was admitted to the Merchant Taylors' School, then a new foundation, on the 26th October 1565.

The headmaster of the school at this time was Richard Mulcaster, the most famous of all Elizabethan schoolmasters. Mulcaster was a zealot. At a time when the English language was regarded by the learned of Europe as an island dialect, he was one of the enthusiasts who deliber-

[1] *Four Letters Confuted*, i, 287.

[2] Almost all that is known of Kyd is gathered into the long and important introduction of F. S. Boas to his edition of *Kyd's Works*, 1901. Although *The Spanish Tragedy* is the most quoted and parodied of all Elizabethan plays, it is only by chance known that Kyd was its author because his name is added to three lines from the play quoted in Heywood's *Apology for Actors*. Nor is the exact date of *The Spanish Tragedy* known. Ben Jonson, in *Bartholomew Fair*, says: 'He that will swear Jeronimo or Andronicus are the best plays yet shall pass unexcepted at here as a man whose judgment shows it is constant and hath stood still these five and twenty or thirty years.' As *Bartholomew Fair* was produced in 1614, *The Spanish Tragedy* dated from the second half of the 1580's.

ately set about creating a new literature which would raise the esteem of English to the level of the Latin tongue. He set down his views in a book called *The Elementary* (1582), 'Which entreateth chiefly of the right writing of our English tongue.' There was, as always, opposition, for Latin scholars would not readily give up their advantages. Mulcaster answered their objections in a fine peroration:

'... For is it not indeed a marvellous bondage to become servants to one tongue for learning's sake, the most of our time, with loss of most time, whereas we may have the very same treasure in our own tongue, with the gain of most time? Our own bearing the joyful title of our liberty and freedom, the Latin tongue remembering us of our thraldom and bondage? I love Rome, but London better; I favour Italy, but England more; I honour the Latin, but I worship the English. I wish all were in ours, which they had from others; neither offer I them wrong, which did the like to others; and by their own precedent do let us understand how boldly we may venture, notwithstanding the opinion of some such of our people as desire rather to please themselves with a foreign tongue, wherewith they are acquainted, than to profit their country in her natural language, where their acquaintance should be.'

This enthusiasm for English he dinned into his pupils and hearers, overwhelming all objections:

'But we have no rare cunning proper to our soil to cause foreigners study it as a treasure of such store. What though? Yet are we not ignorant by the mean thereof to turn to our use all the great treasure, of either foreign soil or foreign language? And why may not the English wits, if they will bend their wills, either for matter or for method in their own tongue, be in time as well sought to by foreign students for increase of their knowledge as our soil is sought to at this same time by foreign merchants for increase of their wealth ? As the soil is fertile, because it is applied, so the wits be not barren if they list to breed.'[1]

Mulcaster's pupils had thus not a little of the missionary spirit, and he can rightly claim some of the credit which belongs to his more famous pupils who include Edmund Spenser and Thomas Kyd. Nothing more is known of Kyd's life before 1586. *The Spanish Tragedy*, in spite of its crudities, was the most popular of all Elizabethan plays. It continued to be acted for over fifty years. It is the first competent stage tragedy in the English language.

Elizabethan audiences were still patient. They enjoyed listening to long speeches. Kyd began leisurely. The play opens with the ghost of Don Andrea sliding on to the stage accompanied by Revenge. The ghost explains the situation. On earth it was Don Andrea, in love with Bel-imperia, but unfortunately slain in the late conflict with Portingal. It describes at length the infernal regions whence it has come with Revenge. The two spirits sit to watch the tragedy. Kyd was reluctant to let his play move. In the first scene he gave another long description of the battle between the Spaniards and the Portingals. Then the plot slowly unfolded. The army comes back from the war. Balthazar, the Portingal prince, is led in between Horatio, the son of old Hieronimo, Marshal of Spain, and Lorenzo, son of the Duke of Castile and brother of Bel-imperia.

Both claim Balthazar's ransom. The King compromises by awarding the ransom to Horatio, the armour to Lorenzo. Horatio comes to Bel-imperia to tell her of the death of her lover—another description. He hands her the scarf of the dead hero and takes his leave. Bel-imperia thereupon finds herself falling in love with Horatio and she dissects her feelings in a naive soliloquy : Andrea is dead : Horatio was his friend : Balthazar, that slew Andrea, was captured by

[1] *Mulcaster's Elementary*, edited by E. T. Campagnac, pp. 269, 272.

Horatio, and is now making love to her : it will be a very pretty vengeance to give herself to his conqueror.

Lorenzo, however, is the complete Machiavellian villain. He becomes friendly with Balthazar and promises that he shall wed Bel-imperia. When Balthazar laments his lack of encouragement from Bel-imperia, Lorenzo bids him be patient, and proceeds to discover why Bel-imperia is so cold. He sets his servant Pedringano to spy, and when next the lovers meet, Pedringano places Lorenzo and Balthazar above to overhear their talk. After a brief speech, they plan to meet again that night, and Bel-imperia names the place as the bower in old Hieronimo's garden.

> Then be thy father's pleasant bower the field,
> Where first we vow'd a mutual amity :
> The Court were dangerous, that place is safe.
> Our hour shall be when Vesper 'gins to rise,
> That summons home distressful travellers.
> There none shall hear us but the harmless birds ;
> Haply the gentle nightingale
> Shall carol us asleep, ere we be ware,
> And, singing with the prickle at her breast,
> Tell our delight and mirthful dalliance :
> Till then each hour will seem a year and more.

Kyd could handle blank verse very prettily. Night falls. Horatio and Bel-imperia come to the bower, and there make love. Pedringano betrays them. Lorenzo and Balthazar rush in. They stab Horatio and hang up the body in the arbour. Then Lorenzo, gagging the outcries of his sister, drags her away.

This episode was regarded by Elizabethan playgoers as the high spot in tragedy.

Scarcely have Bel-imperia's screams been stifled when old Hieronimo enters in his shirt, and with a torch in his hand searches out in the darkness :

> What out-cries pluck me from my naked bed,
> And chill my throbbing heart with trembling fear,
> Which never danger yet could daunt before?
> Who calls Hieronimo? Speak, here I am.
> I did not slumber; therefore 'twas no dream.
> No, no, it was some woman cried for help,
> And here within this garden did she cry,
> And in this garden must I rescue her.
> But stay, what murd'rous spectacle is this?
> A man hang'd up and all the murderers gone:
> And in my bower, to lay the guilt on me.
> This place was made for pleasure, not for death.
> Those garments that he wears I oft have seen:
> Alas, it is Horatio, my sweet son.
> O no, but he that whilom was my son. . . .

It was a most effective passage and Alleyn made the best of it, though Kyd had not yet learned to curb his Muse. There is too much lamentation and the whole speech is too long.

A little later Alleyn had his second great soliloquy. He wanders in, beside himself with grief, crying out:

> Oh eyes, no eyes, but fountains fraught with tears;
> Oh life, no life, but lively form of death;
> Oh world, no world, but mass of public wrongs,
> Confused and filled with murder and misdeeds. . . .

These soliloquies of Hieronimo were not mere windy rhetoric. There is some genuine introspection, a real pathos, and a fine sense of words, for Kyd had imagination. Sometimes it deserted him, and at times the play is incredibly crude, as in the murder of Serberine. Lorenzo, knowing that Serberine may betray him, by a typical Machiavellian trick, plots to rid himself both of Serberine and Pedringano, who is now becoming inconvenient. Lorenzo arranges that Pedringano shall shoot Serberine and later be hanged for the deed. Pedringano enters clasping a large pistol, and after the manner of persons in the earlier Elizabethan tragedies, he tells himself what he is doing:

> Now, Pedringano, bid thy pistol hold;
> And hold on, Fortune, once more favour me,
> Give but success to mine attempting spirit,
> And let me shift for taking of mine aim.
> Here is the gold, this is the gold proposed;
> It is no dream that I adventure for,
> But Pedringano is possessed thereof.
> And he that would not strain his conscience
> For him that thus his liberal purse hath stretched,
> Unworthy such a favour may he fail,
> And, wishing, want, when such as I prevail.
> As for the fear of apprehension,
> I know, if needs should be, my noble Lord
> Will stand between me and ensuing harms:
> Besides, this place is free from all suspect.
> Here therefore will I stay, and take my stand.

He hides. The watch come in and take their places silently. Then Serberine enters, and he too tells himself what he is about:

> Here, Serberine, attend and stay thy pace,
> For here did Don Lorenzo's page appoint
> That thou by his command shouldst meet with him.
> How fit a place, if one were so dispos'd,
> Methinks this corner is to close with one.

Pedringano then steps forth, discharges his pistol, and Serberine is dead. The watchmen look intelligently at each other and observe, 'Hark, gentlemen, this is a pistol shot!' Thereupon they seize Pedringano.

And so the play goes on until Hieronimo at last finds his chance of perfecting a thoroughly artistic vengeance; for vengeance, at least on the stage, demanded not merely an eye for an eye, but something handsome on the credit side. To be entirely satisfactory it must be so arranged that the victim passed out straight to hell without hope of redemption.

Bel-imperia has plotted with the old Marshal. She consents to marry Balthazar. Hieronimo is instructed to prepare a play for the wedding festival. He chooses Lorenzo and Balthazar, Bel-imperia and himself to take the chief parts in the tragedy of ' Soliman and Perseda.' The fathers of Lorenzo and Balthazar sit in the gallery to watch the play, with the rest of the Court. Then in earnest Hieronimo stabs Lorenzo, Bel-imperia stabs Balthazar and kills herself. The Court applaud the realism of the scene, until Hieronimo reveals the true significance of what they have beheld. He is now even with his wrongers child for child, broken heart for broken heart—but in double measure.

The horrified courtiers come down from the gallery and seize Hieronimo. There are more horrors yet. When the old man will not talk they threaten him with torture, but he bites out his tongue.

' Yet he can write,' cries Lorenzo's father.

They bring him a quill pen. As the point is not to his liking, he makes signs for a penknife. Then he leaps at the Duke of Castile, stabs him, and kills himself before anyone can interrupt. The ghost of Don Andrea and Revenge retire satisfied at a good afternoon's work.

It is doubtful whether a modern audience would have the patience to sit through *The Spanish Tragedy*, but despite all its obvious crudities, Kyd had discovered certain elementary principles of drama. The plot of *The Spanish Tragedy* is very finely constructed. The alternation of scene between characters ; the variation of the tension ; the thrilling episodes, murders, public executions, ghosts, madmen, screaming mothers, lamenting fathers, distressed damsels ; all the ingredients of pity and horror are here ; and Kyd worked the plot up to a magnificent climax.

The play went on and on until the Civil War. It was one of those dramas which, in spite of obvious and even comic shortcomings, have an extraordinary longevity, as in more modern times such plays as *The Only Way* or *Charley's Aunt* or *When Knights were Bold* persist through the conservative habits of playgoers and their own vitality. The most famous lines of *The Spanish Tragedy* were parodied mercilessly again and again, but yet with a kind of affection that one feels for the oddities of a favourite teacher.

The Spanish Tragedy set a pattern for all plays of revenge; the bloody deed, the tardy revelation, the obstacles to vengeance, revenge achieved. Even Shakespeare in *Hamlet* observed and kept the pattern.

Alleyn again made a lucky find probably in the autumn of 1587.[1]

This new play was called *Tamburlaine the Great, who from a Scythian shepherd, by his rare and wonderful conquests became a most puissant and mighty monarch, and for his tyranny and terror in war, was termed 'the Scourge of God.'* It was Christopher Marlowe's first drama.[2]

Christopher Marlowe was the son of John Marlowe, shoemaker, of Canterbury, and Catherine Arthur, his wife. John Marlowe was a citizen of some standing; his wife the daughter of a Canterbury rector. They had seven children, most of whom died young. Christopher was baptized on the

[1] The date of *Tamburlaine* can be guessed fairly closely. Greene refers to it in the preface to *Perimedes* (see page 79) printed in 1588. It is not likely to have been produced before Marlowe left Cambridge in the summer of 1587; but it is not known definitely whether *The Spanish Tragedy* or *Tamburlaine* came first.

[2] The bibliography of Marlowe is considerable. The principal documents and records are printed by C. F. Tucker Brooke in The Arden Marlowe: *The Life and Dido*; *Marlowe and his Circle*, by F. S. Boas, gives the best general guide. *Christopher Marlowe*, by John Bakeless, is the latest survey of Marlowe's life. The surname is spelt variously from Marle, Marley, Marlin, Merling, Marling, Morley, to Marlo.

26th February 1564, and was thus two months older than Shakespeare.

Marlowe was brought up with four younger sisters in reasonable comfort. There is no significant record of his childhood, though Canterbury, then—as still—preserved something of the atmosphere of a holy city. It lay on the road between Dover and London; and important personages were constantly passing through. Marlowe was thus brought up in that odour of sanctity which not infrequently turns sour in later life. In 1579 he became a scholar of the King's School at Canterbury, which entitled him to dinner daily at the common table with other members of the Cathedral, and to a new gown annually.

Thence he went up to Corpus Christi College in the University of Cambridge where he matriculated on the 17th March 1581, having been awarded one of the scholarships founded by Archbishop Parker for boys of the King's School. Marlowe was entered at Corpus Christi College as a pensioner.[1]

The records of Corpus Christi College show that Marlowe received payment for his scholarship for the next six years, and spent most of his time in Cambridge. He took his B.A. degree in 1584, and then began to study for his Master's degree. A condition of his scholarship was that he should hold it for three years if he intended to follow a secular career, but that if he proposed to take Holy Orders it might be renewed for a further period of three years. It would thus appear that Marlowe at this time intended to become a cleric. In the spring of 1587 he entered the usual 'sup-

[1] At this time, and until the nineteenth century, there were three classes of student: fellow-commoners, the sons of the wealthy, who shared privileges with the fellows; pensioners or ordinary students; and sizars, poor students who performed various menial tasks in return for their keep and education. Spenser, Greene and Nashe were sizars.

plicat' or formal claim that he was now entitled to the degree. The 'grace' for the degree was granted on the 31st March 1587, but he was not entitled to receive the full degree until the following July. In the interval rumours were circulating that he, like many other disappointed graduates, was proposing to go abroad to one of the continental Catholic colleges for English students which were centres of anti-English propaganda and sedition. Actually, however, he was employed on some secret mission by the Government. This, apparently, was important, for on the 29th June, the Privy Council sent a letter to the University, commanding that the rumours should be ignored:

'Whereas it was reported that Christopher Morley was determined to have gone beyond the seas to Rheims and there to remain, their Lordships thought good to certify that he had no such intent, but that in all his actions he had behaved himself orderly and discreetly, whereby he had done her Majesty good service and deserved to be rewarded for his faithful dealing. Their Lordships' request was that the rumour thereof should be allayed by all possible means, and that he should be furthered in the degree he was to take this next Commencement; because it was not her Majesty's pleasure that any one employed as he had been in matters touching the benefit of his country should be defamed by those who are ignorant in the affairs he went about.' [1]

Shortly afterwards Tamburlaine first stalked across the stage. The play was as sensational a success as *The Spanish Tragedy*, but for quite different reasons. *Tamburlaine* was a feast of rhetoric; nothing like this had ever been heard on the stage before. Marlowe did not suffer from too much

[1] Printed in The Arden Marlowe—*The Life and Dido*, by C. F. Tucker Brooke, p. 32.

modesty, and in the Prologue to the play he made new claims for himself:

> From jigging veins of riming mother wits,
> And such conceits as clownage keeps in pay,
> We'll lead you to the stately tent of war,
> Where you shall hear the Scythian Tamburlaine
> Threatening the world with high astounding terms
> And scourging kingdoms with his conquering sword.

Critics have made much of this pronouncement, as if it were a preface to the first use of blank verse on the English stage, and as if *Tamburlaine* was entirely different from any kind of play that had gone before it. It may be so; but unfortunately so few other stage plays have survived that it is quite impossible to say how far Marlowe was a bold originator. If *The Spanish Tragedy* is earlier in date, then it shows that blank verse had already advanced considerably, for the average level of Kyd's verse is high.

On the other hand the claims made in a prologue are not necessarily more reliable than the claims made in the trailer to a modern film, which, not uncommonly, announces the most Startling, Romantic, Original, Incredible and Stupendous Spectacle that the World has ever seen, when actually the film is a poor imitation of last year's success. But certainly Alleyn never had a better part, and he made the most of it.

Marlowe was not yet a dramatist. *Tamburlaine* is the play of a man who has had little practical experience of the theatre. It is not so much drama as an epic poem, chopped up into chunks and handed round for recitation by various speakers. Most of the speeches are too long, and there is little action; but the language has a gorgeous sonority which no one else had ever touched. Marlowe certainly justified his claim of 'high astounding terms.'

The first part of the play ended with Tamburlaine falling

in love with Zenocrate, and in his declaration of love Marlowe showed what could be done with blank verse. In the second part of the play Tamburlaine continues his conquests, until Zenocrate dies and he is himself only conquered by death.

Marlowe's next play was *The Jew of Malta*. As a drama *The Jew* is a great advance. Marlowe by this time had learnt something of the theatre. He opened his play with a prologue spoken by the ghost of Machiavelli, who claims the Jew as one of his own special pupils. The prologue having withdrawn, the curtains at the back of the stage are pulled aside, and Barrabas, the Jew, is discovered in his counting-house with his treasure about him. He soliloquizes. He is no common miser. The counting of mere gold irks him.

> Give me the merchants of the Indian mines,
> That trade in metal of the purest mould;
> The wealthy Moor, that in the eastern rocks,
> Without control can pick his riches up,
> And in his house heap pearl like pebble stones,
> Receive them free, and sell them by the weight!
> Bags of fiery opals, sapphires, amethysts,
> Jacinths, hard topaz, grass-green emeralds,
> Beauteous rubies, sparkling diamonds,
> And seld-seen costly stones of so great price,
> As one of them, indifferently rated,
> And of a caract of this quantity,
> May serve, in peril of calamity,
> To ransom great kings from captivity.
> This is the ware wherein consists my wealth;
> And thus methinks should men of judgment frame
> Their means of traffic from the vulgar trade,
> And, as their wealth increaseth, so inclose
> Infinite riches in a little room.

This soliloquy shows Marlowe at his best: rich words,

full of colour, and a subtle suggestion of the speaker's character. Marlowe has passed beyond the first primitive stage of soliloquy where the villain comes forward, snarls at the audience and mutters : ' I am the villain, watch me.' There is subtlety about the character, at least in the opening scenes, and as the play continues, the personality of the Jew is developed. He is not merely the villainous miserly hater of all Christians, but a man made gigantic in hate through the wrongs which have been done to him and to his race. Unfortunately the later scenes of the play are not up to its beginning, though the plot was a good rousing melodrama. It was the first play on the ever-popular theme of a villainous foreigner, sinister, rich, unscrupulous, who finally overreaches himself. This play, too, was a success. Marlowe had amply demonstrated to the professional players that education had its value.

Marlowe indeed was always the scholar. He followed Tamburlaine's conquests on the map, and he used his sources conscientiously. He also had a sense of a theme. Both in *Tamburlaine* and *The Jew*—and later in *Dr. Faustus*—he brooded over the theme of power. In *Tamburlaine* the power came by conquest. The Jew was all-powerful because he knew how to win and to use wealth, and also because he was not confined by the moral scruples which hindered, if they did not confine, other men. Faustus sought power in universal knowledge. As the record of his life shows, there is very much of Marlowe in all these plays.

Chapter V

GREENE TURNS PLAYWRIGHT

MARLOWE was notorious in other ways. He became one of the circle of Sir Walter Ralegh's intimates who were accused of the darkest irreligion. Ralegh was much suspected. For a short while after Leicester's death in September 1588, it was generally believed by the outside world that he would become the Queen's favourite and be promoted to the Privy Council and the highest offices of State. Actually he had passed his zenith, and the Queen was already beginning to transfer her affections to the young Earl of Essex. Ralegh finally entered into the ranks of rejected courtiers in 1592, when he married one of the Queen's maids of honour secretly and not without scandal. His disgrace added to the suspicions of his enemies.

Ralegh was always unorthodox; he had no regard for common opinion or for common minds. He encouraged and attracted men of rare ability and unconventional beliefs; his circle included Henry Percy, Earl of Northumberland (known as the Wizard Earl because of his enthusiastic study of science), George Chapman, Matthew Roydon, and Thomas Harriott, one of the greatest of English mathematicians, whom Ralegh had sent as scientific observer to report on Virginia.

Marlowe became one of this coterie. Their discussions were frank, fearless and unconfined within the limits of orthodox theology and science. Ordinary and official people were disturbed. They feared many dangers which might come from a Puritan revolution at home or Jesuit treason from abroad, but at least Puritans, Anglicans and Jesuits all recognized the Scriptures as the foundation of belief, however violently they might differ in their interpretation. Only the most sinister effects could come from a society which openly made a jest of Moses and the Holy Scriptures.

Nashe rather obscurely commented on the group in *Piers Penniless*. In a digression on Pride, he spoke of the pride and self-love of deep scholars who could not be content with the old beliefs but must find new faiths of their own.

' Hence Atheists triumph and rejoice, and talk as profanely of the Bible as of Bevis of Hampton. I hear say there be mathematicians abroad, that will prove men before Adam ; and they are harboured in high places who will maintain it to the death that there are no devils.' [1]

A far more devastating denunciation was made by a Catholic writer (probably Father Robert Parsons, the most violent of the Jesuit propagandists), under the name of D. Andreas Philopater. In 1591 a very severe Edict had been promulgated against Catholics. Philopater commented upon it in a Latin treatise called *Responsio ad Elizabethæ Edictum* (1592). In the course of it Ralegh and his circle were pilloried in one enormous and breathless period, which reads thus in an English translation :

' And certainly if the popular school of Atheism of Walter Ralegh shall have made but little further progress (which he is said to maintain in his own house notoriously and publicly, with a certain necromantic astronomer as tutor, so that no small crowds of noble youth have learned to mock both the Old Law of Moses and the New Law of Christ Our Lord

[1] *The Works of Thomas Nashe*, edited by R. B. McKerrow, i, 172.

GREENE TURNS PLAYWRIGHT

with certain witty jests and quips, and to laugh at them in their society), if this school, I say, should take root and strength, and Ralegh himself should be chosen to the Senate, whereby he may direct also the business of the Commonwealth (which all expect, and not without the highest probability, since he holds first place in the Queen's eyes after Dudley and Hatton, and all see that from almost all the crowd of soldiers from Ireland he has been made chief man and powerful without any previous merits by the favour of the Queen alone); what else, I say, may be expected than that we may even see at some time some Edict ordained by that magician and epicurean tutor of Ralegh, and proclaimed in the Queen's name, whereby openly all divinity, all immortality of the soul and expectation of another life may be lucidly, clearly, briefly, and beyond a peradventure, denied, and those accused of high treason as if they were troublers of the commonwealth who have any occasion for scruple against a doctrine of that nature, so easy-going and kindly to those who wallow in the vices of the flesh.'

Shortly after, a summary of the *Responsio* was issued in English under the title of *An Advertisement written to a Secretary of my Lord Treasurer's of England, by an English Intelligencer as he passed through Germany towards Italy*. The book was printed abroad and was a cunning attempt to circulate the *Responsio* in the innocent guise of a warning to Protestants. The paragraph about Ralegh is summarized thus:

' Of Sir Walter Ralegh's school of Atheism by the way, and of the conjurer that is master thereof, and of the diligence used to get young gentlemen to this school, wherein both Moses and our Saviour, the Old and New Testaments are jested at, and the scholars taught among other things, to spell God backward.' [1]

[1] p. 18.

Anyone who belonged to such a set was likely to be a marked man : and in other ways Marlowe had been in the public eye.

In the autumn of 1589 he was in trouble with the authorities.[1] One of his friends was Thomas Watson, the poet. Watson had quarrelled with a certain William Bradley, who had sought protection from the courts against Watson because he went in fear of his life.

In the afternoon of the 18th September 1589, Bradley met Marlowe in Hog Lane, outside Cripplegate. Swords and daggers were drawn, and the two men were fighting when Watson appeared. As soon as Bradley saw Watson, he cried out : ' Art thou now come ? Then I will have a bout with thee.'

He left Marlowe, and with sword in one hand, dagger in the other, attacked Watson so furiously that he was forced to give back until he was driven to the edge of a ditch. Watson was now in great danger, and fought back desperately. He thrust at Bradley and ran him through, giving him a mortal wound on the breast. Marlowe and Watson were arrested and taken to Newgate. Next day the coroner's jury decided that Watson had killed Bradley in self-defence ; but both the accused were remanded at Newgate pending a pardon. Marlowe remained a prisoner until the 1st October 1589, when he was able to find two substantial securities who undertook in a bail of £40 that he would stand to trial. Watson was pardoned on the 10th February 1590.

Marlowe's next play was apparently *Edward the Second*. He now attempted to write one of the plays of English history which were becoming popular. As a play it was more successful than its predecessors. In Edward, Marlowe

---

[1] This episode was rescued from obscurity by Dr. Mark Eccles and published in his *Christopher Marlowe in London*.

produced a person of real character, and the play has a tragic theme. It is not merely a set of incidents.

Meanwhile Greene was still turning out novels, but as yet he had not been persuaded to write for the stage. As a University man he regarded stage players as beneath contempt; and in the 'Address to the Gentlemen Readers' of *Perimedes the Blacksmith*, 1588, he complained darkly of insults which had been offered him on the stage, but disdained to answer them except in print.

'I keep my old course,' he wrote in the 'Address to the Gentlemen Readers,' 'to palter up something in prose, using mine old poesy still, *Omne tulit punctum*; although lately two gentlemen poets made two madmen of Rome beat it out of their paper bucklers, and had it in derision, for that I could not make my verses jet upon the stage in tragical buskins, every word filling the mouth like the faburden of Bow Bell, daring God out of heaven with that atheist Tamburlaine, or blaspheming with the mad priest of the Sun; but let me rather openly pocket up the Ass at Diogenes' hand, than wantonly set out such impious instances of intolerable poetry, such mad and scoffing poets, that have prophetical spirits, as bred of Merlin's race, if there be any in England that set the end of scholarism in an English blank verse, I think either it is rather the humour of a novice that tickles them with self-love or too much frequenting the hot-house, to use the German proverb, hath sweat out all the greatest part of their wits, which wastes *gradatim*, as the Italians say, *Poco à poco*. If I speak darkly, gentlemen, and offend with this digression, I crave pardon, in that I but answer in print what they have offered on the stage.'[1]

There seems indeed to have been some kind of feud between Greene and his friends and those who were writing

[1] *Perimedes the Blacke-smith*, in *The Prose Works of Robert Greene*, edited by A. B. Grosart, vii, 8.

plays for the common stages. In the following year Greene wrote *Menaphon*, one of his best novels. It was introduced in a long and enigmatical preface by Thomas Nashe. Nashe also attacked playwrights, though when he was being deliberately obscure he succeeded impenetrably. *Menaphon* was also introduced by a poem of ' Thomas Brabine, Gent. In praise of the Author ' who repeats the challenge to the play-makers.

> Come forth you wits that vaunt the pomp of speech,
> And strive to thunder from a stage-man's throat :
> View *Menaphon* a note beyond your reach ;
> Whose sight will make your drumming descant dote :
> Players avaunt, you know not to delight :
> Welcome, sweet shepherd, worth a scholar's sight.[1]

The trouble apparently was that in Greene's opinion educated men demeaned themselves by writing for unlearned actors. The objection was not entirely free from a quite sordid jealousy because the actors were so manifestly prosperous. But Greene never suffered from the narrow-minded vice of consistency, especially when he was hard up. Within a few weeks he came to terms with the despised players. In *The Groatsworth of Wit*, which was, he admits, to a large extent his own life, he tells how Roberto, the hero of the story, was persuaded to turn dramatist. Allowing for a little writing up, the account may well be true. Roberto, having been reduced to the utmost misery and poverty, sits down by a hedge and laments his unhappy lot aloud :

' On the other side of the hedge sat one that heard his sorrow, who getting over, came towards him and brake off his passion. When he approached, he saluted Roberto in this sort.

---

[1] *Menaphon*, and *A Margaret of America*, edited by G. B. Harrison, p. 20.

' " Gentleman," quoth he, " (for so you seem), I have by chance heard you discourse some part of your grief, which appeareth to be more than you will discover, or I can conceit. But if you vouchsafe such simple comfort as my ability may yield, assure yourself that I will endeavour to do the best that either may procure you profit or bring you pleasure ; the rather for that I suppose you are a scholar, and pity it is men of learning should live in lack."

' Roberto wondering to hear such good words, for that this iron age affords few that esteem of virtue, returned him thankful gratulations, and, urged by necessity, uttered his present grief, beseeching his advice how he might be employed.

' " Why, easily," quoth he, " and greatly to your benefit ; for men of my profession get by scholars their whole living."

' " What is your profession ? " said Roberto.

' " Truly, sir," said he, " I am a player."

' " A player," quoth Roberto, " I took you rather for a gentleman of great living, for if by outward habit men should be censured, I tell you, you would be taken for a substantial man."

' " So I am where I dwell," quoth the player, " reputed able at my proper cost, to build a windmill. What though the world once went hard with me, when I was fain carry my playing fardle a foot back ; *Tempora mutantur*, I know you know the meaning of it better than I, but I thus conster it, it's otherwise now ; for my very share in playing apparel will not be sold for two hundred pounds."

' " Truly," said Roberto, " it is strange that you should so prosper in that vain practice, for it seems to me your voice is nothing gracious."

' " Nay, then," said the player, " I mislike your judgment ; why, I am as famous for Delphrigus, and the King of Fairies, as ever was any of my time. The twelve labours of Hercules have I terribly thundered on the stage, and played three scenes of the devil on the highway to Heaven."

'" Have ye so ? " said Roberto, " then I pray you pardon me."

'" Nay, more," quoth the player, " I can serve to make a pretty speech, for I was a country author, passing at a Moral, for 'twas I that penned the *Moral of Man's Wit*, the *Dialogue of Dives*, and for seven years' space was absolute interpreter of the puppets. But now my Almanack is out of date.

> ' The people make no estimation,
> Of moral's teaching education.'

Was not this pretty for a plain rhyme extempore ? If ye will ye shall have more."

'" Nay, it's enough," said Roberto, " but how mean you to use me ? "

'" Why, sir, in making plays," said the other, " for which you will be well paid, if you will take the pains."

' Roberto perceiving no remedy, thought best in respect of his present necessity, to try his wit, and went with him willingly.'[1]

Greene thus decided to swallow his pride and to turn playwright. As before when he had first set out as a novelist, he carefully considered what the public wanted. Then he got to work to imitate Marlowe's style as closely as he could. His first play was apparently *The Comical*[2] *History of Alphonsus, King of Aragon*. The play is not so bad as the few critics who have read it have declared. As a crude melodrama intended for unsophisticated and gaping groundlings, it had its merits. Greene had always a shrewd

---

[1] *The Groatsworth of Wit*, in *Bodley Head Quartos*, vi, 32.

[2] ' Comical ' at this date means ' not tragical ' ; there was, as yet, no suggestion of intentional hilarity in the word.

idea of the tastes of his admirers. He easily caught the crudities of the *Tamburlaine* style. It was not difficult. Its grandeurs eluded him; but he had instinctively realized the possibilities of the stage, and that in a drama the eye needs feeding as much as the ear. *Alphonsus* survives in three copies only. It was printed by Thomas Creede in 1599. The text is interesting because of its stage directions, which suggest that it was printed direct from an author's manuscript and that he was rather a literary man, visualizing his play, than anyone actually writing in the theatre itself.

Greene opened with an induction, one of the first surviving specimens of those literary critical inductions which had a revived vogue ten years later. He began with the stage direction:

After you have sounded thrice, let Venus be let down from the top of the stage, and when she is down, say : . . .

'Poets are scarce,' she begins, and therefore the deeds of Alphonsus have not received their due. She will take their place. Hereupon:

Enter Melpomene, Clio, Erato, with their sisters, playing all upon sundry instruments, Calliope only excepted, who coming last, hangeth down the head, and plays not of her instrument.

The Muses wrangle, and then agree that they will go with Venus to the top of Parnassus hill

> . . . And there together do our best devoir
> For to describe Alphonsus' warlike fame:
> And in the manner of a Comedy,
> Set down his noble valour presently.

Then the play begins. Carinus, true but exiled King of Aragon, confides in his son Alphonsus, who is fired to doughty deeds. He is disguised as a common soldier. He overcomes Albinius, who had thought him dead, but becomes his sworn and loyal vassal. Albinius, without revealing his true name, shows him to Belinus, King of Naples. Alphonsus offers to serve the King, who is at war with the usurping King of Aragon as long as he may keep whatever he wins by his sword. Alphonsus slays the usurper and claims his reward. Belinus reluctantly crowns him King of Aragon. Not content with that, Alphonsus immediately demands that Belinus shall do him homage. The King is not unnaturally annoyed. Wars follow, and Belinus is forced to run away. He flees to Amurack, the Turkish King, and seeks his aid. The action then shifts to Amurack's court.

Greene had a fancy for the occult in his plays. Amurack is lulled asleep by Medea (whose presence here is surprising), as his wife Fausta and Iphigina his daughter sit by. Medea conjures, calls up the spirit of Calchas, and by her charms, Amurack in his sleep foretells the future: that Alphonsus will destroy Belinus and his army, and ultimately marry Iphigina. If well played, this would make a very effective scene. The two ladies are so angry at this revelation that they rage at him. He wakes and drives them away from him in fury. They fly from the court and raise an army of Amazons to fight Alphonsus.

The fourth Act begins, after an explanatory prologue by Venus, with another occult scene:

Let there be a brazen Head set in the middle of the place behind the stage, out of the which cast flames of fire, drums rumble within.

The head—it is Mahomet's—speaks, rebuking the Turks for their dilatoriness. The Act ends with the defeat of Amurack, or as explained in the stage directions:

Amurack draw thy sword: Alphonsus and all the other Kings draw theirs: strike up alarum: fly Amurack and his company. Follow Alphonsus and his company.

The last Act, after brief intervention by Venus who explains that Alphonsus was victor, begins:

Strike up alarum: fly Amurack, follow Alphonsus, and

take him prisoner : carry him in. Strike up alarum : fly Crocon and Faustus. Enter Fausta and Iphigina, with their army, and meet them :

Iphigina then tries her luck, and at once makes Alphonsus flee. She overtakes him and they stand facing each other. Alphonsus is infected with love. He asks her to marry him, promising her vast power and wealth. She scorns his offer. He is enraged :

> Nay then, proud peacock, since thou art so stout
> As that entreaty will not move thy mind
> For to consent to be my wedded spouse,
> Thou shalt, in spite of Gods and Fortune too,
> Serve high Alphonsus as a concubine.
> IPHIGINA : I'll rather die than ever that shall hap.
> ALPHONSUS : And thou shalt die unless it come to pass.

His blood is up, and he pursues her lustily from the field. All his enemies are now captives and they are paraded before him, bound. Alphonsus promises to release Amurack and Fausta if they will consent to bestow Iphigina on him. But the great-hearted Turk spits back defiance, and things look black for his family.

At this point old Carinus appears clad in pilgrim's weeds. He quickly takes in the situation and realizes that his son's knowledge of women is elementary and his wooing too precipitate. With a little persuasion he makes Iphigina (who has something of Pamela in her nature) confess that as his wife she is prepared to love Alphonsus. Fausta agrees, but Amurack's consent is also necessary. He is brought back. After a brief internal struggle, in which he weighs up the alternatives, he decides that since Alphonsus is after all a king's son, and not, as he had supposed, a beggar's brat, he may with decency hand Iphigina over to him. All ends happily. Venus collects the Muses once more and bids them farewell, after which :

Exit Venus : or if you can conveniently, let a chair come down from the top of the stage and draw her up.

Greene then wrote *A Looking Glass for London*, in which he collaborated with Thomas Lodge. Lodge also had seen life. He was about the same age as Greene, and the son of a wealthy city merchant. His father had distinguished himself by becoming Lord Mayor of London and then going bankrupt. The son also had been imprisoned for debt. After this he had gone voyaging. The collaboration produced an excellent melodrama which would make a perfect scenario for a Hollywood film. There is everything here to delight the Saturday night film-goer : luxury, magnificence, luscious scenes of illicit love, magic and mystery, rowdy scenes, tavern scenes, a first-class clown, a song or two, the highest of moral lessons, and an edifying conclusion.

The story dramatizes the Book of Jonah with details filled up from imagination and the bitter personal experiences of the authors. It starts well. Rasni, King of Nineveh, falls in love with his sister, and insists on marrying her. The wedding is to be sumptuous and magnificent, and, lacking modern stage equipment and capital, Greene provided the luxury in poetry.

> Lordings, I'll have my wedding sumptuous,
> Made glorious with the treasures of the world.
> I'll fetch from Albia shelves of margarites,
> And strip the Indies of their diamonds,
> And Tyre shall yield me tribute of her gold,
> To make Remilia's wedding glorious.
> I'll send for all the damsel Queens that live
> Within the reach of Rasni's government,
> To wait as handmaids on Remilia,
> That her attendant train may pass the troop
> That gloried Venus at her wedding day.

The King and his train having departed, the prophet

Oseas is wafted on to the scene by an angel, and ' set down over the stage in a throne,' where he looks on and comments austerely at every pause in the action. The general wickedness of the Ninevites is then shown in a series of realistic prose scenes : the clown, the smith's man, comes in with ruffianly companions on the way to a debauch in the tavern : the usurer tricks a young gentleman of his money, and a poor old man of his cow.

Then comes the magnificent scene of Remilia's marriage. She is tricked out in her fine clothes, painted and perfumed, and waits for the bridegroom. Rasni approaches, commands his magi to produce an arbour for his love, but lightning comes from heaven, and Remilia is struck dead and black.

The debtors try to obtain justice from the usurer, but the judge is bribed and they are foiled. The clown and his crew get so drunk that a murder is committed. King Rasni consoles himself with Alvida, the wife of the King of Paphlagonia, whom she forthwith poisons, to the delight of Rasni. From the gallery Oseas underlines the moral :

> London, behold the cause of others' wrack,
> And see the sword of justice at thy back.
> Defer not off, to-morrow is too late ;
> By night he comes perhaps to judge thy state.

At this point Jonah, the prophet, is introduced. The Angel summons him from Nineveh, and he books his passage. The victims of the usurer are reduced to poverty. Their son Radagon, who is now become pimp to the King, scorns them, but his old father curses him ' and a flame of fire appeareth and Radagon is swallowed.' The clown makes love to his master's wife and drives him out. Then come in the merchants of Tarsus and some sailors, wet from the sea, to relate how Jonah was heaved overboard.

The next scene begins with the direction : *Jonas,*

the prophet, cast out of the whale's belly upon the stage, a dramatic entry which stirs the curiosity about the mechanics of its production ; for this was plainly no common entrance. The wickedness of Nineveh is now reaching its climax. Alvida ' in rich attire ' encourages the King of Cilicia to be her lover, but judiciously faints when Rasni approaches and so deceives him. Signs and portents accumulate. The priests of the Sun warn Rasni of doom to come : *A hand from out a cloud threateneth a burning sword.* Wickedness abounds, and then Jonah appears and at once calls on the men of Nineveh to repent. His preachings amongst the people are immediately successful ; in the palace Rasni and Alvida and the Court hold a riotous banquet. Drink flows. Jonah enters and cries out his message :

> Repent, repent, ye men of Nineveh, repent,
> The Lord hath spoke, and I do cry it out,
> There are as yet but forty days remaining,
> And then shall Nineveh be overthrown,
> Repent, ye men of Nineveh, repent !

Rasni and his courtiers are overcome with remorse ; the usurer repents ; everyone makes for the temple. The King ordains a fast.

Only the clown is unmoved. He comes in wearing a huge pair of slops. Down one leg he has hidden a bottle of beer, down the other a great hunk of beef. He has no use for the King's proclamation. He could prettily away with praying, but for fasting, 'tis so contrary to his nature that he would rather suffer a long hanging than a short fast. ' And yet in faith,' he muses, ' I need not find fault with the proclamation, for I have a buttery and a pantry and a kitchen about me. For proof, *ecce signum* ! this right slop is my pantry—behold a manchet (*draws it out*) ; this place is my kitchen, for, lo, a piece of beef (*draws it out*). Oh, let me repeat that sweet word again : " For, lo ! a piece of beef." This is my buttery, for see, see, my friends, to my great joy, a bottle of beer (*draws it out*). Thus, alas, I make shift to wear out this fasting ; I drive away the time ; but there go searchers about to seek if any man breaks the King's command. O, here they be, in with your victuals, Adam ' (*puts them back into his slops*).

Enter two Searchers.

1st Searcher. How duly the men of Nineveh keep the proclamation ! How are they armed to repentance ! We have searched through the whole city and have not as yet found one that breaks the fast.

2nd Searcher. The sign of the more grace. But stay, here sits one, methinks at his prayers ; let us see who it is.

1st Searcher. 'Tis Adam, the smith's man. How now, Adam ?

Clown. Trouble me not : ' Thou shalt take no manner of food, but fast and pray.'

1st Searcher. How devoutly he sits at his orisons ! But, stay, methinks I feel a smell of some meat or bread about him.

2nd Searcher. So thinks me too. You, sirrah, what victuals have you about you ?

Clown. Victuals ! Oh horrible blasphemy ! Hinder me not of my prayer, nor drive me not into a choler. Victuals ! Why, heardst thou not the sentence, ' Thou shalt take no food, but fast and pray ' ?

The searchers nevertheless feel him, and in spite of his plea that ' *modicum non nocet ut medicus daret* ' they carry him off to be hanged.

So Nineveh repents and all the sinners make amends. Rasni and Alvida are respectably married ; the usurer returns the goods that he has embezzled.

Then Jonah comes forward to the edge of the stage to underline the lesson once more : As Nineveh, so London ; an adulterous town, full of corruption, whoredom, drunkenness and pride. . . .

London, awake, for fear the Lord do frown;
I set a looking glass before thine eyes.
O turn, O turn, with weeping to the Lord,
And think the prayers and virtues of thy Queen
Defers the plague which otherwise would fall.
Repent, O London, lest for thine offence
Thy shepherd fail, whom Mighty God preserve,
That she may bide the pillar of His Church
Against the storms of Romish Antichrist.
The hand of Mercy overshed her head,
And let all faithful subjects say, Amen.

Marlowe might write the mightier line, but here were two experts who knew just how to plan a two hours' entertainment which would keep the audience thrilled and happy, to send them away well-filled and feeling good.

Greene's next play apparently was called *Orlando Furioso*. It contained a fat part for Alleyn, and Greene imitated the verse of Tamburlaine closely, so that the play is full of those rhetorical braveries in which Marlowe delighted, but it lacks any speech of distinction. There is less action and more talk than in the other plays. It gave Alleyn a typical part, for Orlando is by turns warrior, lover and lunatic, and furious in each guise. On the whole it is an uninteresting play, except that Sacrepant, the villain, is a faint shadow of later and greater villains to come.

It may be, however, that Greene has been wronged by the printer, for the text which was first published in 1594 is very bad.[1] During the lean months following the plague of 1592 and 1593 the players sold many play-books to the printers, and neither party was always too scrupulous of the

[1] There are several matters of bibliographical interest in *Orlando Furioso*. The actual script of Alleyn's part in the play exists in the Dulwich Collection, and is reprinted in the *Henslowe Papers*, p. 155. Dr. Greg also examined text and script in 'Two Elizabethan Stage Abridgments: *The Battle of Alcazar* and *Orlando Furioso*," Malone Society, 1922.

author's interests in the matter, for most of the texts then published were careless and corrupt.

Another of Greene's plays was *The Honourable History of Friar Bacon and Friar Bungay*, which was first played by the Queen's Men. Again Greene chose an occult theme. *Friar Bacon* was his most ambitious and varied play. In it he combined several stories, and mixed the moods with some skill, giving contrast of emotions and situations. The story was vaguely historical. Roger Bacon was real enough, but round his name had gathered many legends. Edward, Prince of Wales, who married Eleanor of Castile, was likewise historical, but the story of the play, including the love of the knight of high degree for the lowly maiden, was all legend. Greene shamelessly gave his creatures historical names to enhance their interest with an uncritical and unlearned audience. In one way the play was an innovation. For the first time in English drama there appears a new atmosphere, idyllic, pastoral and yet English. Greene had evoked this atmosphere in his novels, but usually it was set in Arcadia. Now he brought it on to the English stage. He opened with Prince Edward, deep in a dump because of his love for fair Margaret, the keeper's daughter of Freshingfield, but roused to vent his feelings in an ecstatic description of her charms :

> When as she swept like Venus through the house,
> And in her shape fast folded up my thoughts,
> Into the milkhouse went I with the maid,
> And there amongst the cream bowls she did shine,
> As Pallas 'mongst her princely housewifery.
> She turned her smock over her lily arms,
> And dived them into milk to run her cheese :
> But, whiter than the milk, her crystal skin,
> Checked with lines of azure, made her blush,
> That art or nature durst bring for compare.

The story was far from new. Lacey must woo the girl for the Prince, but he is in love himself, and wins her in disguise, to be his own wife. But Margaret is another of Greene's Good Girls, and therefore she must endure a deal of sorrow before it all comes right in the end. Prince Edward is shown the love of Lacey and Margaret through Friar Bacon's magic glass, and just as Bungay is about to marry them, Bacon's magic interposes and the Friar is struck dumb. So Margaret must have another disappointment, when Lacey pretends that he is finished with her, and sends his man with gold to recompense her disappointments. To one of her nature there are only two possible sequels—the cloister or suicide. Fortunately she chooses the cloister, and Lacey is able to rescue her from the irrevocable in the nick of time.

This story is broken up into episodes by a series of scenes showing the legend of Friar Bacon. Bacon vindicates English learning at the Court of King Henry. Before the King and the Emperor, Friar Bungay and the German magician Vandermast show off their skill. Bungay conjures the tree of the Hesperides with dragons shooting fire. Vandermast counters by calling up Hercules to break down Bungay's tree. At this moment Greene achieves a fine dramatic effect; Vandermast begins to brag of his prowess. Bacon enters and takes no notice of him. The bombastic German is decisively deflated. He asks in an awe-struck voice:

'What art thou that questions thus?'

The reply is in four words—'Men call me Bacon.'

It is enough.

Greene was the first dramatist to discover the effect of restraint.

Greene continued with other stories of Bacon; how he made a brazen head which should prophesy; and how the moment comes when Bacon and Bungay have watched for sixty days, and Bacon cannot keep awake any longer, but must needs leave the watching to Miles, his pupil. And then the head speaks thrice, to Miles's infinite contempt: 'Time is,' 'Time was,' 'Time is past.'

It might have been a solemn moment, but Greene made it wholly comical, for to him there was no deep tragic significance in Bacon's occult studies. Miles is dismissed, and ultimately encounters one of his master's devils. He puts on spurs, mounts the devil's back, and rides off triumphant to hell. Meanwhile Bacon is brought to a sudden realization of the evil of necromancy. By means of his glass he shows two young scholars that their fathers are fighting to the death. The youths fall on each other, and all are killed. So Bacon breaks his glass, prays for forgiveness, and turns henceforward to pure devotion. It is a very different mood and treatment from Marlowe's handling of the grimmer story of Dr. Faustus.

And so to a spectacular ending, with Lacey married to Margaret, and the State Wedding of Edward and Eleanor.

After the Queen's Men had dispersed the play was taken over by the Admiral's and played at the Rose with considerable success.[1]

[1] *Friar Bacon* gives another warning against jumping to hasty conclusions. There are a number of parallels between *Friar Bacon* and *Dr. Faustus* which could hardly be accidental. A long line of critics have argued that since Marlowe was the greater poet, Greene must have been the imitator: *argal, Friar Bacon* was later in date than *Dr. Faustus*. And this belief would have persisted had it not been shown that Marlowe's *Dr. Faustus* was written in 1592 (see page 114).

Chapter VI

THE DEATH OF GREENE

IN the first weeks of 1592 there was great activity at the Rose Theatre, which was owned by Philip Henslowe. Edward Alleyn was coming to play there with Lord Strange's Men. Henslowe had started life in the leather trade as apprentice to a certain Master Woodward, and thereafter followed the course marked out for the good apprentice. When his master died, he married the widow, and took over the considerable property which had accumulated. Henslowe had various ventures. He raised money by pawnbroking, and as a landlord he collected his rents from brothels. About five years earlier he had built the Rose Theatre on the Bankside.

The coming of Alleyn to the Rose was an important event in the history of Elizabethan drama and of the stage. Alleyn stayed. A few months later he married Joan Woodward, Henslowe's step-daughter, and thereafter the two men worked together. When Henslowe died he left his property to Alleyn, and when Alleyn died a rich man in 1626, he left much of his property, together with his books, pictures and papers, to his foundation, Dulwich College, where, by extreme good fortune, they still remain. The Henslowe Papers are the most important collection of documents in the history of the English stage. Amongst them is Henslowe's *Diary*, his account-book for the years 1592–1602. In the earlier part of the *Diary* Henslowe recorded the plays acted daily at his playhouse and the money which he received. Later he became banker for the players who acted at his playhouse, and then recorded the sums laid out for plays, costumes, properties, licences, and the like.

Lord Strange's Men began their season on the 19th February. Their first plays were Greene's *Friar Bacon*, *Muly Mulocco*, Greene's *Orlando*, Kyd's *Spanish Tragedy*, *Sir John Mandeville*, *Harry of Cornwall*, Marlowe's *Jew of Malta*, *Chloris and Orgasto*, *Pope Joan*, and *Machiavel*. On the 3rd March, Henslowe's receipts suddenly leaped up from an average of about 25*s*. an afternoon to £3 16*s*. 8*d*. The occasion was a new play called *Harry the Sixth*. It was apparently the work of a new writer called William Shakespeare.[1]

Meanwhile Greene seems to have ceased writing for theatres. The conny catching books were doing very well. *The Notable Discovery* had been reprinted. The *Second Part of Conny Catching* also was popular, and was reprinted almost at once as the *Second and Last Part of Conny Catching*.

The Notable Discovery dealt chiefly with card sharping, 'cross-biting' (that is, the various ways by which gentlemen of means were lured into brothels and there robbed), and the tricks of colliers who gave short weight. Greene's method was to write a short account of the particular form of rascality, and then to illustrate it by sundry merry tales. The moral tone which was conspicuous in the first part disappeared as the series went on. At first Greene's friends and admirers were a little uneasy. *The Notable Discovery* was written in a plain, straightforward style; and hitherto

[1] The facts of Shakespeare's early life are fragmentary, and scholars interpret them diversely. Some believe that he began to write as early as 1587, others (to which party I belong), that this is his first appearance as a dramatist. It is not likely that there were two popular *Henry the Sixth* plays and, as the receipts in the *Diary* and Nashe's remarks (see p. 100) show, it was a popular play.

they had admired Greene for the elaborate artificiality of his prose. In the *Second Part* he met their criticisms :

' Here, by the way, give me leave to answer an objection, that some inferred against me ; which was that I showed no eloquent phrases, nor fine figurative conveyance in my first book as I had done in other of my works. To which I reply that το πρεπον, a certain decorum, is to be kept in everything, and not to apply a high style in a base subject. Beside, the faculty is so odious, and the men so servile and slavish minded, that I should dishonour that high mystery of eloquence, and derogate from the dignity of our English tongue, either to employ any figure or bestow one choice English word upon such disdained rakehells as those Conny Catchers. Therefore humbly I crave pardon, and desire I may write basely of such base wretches who live only to live dishonestly.' [1]

In the *Third and Last Part of Conny Catching*, which was entered on the 7th February 1592, Greene claimed that he was retailing actual instances which were founded on the experiences and the observations of a City magistrate.

By this time, so he declared, the conny catchers were becoming alarmed and prepared for counter-attack. If true, it was a good advertisement. On the 21st April *The Defence of Conny Catching* was entered. It claimed to be written by ' Cuthbert Conny Catcher,' and the device printed on the title page was a rabbit rampant, defending itself with sword and buckler, a gauntlet flung down in challenge at its feet.[2]

' Cuthbert Conny Catcher ' took the line that Greene

[1] The *Second Part of Conny Catching*, in *Bodley Head Quartos*, i, 7.

[2] Some critics, notably M. Pruvost, believe that Greene himself was the author of the pamphlet ; and certainly there are some mysteries about it. M. Pruvost argues the case at length in Chapter XI, section iii, of his book.

was concerning himself only with the small fry, and dared not touch the real robbers of the commonwealth. He further added a hint that unless Greene ceased his disclosures, he would find himself in trouble. He then proceeded to tell a number of merry (and very ribald) tales of his own.

Greene, however, was not deterred. His next pamphlet was *A Disputation between a He Conny Catcher and a She Conny Catcher whether a thief or a whore is most hurtful in cozenage to the Commonwealth*. The lady wins the argument.

This time Greene did not hesitate to give names. The conny catchers, he declared, had tried to kill him. ' All the crew,' he said, ' have protested my death, and to prove they meant good earnest, they beleaguered me about in the Saint John's Head within Ludgate, being at supper. There were fourteen or fifteen of them met, and thought to have made that the fatal night of my overthrow, but that the courteous citizens and apprentices took my part; and so two or three of them were carried to the Counter, although a gentleman in my company was sore hurt. I cannot deny but they begin to waste away about London, and Tyburn (since the setting out of my book) hath eaten up many of them, and I will plague them to the extremity. Let them do what they will with their bilbo blades, I fear them not. And to give them their last adieu, look shortly, countrymen, for a pamphlet against them, called *The Black Book*. . . . Beside, you shall see there what houses there be about the suburbs and town's end, that are receivers of cutpurses' stolen goods, lifts and such like. And lastly, look for a bead-roll or catalogue of all the names of the foists, nips, lifts and priggers in and about London : and although some say I dare not do it, yet I will shortly set it abroad, and whosoever I name or touch, if he think himself grieved, I will answer him before the honourable Privy Council.' [1]

[1] *A Disputation*, etc., in *Bodley Head Quartos*, iii, 40.

To the *Disputation* Greene added an account of 'the conversion of an English Courtesan reformed this present year 1592.' It was a very edifying story. A young clothier, falling genuinely in love with the courtesan, seeks to convert her. He comes to her as a customer, but he demands complete darkness, and will not easily be satisfied. At length she leads him to an attic. 'Somebody may by fortune see us,' says he. 'In faith,' she answers, 'none but God.' The young man, seizing on this cue, gives her such an effective discourse that she repents, and afterwards marries him. It was a moving tale and well told. Unfortunately it was not a new tale: a similar repentance had already been attributed to Thais, mistress of Alexander the Great. The young clothier may perhaps have been well read, but more probably Greene was merely being a good journalist.

Greene's promise to produce a *Black Book* was exciting, both to the general public and to the conny catchers. On the 21st August there was entered in the Stationers' Register, *The Repentance of a Conny Catcher, with the Life and Death of Mourton and Ned Brown, two noble Conny Catchers, the one lately executed at Tyburn, the other at Aix in France.* Whatever may have been his motives in the beginning, by this time Greene had realized that the conny catching pamphlets were best sellers. After the books had been entered in the Register *The Life and Death of Ned Brown* was issued as a separate volume, with the exciting title of *The Black Book's Messenger,* in the hope of catching the unwary. But the supply of London tales was now running short, and most of Ned Brown's exploits are manifest fictions. Some indeed were borrowed from his enemies' *Defence of Conny Catching.*

Greene and Nashe were seeing a good deal of each other at this time. Nashe had just completed one of the most popular and successful of all Elizabethan pamphlets. It was called *Piers Penniless, His Supplication to the Devil.* The book was entered on the 8th August 1592 ; three editions came out in 1592, a fourth in 1593, and a fifth in 1595. *Piers Penniless* was a rambling, digressive satire on anything and everything that interested English readers in the summer of 1592, from usurers, drunkards and Scottish witches to the late Martinist excitements.

In form it was a letter to the Devil. Piers, finding that no one cares for poor scholars, now that Sir Philip Sidney is dead, draws up a petition to the Devil to remove some of the old usurers that money may flow more freely ; but the Devil is busy in the north, where King James of Scotland has been weighing the truth of the astonishing revelations of the Berwick witches. So Piers gives his petition to a Knight of the Post—a professional perjurer—as one likely to know where to find the Devil at all times.

The supplication itself was a return in form to the old allegory of the Seven Deadly Sins, under each of which Nashe was able to gather modern representatives to be chastised in his own peculiar and fruity verbosity. The sin of sloth brought him to plays ; the enemy of sloth is emulation.

' That State or Kingdom that is in league with all the world, and hath no foreign sword to vex it, is not half so strong or confirmed to endure as that which lives every hour in fear of invasion. There is a certain waste of the people for whom there is no use but war ; and these men must have some employment still to cut them off : *Nam si foras hostem non habent, domi invenient* ; if they have no service abroad, they will make mutinies at home. Or if the affairs of the State be such as cannot exhale all these corrupt excrements, it is very expedient they have some light toys to busy their heads withal, cast before them as bones to gnaw upon, which may keep them from having leisure to intermeddle with higher matters.

'To this effect, the policy of plays is very necessary, howsoever some shallow brained censurers (not the deepest searchers into the secrets of government) mightily oppugn them. For whereas the afternoon being the idlest time of the day, wherein men that are their own masters (as gentlemen of the Court, the Inns of the Court, and the number of captains and soldiers about London) do wholly bestow themselves upon pleasure, and that pleasure they divide (how virtuously it skills not) either into gaming, following of harlots, drinking, or seeing a play. Is it not then better (since of four extremes all the world cannot keep them but they will choose one) that they should betake them to the least, which is plays? Nay, what if I prove plays to be no extreme, but a rare exercise of virtue? First, for the subject of them (for the most part) it is borrowed out of our English Chronicles, wherein our forefathers' valiant acts (that have lain long buried in rusty brass and worm-eaten books) are revived, and they themselves raised from the grave of Oblivion and brought to plead their aged honours in open presence; than which, what can be a sharper reproof to these degenerate effeminate days of ours?

'How would it have joyed brave Talbot (the terror of the French) to think that after he had lain two hundred years in his tomb, he should triumph again on the stage, and have his bones new embalmed with the tears of ten thousand spectators at least (at several times) who in the tragedian that represents his person, imagine they behold him fresh bleeding?

'I will defend it against any collian or clubfisted usurer of them all, there is no immortality can be given a man on earth like unto plays. What talk I to them of immortality, that are the only underminers of honour, and do envy any man that is not sprung up by base brokery like themselves? They care not if all the ancient houses were rooted out, so that, like the Burgomasters of the Low Countries, they might share the government amongst them as States, and be quartermasters of our monarchy. All arts to them are vanity; and if you tell them what a glorious thing it is to have Henry the Fifth represented on the stage, leading the French King prisoner and forcing both him and the Dolphin to swear fealty. " Ay, but," will they say, " what do we get by it?" Respecting neither the right of Fame that is due to true nobility deceased, nor what hopes of eternity are to be proposed to adventurous minds to encourage them forward, but only their execrable lucre and filthy unquenchable avarice.

'They know when they are dead they shall not be brought upon the stage for any goodness, but in a merriment of the Usurer and the Devil, or buying arms of the Herald, who gives them the lion without tongue, tail or talons, because his master whom he must serve is a townsman and a man of peace, and must not keep any quarrelling beasts to annoy his honest neighbours.

'In plays, all cozenages, all cunning drifts overgilded with outward holiness, all stratagems of war, all the cankerworms that breed on the rust of peace, are most lively anatomized: they show the ill success of treason, the fall of hasty climbers, the wretched end of usurpers, the misery of civil dissension, and how just God is evermore in punishing of murder. And to prove every one of these allegations, could I propound the circumstances of this play and that play, if I meant to handle this theme otherwise than *obiter*. What should I say more? They are sour pills of reprehension, wrapped up in sweet words. Whereas some petitioners of the Council against them object, they corrupt the youth of the City and withdraw 'prentices from their work; they heartily wish they might be troubled with none of their youth nor their 'prentices; for some of them (I mean the ruder handicrafts' servants) never come abroad, but they are in danger of undoing; and as for corrupting them when they come, that's false; for no play they have encourageth any man to tumults or rebellion, but lays before such the halter and the gallows; or praiseth or approveth pride, lust, whoredom, prodigality or drunkenness, but beats them down utterly. As for the hindrance of trades and traders of the City by them, that is an article foisted in by the vintners, alewives and victuallers, who surmise, if there were no plays, they should have all the company that resort to them lie boozing and beer-bathing in their houses every afternoon. Nor so, nor so, good brother bottle-ale; for there are other places besides where money can bestow itself. The sign of the smock will wipe your mouth clean; and yet I have heard ye have made her a tenant to your tap-houses. But what shall he do that hath spent himself? Where shall he haunt? Faith, when Dice, Lust, and Drunkenness and all have dealt upon him, if there be never a play for him to go to for his penny, he sits melancholy in his chamber, devising upon felony or treason, and how he may best exalt himself by mischief.'[1]

It was the most vigorous counter-attack against the enemies of the players ever penned; and it caused sufficient stir for even the Common Council of the City to notice it. When next they complained against plays they deigned to consider Nashe's arguments.

Meanwhile Greene had also tried his hand at this kind of fiction. He too reverted to social satire in the form of allegory. On the 21st July was entered *A Quip for an Upstart Courtier or A Dispute between Cloth Breeches and Velvet Breeches*, in which the old-fashioned countryman

[1] *Piers Penniless*, edited by R. B. McKerrow, i, 211–14.

and the new-fangled courtier describe their own particular merits.

It happened that Gabriel Harvey's brother Richard, who unluckily ventured to publish an *Astrological Discourse*, fell foul of Greene and his friends. He had even been so rash as to refer to poets and writers in London who had taken part in the Marprelate business as ' piperly make-plays and make-bates.'

Harvey's father was a well-known rope-maker at Saffron Walden, and so Greene introduced a passage on the family.

' " And whither are you agoing," quoth I ?

' " Marry sir," quoth he, " first to absolve your question, I dwell in Saffron Walden, and am going to Cambridge to three sons I keep there at school, such apt children, sir, as few women have groaned for, and yet they have ill luck. The one, sir, is a divine, to comfort my soul ; and he indeed though he be a vainglorious ass, as divers youths of his age be, is well given to the show of the world, and writ a late *The Lamb of God*, and yet his parishioners say he is a limb of the devil, and kisseth their wives with holy kisses ; but they had rather he should keep his lips for Madge his mare. The second, sir, is a physician or a fool, but indeed a physician, and had proved a proper man if he had not spoiled himself with his astrological discourse of the terrible conjunction of Saturn and Jupiter. For the eldest, he is a civilian, a wondrous witted fellow, sir reverence sir, he is a Doctor, and as Tubalcain was the first inventor of music, so he, God's benison light upon him, was the first that invented English hexameter. But see how in these days learning is little esteemed, for that and other familiar letters and proper treatises he was orderly clapped in the Flect. But, sir, a hawk and a kite may bring forth a coystrel, and honest parents may have bad children."

' "Honest with the devil," quoth the collier.'[1]

When the book appeared in print Greene was uneasy. Harvey, for all his faults, had influential friends, and the slander was gross, though Nashe declared that Greene had been persuaded by his doctor to revise the book. Accordingly the passage was suppressed in most copies.

Gabriel Harvey was goaded beyond endurance. He had business in London and he determined to claim damages from Greene for slander; but he was too late.

Greene's life had always been gay. Early in August he and Thomas Nashe and one Will Monox met together and gorged themselves on pickled herrings and Rhenish wine. It was not good fare for one whose organs were already overtaxed. The plague was about. The players had gone into the country; Nashe followed them; Greene was left alone. He was quite penniless. In this state he suffered agonies of remorse for his wasted life, his only consolation being that he might have done some good by laying open the most horrible cozenages and common conny catchers, cozeners and cross-biters. Indeed, but for the charity of those who gave him lodging, he would have starved to death in the streets. The thought of his deserted wife tormented him sorely.

'But, oh my dear wife,' he lamented, 'whose sight and company I have refrained these six years, I ask God and thee forgiveness for so greatly wronging thee, of whom I seldom or never thought until now. Pardon me, I pray you, wheresoever thou art, and God forgive me all my offences.'[2]

Accordingly he wrote a letter begging her to take care of their son. Shortly afterwards a friend came in to say that

---

[1] This passage exists only in one extant copy, now in the Huntington Library. In Grosart's edition of *Greene's Works* (xi, 259) the passage should have occurred after 'other cause pretended' (line 25).

[2] *Repentance*, p. 26.

she sent him her commendations, and in answer he sent a farewell letter:

'Sweet wife, As ever there was any good will or friendship between thee and me, see this bearer (my host) satisfied of his debt. I owe him ten pounds, and but for him I had perished in the streets. Forget and forgive my wrongs done unto thee, and Almighty God have mercy on my soul. Farewell till we meet in heaven, for on earth thou shalt never see me more. This 2 of September, 1592.

Written by thy dying husband,
ROBERT GREENE.'[1]

He died a few hours afterwards.

When Gabriel Harvey heard that his enemy was dead, he hurried down to Greene's lodging to learn at first hand from the neighbours the particulars of Greene's last hours. The lurid details of the deathbed scene gave him great satisfaction. Two days later he wrote a long account of what he had seen and heard to his friend, Master Christopher Bird of Saffron Walden, which he afterwards had the vile taste to publish, with much unctuous gloating and moralizing by the way.

'I was suddenly certified that the King of the Paper Stage (so the gentleman termed Greene) had played his last part, and was gone to Tarlton; whereof, I protest, I was nothing glad, as was expected, but unfeignedly sorry; as well because I could have wished he had taken his leave with a more charitable farewell; as also because I was deprived of that remedy in law that I intended of him in the behalf of my father, whose honest reputation I have many duties to tender. Yet to some conceited wit, that could take delight to discover knaveries, or were a fit person to augment the History of Conny catchers, O Lord, what a pregnant occasion were here presented to display lewd vanity in his

[1] *Repentance.*, p. 32.

lively colours, and to decipher the very mysteries of that base art. Petty cozeners are not worth the naming: he, they say, was the Monarch of Cross-biters and the very Emperor of Shifters.'[1]

After a crescendo of abuse,[2] Harvey continued self-righteously:

'Truely I have been ashamed to hear some ascertained reports of his most woeful and rascal estate: how the wretched fellow, or shall I say the Prince of beggars, laid all to gage for some few shillings: and was attended by lice: and would pitifully beg a penny-pot of Malmesy: and could not get any of his old acquaintance to comfort or visit him in his extremity but Mistress Appleby and the mother of Infortunatus. Alas, even his fellow-writer, a proper young man, if advised in time, that was a principal guest at that fatal banquet of pickled herring (I spare his name, and in some respects wish him well), came never more at him: but either would not, or happily could not perform the duty of an affectionate and faithful friend. The poor Cordwainer's wife was his only nurse, and the mother of Infortunatus his sole companion, but when Mistress Appleby came, as much to expostulate injuries with her as to visit him. God help good fellows when they cannot help themselves. Slender relief in the predicament of privations and feigned habits. Miserable man, that must perish or be succoured by counterfeit or impotent supplies. I once bemoaned the decayed and blasted estate of M. Gascoigne, who wanted not some commendable parts of conceit and endeavour, but unhappy M. Gascoigne, how lordly happy in comparison of most unhappy M. Greene? He never envied me so much as I pitied him from my heart, especially when his hostess Isam,

---

[1] *Four letters and certain Sonnets, especially touching Robert Greene and other parties by him abused*, in *Bodley Head Quartos*, ii, 18.
[2] Quoted on p. 60.

THE DEATH OF GREENE

with tears in her eyes, and sighs from a deeper fountain (for she loved him dearly), told me of his lamentable begging of a penny-pot of Malmesy ; and sir reverence, how lousy he, and the mother of Infortunatus [1] were (I would her surgeon found her no worse than lousy) ; and how he was fain, poor soul, to borrow her husband's shirt whiles his own was a washing ; and how his doublet and hose and sword were sold for three shillings : and beside, the charges of his winding sheet, which was four shillings : and the charges of his burial yesterday in the New Churchyard near Bedlam, which was six shillings and fourpence : how deeply he was indebted to her poor husband ; as appeared by his own bond of ten pounds, which the good woman kindly showed me ; and beseeched me to read the writing beneath, which was a letter to his abandoned wife, in the behalf of his gentle host, not so short as persuasible in the beginning, and pitiful in the ending.' [2]

Such was the end of Robert Greene, whom (to Harvey's sniggering amusement) ' his sweet hostess for a tender farewell crowned with a garland of bays, to show that a tenth Muse honoured more being dead, than all nine honoured him alive.'

Other vultures were soon attracted. Greene had left various manuscripts. He had begun a novel which was largely autobiographical, called *Greene's Groatsworth of Wit, bought with a million of Repentance*. It was unfinished. He had written a letter in the miseries of these last days ' To those Gentlemen his quondam acquaintance that spend their wits in making plays,' for Greene felt very bitterly about the players. Scholars such as himself supplied them with plays

---

[1] The boy did not survive his father long. He died, probably of the plague, in the following summer, and his burial is recorded in the register of St. Leonard's, Shoreditch, on the 12th August.
[2] *Four Letters*, pp. 20-3.

by which they made their fortunes, but they left him to die in poverty. He had written plays; let them be warned by his example. No one was named in the letter, but three were definitely indicated.

To the first he wrote:

'Wonder not, for with thee I will first begin, thou famous gracer of tragedians, that Greene, who hath said with thee (like the fool in his heart) there is no God, should now give glory unto His greatness, for penetrating is His power; His Hand lies heavy upon me; He hath spoken unto me with a voice of thunder, and I have felt He is a God that can punish enemies. Why should thy excellent wit, His gift, be so blinded, that thou shouldst give no glory to the Giver? Is it pestilent Machiavellian policy that thou hast studied? O peevish folly! What are his rules but mere confused mockeries, able to extirpate in small time the generation of mankind.'[1]

Anyone reading the letter would recognize it for Marlowe.

'Defer not with me,' Greene ended his paragraph, 'till this last point of extremity: for little knowest thou how in the end thou shalt be visited.'

Next he addressed briefly 'young Juvenal, that biting young satirist that lastly with me together writ a comedy.' This was a fairly clear reference to Nashe, but the comedy has perished.

Then in more general terms he referred to a third driven like himself ' to extreme shifts,' who was probably Lodge.

'Base-minded men all three of you, if by my misery you be not warned: for unto none of you like me sought those burrs to cleave, those puppets, I mean, that spake from our mouths, those antics garnished in our colours. Is it not strange that I, to whom they all have been beholding—is it not like that you to whom they all have been beholding—

[1] *Greene's Groatsworth of Wit*, in *Bodley Head Quartos*, vi, 43.

shall, were ye in that case as I am now, be both at once of them forsaken?

'Yes, trust them not. For there is an upstart crow, beautified with our feathers, that with his *Tiger's heart wrapped in a player's hide* supposes he is as well able to bombast out a blank verse as the best of you; and, being an absolute *Johannes fac totum*, is in his own conceit the only Shake-scene in a country. O that I might entreat your rare wits to be employed in more profitable courses; and let those apes imitate your past excellence, and never more acquaint them with your admired inventions. I know the best husband of you all will never prove an usurer, and the kindest of them all will never prove a kind nurse; yet, whilst you may, seek you better masters, for it is pity men of such rare wits should be subject to the pleasure of such rude grooms.'[1]

Greene had also written a little fragment, a fable of an ant and a grasshopper—part prose, part verse. All these, together with a copy of the letter written to his wife, came into the hands of Henry Chettle, who put them together for William Wright the printer. The *Groatsworth* was entered for publication on the 20th September. On the 6th October Cuthbert Burby entered *The Repentance of Robert Greene, Master of Arts*.

Some have doubted whether both books are genuine. *The Repentance* certainly reads like a genuine document, but yet it is very like the *Confessions of Ned Browne* and it owes not a little to Lyly's *Euphues and his England*. If it was a fake, then the forger was able, not only to imitate Greene's style (which would not be difficult), but to write with real feeling. Genuine or not, it is a remarkable piece of introspection, to be compared with the similar but much more elaborate revelation of John Bunyan in *Grace Abounding*.

[1] *Groatsworth*, p. 45.

In either case, the facts are likely to be true. At the same time several printers took this chance of collecting scraps of Greene's work and passing them off as his dying words. The publisher of Greene's *Vision*, for instance, informs his readers that there are many feigned *Repentances*, and adds to their number by pretending that this volume is Greene's last work, when on internal evidence it is obviously more than two years old.

The *Groatsworth* caused trouble. Some said that Nashe had written it, but this he denied indignantly. In the preface to a new edition of *Piers Penniless*, in which he called it ' a scald, trivial lying pamphlet,' he declared with a mighty oath that not the least word or syllable was his writing, nor had he been in any way privy to the penning of it.

Shakespeare, who was presumably intended as the ' only Shake-scene,' and Marlowe also seem to have protested. Soon afterwards Chettle himself published a book called *Kindheart's Dream*, published also by Wright, and entered on the 8th December. In the preface to the gentlemen readers he explained his part in Greene's work.

' About three months since died M. Robert Greene, leaving many papers in sundry booksellers' hands, among other his *Groatsworth of Wit*, in which a letter written to divers play-makers is offensively by one or two of them taken, and because on the dead they cannot be avenged, they wilfully forge in their conceits a living author ; and after tossing it to and fro, no remedy but it must light on me. How I have all the time of my conversing in printing hindered the bitter inveighing against scholars it hath been very well known, and how in that I dealt I can sufficiently prove. With neither of them that take offence was I acquainted, and with one of them I care not if I never be ; the other, whom at that time I did not so much spare, as since I wish I had, for that as I have moderated the heat of living writers,

THE DEATH OF GREENE

and might have used my own discretion, especially in such a case, the author being dead, that I did not, I am as sorry as if the original fault had been my fault, because myself have seen his demeanour no less civil than he excellent in the quality he professes. Besides, divers of worship have reported his uprightness of dealing, which argues his honesty, and his facetious grace in writing that approves his art. For the first, whose learning I reverence, and at the perusing of Greene's book, stroke out what then in conscience I thought he in some displeasure writ ; or had it been true, yet to publish it was intolerable ; him I would wish to use me no worse than I deserve. I had only in the copy this share ; it was ill written, as sometime Greene's hand was none of the best ; licensed it must be, ere it could be printed, which could never be if it might not be read. To be brief, I writ it over, and as near as I could, followed the copy, only in that letter I put something out, but in the whole book not a word in, for I protest it was all Greene's, not mine nor Master Nashe's, as some unjustly have affirmed. Neither was he the writer of an Epistle to the second part of *Gerileon*, though by the workman's error T. N. were set to the end ; that I confess to be mine, and repent it not.'[1]

Meanwhile, after the promising start in February 1592, Lord Strange's Men had continued playing at the Rose, right through March and April, thereby disregarding the usual restriction which forbade playing in Lent. They continued until the middle of June. On the 11th June there was serious rioting in Southwark. One of the Knight Marshal's men was sent to serve a warrant on the servant of a felt-maker. The officer was unnecessarily high-handed in making the arrest and was resisted. Other arrests were made. Hereupon the felt-maker's apprentices planned a rescue.

As it happened there was a new play at the Rose called

[1] *Kindheart's Dream*, in *Bodley Head Quartos*, iv.

The Knack to know a Knave, and this gave excuse for a large gathering to assemble without attracting suspicion. After the play was over the apprentices marched off to the Marshalsea and shouted for their man. The rioting became so serious that the Lord Mayor himself and one of the sheriffs were called out to deal with it.

The Privy Council were alarmed by the reports which reached them. The apprentices usually went wild on Midsummer Night, and grave trouble was likely. They sent to warn the magistrates in London and the suburbs to cause an extra watch to be kept, and to close the playhouses until Michaelmas. Lord Strange's men considered that they had a grievance; for the playhouse to be closed so suddenly was mighty inconvenient. Fortunately they were not without allies. The watermen of the Thames did a good business in transporting the playgoers from one side of the river to the other; they too were innocent victims of the violence of the felt-makers. The players petitioned the Council:

'Our duties in all humbleness remembered to your Honours. For as much (Right Honourable) our Company is great, and thereby our charge intolerable in travelling the country, and the continuance thereof will be a means to bring us to division and separation, whereby we shall not only be undone, but also unready to serve her Majesty when it shall please her Highness to command us. And for that the use of our playhouse on the Bankside, by reason of the passage to and from the same by water, is a great relief to the poor watermen there. And our dismission thence now in this long vacation is to those poor men a great hindrance, and in manner an undoing, as they generally complain. Both our and their humble petition and suit therefore to your good Honours is that you will be pleased of your special favour to recall this our restraint, and permit us the use of the said playhouse again. And not only ourselves but also a great number of poor men shall be especially bounden to pray for your Honours.

> Your Honours' humble supplicants,
> The Right Honourable the Lord Strange,
> His servants and players.'

At the same time the watermen sent their petition to the Lord Admiral :

'In most humble manner complaineth and showeth unto your good Lordship your poor suppliants and daily orators Philip Henslowe, and others the poor watermen on the Bankside. Whereas your good Lordship hath directed your warrant unto her Majesty's Justices for the restraint of a playhouse belonging unto the said Philip Henslowe, one of the grooms of her Majesty's chamber, so it is, if it please your good Lordship, that we, your said poor watermen, have had much help and relief for us, our poor wives and children, by means of the resort of such people as come unto the said playhouse ; it may therefore please your good Lordship, for God's sake and in the way of charity, to respect us your poor watermen, and to give leave unto the said Philip Henslowe to have playing in his said house during such time as others have, according as it hath been accustomed. And in your Honour's so doing you shall not only do a good and a charitable deed, but also bind us all according to our duties, with our poor wives and children daily to pray for your Honour in much happiness long to live.'

The hearts of the Lords of the Council were softened. Late in the summer they issued a letter to the Justices of the Peace concerned.

'Whereas not long since upon some considerations we did restrain the Lord Strange his servants from playing at the Rose on the Bankside, and enjoined them to play three days at Newington Butts, now, forasmuch as we are satisfied that by reason of the tediousness of the way and that of long time plays have not there been used on working days, and that a number of poor watermen are thereby relieved, you shall permit and suffer them or any other there to exercise themselves in such sort as they have done heretofore. And that the Rose may be at liberty without any restraint, so long as it shall be free from infection of sickness, any commandment from us heretofore to the contrary notwithstanding.'[1]

The relief came too late. An epidemic of plague had already broken out. It continued throughout the autumn very severely and carried off more than 11,000 victims. So Lord Strange's Men were obliged to pack their playing apparel and once more to take to the road.

About this time Marlowe wrote his greatest play : *The Tragical History of Dr. Faustus.*[2]

Unfortunately the text is very corrupt. The play has less than 1,500 lines, compared with an average of 2,500 for *Edward the Second* and *The Jew of Malta* ; and critics like to believe that much of the clowning in the middle scenes was written by someone else. The play was a dramatization of *The History of the damnable life and deserved death of Dr. John Faustus*, published in German in 1587, translated into English by ' P. F., Gent.' in 1592. Marlowe followed his source closely, but his own life was reflected in the story. He had himself much in common with the ' studious artisan ' who perused all forms of academic knowledge, found them barren, and was tempted to reach his ideal by forbidden paths. *Dr. Faustus* has some of Marlowe's greatest verse and his most cherished opinions.

[1] *Henslowe Papers*, pp. 42–4.
[2] It was for long believed that *Faustus* followed *Tamburlaine*. Dr. F. S. Boas, however, in his edition of *Faustus* in the *Arden Marlowe*, has shown that it could not have been written earlier than the summer of 1592, as the source book which clearly Marlowe used was not available.

As with the *Jew of Malta*, Marlowe began his play with the hero discovered. Faustus is in his study, contemplating academic knowledge, rejecting in turn logic, medicine and divinity, and finding himself attracted by the doctrine of 'What will be shall be.' So Faustus takes to necromancy and risks his soul. At this point Marlowe reverted to the methods of the morality play. Wishing to show the struggle in Faustus' mind, he introduced a good angel and a bad angel, each trying to convince him. Faustus yields to temptation, summons Mephistophilis, and then, being still the scholar, seeks from him the solution of some of those problems which perpetually recurred to the academic mind: such as the nature and place of hell and the lot of the spirits of the infernal world—matters akin to those which Marlowe had himself discussed with Ralegh and his circle.

FAUSTUS. And what are you that live with Lucifer?
MEPHISTOPHILIS. Unhappy spirits that fell with Lucifer,
Conspir'd against our God with Lucifer,
And are for ever damn'd with Lucifer.
FAUSTUS. Where are damn'd?
MEPHISTOPHILIS. In hell.
FAUSTUS. How comes it then that thou art out of hell?
MEPHISTOPHILIS. Why this is hell, nor am I out of it:
Think'st thou that I, that saw the face of God,
And tasted the eternal joys of heaven,
Am not tormented with ten thousand hells,
In being depriv'd of everlasting bliss?

Up to the point where Faustus signs away his soul the tragedy remains at a high level, but thereafter Faustus and the play degenerate, and become merely vulgar and sensual. Faustus enjoys his powers, but uses them mostly to play silly tricks, except when he calls up Helen of Troy to be his paramour and greets her with the immortal lines:

> Was this the face that launch'd a thousand ships
> And burnt the topless towers of Ilium?

At the end the play again rises to heights unsurpassed. The time has come for Faustus to fulfil his bargain with Lucifer, his twenty-four years' lease of his own soul has lapsed, and he is left alone, with but one poor hour to live, to damnation eternal. In this long soliloquy Marlowe probed terror to the depths. It is a magnificent display of mortal agony; but it needed an actor of Alleyn's calibre.

Fragmentary and imperfect as the text is, *Dr. Faustus* is yet Marlowe's greatest play, for it has a real depth of psychological insight. Marlowe succeeded in lifting the tragic drama above mere incident, and in creating a play which reveals the tragedy of intellectual ambition. He showed the temptations and the sufferings of an acute mind with real subtlety, and he demonstrated what poetry could do for the theatre.

Chapter VII

THE DEATH OF MARLOWE

In January 1593 the plague again appeared, and at the end of the month the Privy Council prohibited all plays, bear-baiting and other assemblies for sport.

On the 19th February a parliament was summoned which sat for seven weeks. It was an uneasy session, for religious feeling was running high. Some members even brought in a bill to curtail the powers of the bishops; and from the other side a bill against recusants was proposed and hotly debated. There was a general fear in official quarters that some vast but undefined subversive movement was stirring. The utterances of extreme puritans were scrutinized, and found to be alarming and revolutionary. Little incidents accumulated.

On the 9th March a meeting of Barrowists—one of the extreme puritan sects—was surprised at Islington. Barrow himself, and Greenwood, another leader, were arrested and hanged on the 6th April. Mysterious propaganda against the Government was being put out, and it seemed as if the troubles of Martin Marprelate were about to start all over again. Libels against foreigners living in London, particularly the Dutch, appeared on walls.

'Be it known'—one of them ended—'to all Flemings and Frenchmen, that it is best for them to depart out of the realm of England, between this and 9th of July next. If not, then to take what follows. For there shall be many a sore stripe. Apprentices will rise to the number of 2336. And all prentices and journeymen will down with Flemings and Strangers.'[1]

On the 22nd April the Council appointed a special commission to go into the matter ; but in spite of their efforts, the libelling continued, and on the 11th May a libel more threatening and malicious than the rest appeared on the wall of the Dutch Church. The Council urged the commissioners to greater efforts. They were given powers to search and arrest any persons suspected, to enter their studies, break open their chests, peruse their papers. They might even use torture to extract the truth.

The Lord Mayor immediately proceeded to round up suspects, and, amongst others, Thomas Kyd found himself in Bridewell prison. When the officers examined his papers they discovered nothing which would throw light on the libels against the Dutch, but they came on something much more exciting—some pages of a disputation denying the divinity of Christ. Kyd was asked to explain the presence of this incriminating document. He was even tortured to encourage his memory, but the only explanation he could give was that the incriminating document had been accidentally left with his papers by Marlowe when they were sharing a study some two years before.

The Lords of the Council, particularly Sir John Puckering, the Lord Keeper, were hot on the trail. Marlowe was notorious : he was favoured by Sir Walter Ralegh. Ralegh was a known malcontent : within these last weeks in the House of Commons he had publicly and persuasively opposed the recent Bill against the Brownists : it was altogether very suspicious. On the 18th May a warrant was issued to ' Henry Maunder, one of the messengers of her Majesty's Chamber, to repair to the house of Mr. Thomas Walsingham in Kent, or to any other place where he shall understand

[1] I *Elizabethan Journals*, p. 237.

Christopher Marlowe to be remaining, and by virtue thereof to apprehend and bring him to the Court in his company. And in case of need to require aid.'

Two days later it was recorded that ' Christopher Marley of London, gentleman, being sent for by warrant from their Lordships, hath entered his appearance accordingly for his indemnity therein, and is commanded to give his daily attendance on their Lordships until he shall be licensed to the contrary.[1]

Meanwhile the Lord Keeper sent out his spies to see what could be discovered about Marlowe, his associates and his opinions. Soon a certain Richard Baines handed in a long, variegated and dreadful list of accusations which were considered so important that a copy was made and submitted to the Queen.

' A note containing the opinion of one Christopher Marly concerning his damnable judgment of religion and scorn of God's Word.

' That the Indians and many authors of antiquity have assuredly written of above sixteen thousand years agone, whereas Adam is proved to have lived within six thousand years.

' He affirmeth that Moses was but a juggler, and that one Heriots [i.e. Harriott], being Sir W. Ralegh's man, can do more than he.

' That Moses made the Jews to travel 40 years in the wilderness, which journey might have been done in less than one year, ere they came to the promised land, to the intent that those who were privy to most of his subtleties might perish, and so an everlasting superstition remain in the hearts of the people.

' That the first beginning of religion was only to keep men in awe.

[1] *Acts of the Privy Council*, edited by J. R. Dasent, xxiv, 244.

'That it was an easy matter for Moses being brought up in all the arts of the Egyptians to abuse the Jews, being a rude and gross people.

'That Christ was a bastard and His mother dishonest.

'That He was the son of a carpenter, and that if the Jews among whom He was born did crucify Him they best knew Him and whence He came.

'That Christ deserved better to die than Barrabas, and that the Jews made a good choice, though Barrabas were both a thief and a murderer.

'That if there be any God or any good religion, then it is in the papists, because the service of God is performed with more ceremonies, as elevation of the Mass, organs, singing men, shaven crowns, etc. That all Protestants are hypocritical asses.

'That if he were put to write a new religion, he would undertake both a more excellent and admirable method, and that all the New Testament is filthily written.

'That the woman of Samaria and her sister were whores and that Christ knew them dishonestly.

'That St. John the Evangelist was bedfellow to Christ and leaned always in his bosom; that he used him as the sinners of Sodoma.

'That all they that love not tobacco and boys were fools.

'That all the apostles were fishermen and base fellows neither of wit nor worth; that Paul only had wit but he was a timorous fellow in bidding men to be subject to magistrats against his conscience.

'That he had as good right to coin as the Queen of England, and that he was acquainted with one Poole [i.e. Poley], a prisoner in Newgate, who hath great skill in mixture of metals; and having learned some things of him, he meant, through the help of a cunning stamp-maker, to coin French crowns, pistolets and English shillings.

'That if Christ would have instituted the sacrament with more ceremonial reverence it would have been had in more admiration ; that it would have been much better being administered in a tobacco pipe.

'That the Angel Gabriel was bawd to the Holy Ghost, because he brought the salutation to Mary.

'That one Richard Cholmley hath confessed that he was persuaded by Marlowe's reasons to become an atheist.

'These things, with many other, shall by good and honest witness be approved to be his opinions and common speeches ; and that this Marlowe doth not only hold them himself, but almost into every company he cometh he persuadeth men to atheism, willing them not to be afeared of bugbears and hobgoblins, and utterly scorning both God and His ministers, as I, Richard Baines, will justify and approve, both by mine oath and the testimony of many honest men ; and almost all men with whom he hath conversed any time will testify the same ; and, as I think, all men in Christianity ought to endeavour that the mouth of so dangerous a member may be stopped. He saith likewise that he hath quoted a number of contrarieties out of the Scripture, which he hath given to some great men who in convenient time shall be named. When these things shall be called in question the witness shall be produced.

RICHARD BAINES.'[1]

Next Puckering sent to find more about this Richard Cholmeley whom Marlowe was said to have converted. The report of Cholmeley's words and behaviour was equally damnable.

'Remembrances of words and matter against Richard Cholmeley.

'That he speaketh in general all evil of the Council,

[1] Printed from Harleian MSS. 6848, f. 185, in *The Life and Dido*. Edited by C. F. Tucker Brooke, *The Arden Marlowe*, p. 100.

saying that they are all atheists and Machiavellians, especially my Lord Admiral.

'That he made certain libellous verses in commendation of papists and seminary priests very greatly inveighing against the State, among which lines this was one :

Nor may the Prince deny the Papal Crown.

'That he had a certain book (as he saith) delivered him by Sir Robert Cecil, of whom he giveth very scandalous reports ; that he should incite him to consider thereof and to frame verses and libels in the commendation of constant priests and virtuous recusants. This book is in custody and is called an Epistle of Comfort, and is printed at Paris.

'That he rails at Mr. Topcliffe,[1] and hath written another libel jointly against Sir Francis Drake and Justice Young, whom he saith he will couple up together because he hateth them alike.

'That when the mutiny happened after the Portingal voyage in the Strand, he said that he repented him of nothing more than that he had not killed my Lord Treasurer with his own hands, saying that he could never have done God better service. This was spoken in the hearing of Francis Clarke and many other soldiers.

'That he saith he doth entirely hate the Lord Chamberlain and hath good cause so to do.

'That he saith and verily believeth that one Marlowe is able to show more sound reasons for atheism than any divine in England is able to give to prove divinity, and that Marlowe told him that he hath read the atheist lecture to Sir Walter Ralegh and others.

[1] Topcliffe was in charge of the anti-Catholic spy system : an unpleasant person.

'That he so highly esteemeth his own wit and judgment that he saith that no men are sooner deceived and abused than the Council themselves, and that he can go beyond and cozen them as he list; and that if he make any complaint in behalf of the Queen he shall not only be presently heard and entertained, but he will so urge the Council for money that without he have what he list, he will do nothing.

'That being employed by some of her Majesty's Privy Council for the apprehension of papists and other dangerous men, he used as he saith to take money of them, and would let them pass in spite of the Council.

'That he saith that William Parry was hanged, drawn and quartered but in jest; that he was a gross ass over-reached by cunning, and that in truth he never meant to kill the Queen more than himself had.'[1]

Puckering wished to learn more. His spy produced a second report.

'Right Worshipful, Whereas I promised to send you word when Cholmeley was with me, these are to let you understand that he hath not yet been with me, for that he doth partly suspect that I will bewray his villainy and his company. But yesterday he sent two of his companions to me to know if I would join with him in familiarity and become of their damnable crew. I soothed the villains with fair words in their follies, because I would thereby dive into the secrets of their devilish hearts that I might the better bewray their purposes to draw her Majesty's subjects to be atheists. Their practice is after her Majesty's decease to make a king among themselves and live according to their own laws; and this, saith Cholmeley, will be done easily, because they be and shortly will be by his and his fellows' persuasions, as many of their opinion as of any

[1] Harleian MSS. 6848, f. 190.

other religion. Mr. Cholmeley his manner of proceeding in seducing the Queen's subjects is first to make slanderous reports of the most noble peers and honourable Councillors, as the Lord Treasurer, the Lord Chamberlain, the Lord Admiral, Sir Robert Cecil. These, saith he, have profound wits, be sound atheists, and their lives and deeds show that they think their souls do end, vanish, and perish with their bodies.'

The informer then repeats Cholmeley's blasphemies, which were much the same as Marlowe's, and concludes : ' This cursed Cholmeley hath 60 of his company, and he is seldom from his fellows. And therefore I beseech your Worship have a special care of yourself in apprehending him, for they be resolute murdering minds.'

Marlowe's case, however, was taken out of the hands of the Privy Council. On the 30th May at Deptford, Marlowe, in company with Ingram Frizer, Nicholas Sheres and Robert Poley, met together in a room in the house of a certain Mistress Eleanor Bull, widow, at ten in the morning. They dined. After dinner they walked in the garden. About six o'clock they came back into the room and supped. Marlowe lay down on a bed, and Frizer sat at the table between Sheres and Poley, with his back towards the bed. Frizer and Marlowe began to quarrel. Malicious words passed because they could not agree on the payment of the reckoning. Marlowe lost his temper, sprang up, drew Frizer's dagger, which was hanging at his back, and struck him on the head. Frizer, being wedged in between the other two, could not escape. He seized Marlowe's wrist and tried to force the dagger out of his hand, but in the struggle Marlowe was jabbed in the eye, ' of which mortal wound,' according to the report of the coroner, ' the aforesaid Christopher Morley then and there instantly died.' An inquest was held the next day, and the jury, having heard

THE DEATH OF MARLOWE

what the survivors had to say, decided that Frizer had acted in defence of his own life.[1]

Marlowe was buried in the churchyard at Deptford ; the entry in the register records *Christopher Marlow, slaine by ffrancis ffrezer: the 1 of June.* The next day—as it happened—John Penry, reputed author of the Martin Marprelate pamphlets was hanged at St. Thomas Watering.

Marlowe's death gave great satisfaction to the godly. Three years later Thomas Beard, a puritan writer, produced a book called *The Theatre of God's Judgment,* a vast collection from sacred, ecclesiastical and profane authors of the ' admirable judgments of God upon the transgressors of His commandments.' Most of the examples were taken from learned authors. Marlowe was one of the few modern instances, and found his place in the section devoted to Epicures and Atheists.

' Not inferior to any of the former in atheism and impiety, and equal to all in manner of punishment was one of our own nation, of fresh and late memory, called Marlin [in the marginal note spelt *Marlow*], by profession a scholar, brought up from his youth in the University of Cambridge, but by practice a playmaker, and a poet of scurrility, who, by giving too large a swing to his own wit, and suffering his lust to have the full reins, fell, not without just desert, to that outrage and extremity that he denied God and his Son Christ, and not only in word blasphemed the Trinity, but also (as it is credibly reported) wrote books against it, affirming our Saviour to be but a deceiver, and Moses to be but a conjurer and seducer of the people, and the Holy Bible to be but vain and idle stories, and all religion but a device of policy.

---

[1] The record of the inquest, from which these details are taken, was the brilliant discovery of Professor Leslie Hotson, who published his finds as *The Death of Christopher Marlowe,* 1925.

'But see what a hook the Lord put in the nostrils of this barking dog. It so fell out, that in London streets as he purposed to stab one whom he owed a grudge unto with his dagger, the other party perceiving so avoided the stroke, that withall catching hold of his wrist, he stabbed his own dagger into his own head, in such sort, that notwithstanding all the means of surgery that could be wrought, he shortly after died thereof. The manner of his death being so terrible (for he even cursed and blasphemed to his last gasp, and together with his breath an oath flew out of his mouth) that it was not only a manifest sign of God's judgment, but also an horrible and fearful terror to all that beheld him. But herein did the justice of God most notably appear, in that He compelled his own hand which had written those blasphemies to be the instrument to punish him, and that in his brain, which had devised the same. I would to God (and I pray it from my heart) that all atheists in this realm, and in all the world beside, would by the remembrance and consideration of this example, either forsake their horrible impiety or that they might in like manner come to destruction: and so that abominable sin which so flourisheth among men of greatest name, might either be quite extinguished and rooted out, or at least smothered and kept under, that it durst not show its head any more in the world's eye.'

Kyd's position was now precarious, as only Marlowe could have proved his innocence. He therefore wrote a pathetic letter to the Lord Keeper Puckering laying the blame on the dead Marlowe, and excusing himself for not having spoken out sooner by his respect for Marlowe's illustrious friends.

After suggesting that he is afraid the Lord Keeper will suspect him of 'Atheism, a deadly thing which I was undeserved charged withal,' he goes on to explain his relations with Marlowe:

THE DEATH OF MARLOWE

'When I was first suspected for that libel that concerned the State, amongst those waste and idle papers, which I cared not for, and which, unasked, I did deliver up, were found some fragments of a disputation touching that opinion affirmed by Marlowe to be his, and shuffled with some of mine, unknown to me, by some occasion of our writing in one chamber two years since.

'My first acquaintance with this Marlowe rose upon his bearing name to serve my Lord, although his Lordship never knew his service but in writing for his players, for never could my Lord endure his name or sight, when he had heard of his conditions, nor would indeed the form of divine prayers used duly in his Lordship's house have quadred with such reprobates . . .'

'For more assurance that I was not of that vile opinion, let it but please your Lordship to enquire of such as he conversed withal, that is (as I am given to understand) with Harriott, Warner, Roydon and some stationers in Paul's Churchyard, whom I in no sort can accuse nor will excuse by reason of his company; of whose consent if I had been, no question by I also should have been of their consort, for *ex minimo vestigio artifex agnoscit artificem.*' [1]

Kyd wrote another letter to Puckering. He mentioned some of Marlowe's loose talk in the same strain as Baines' charges, and adds a remark that Marlowe 'would persuade with men of quality to go unto the King of Scots, whither I hear Royden is gone, and where, if he had lived he told me when I saw him last, he meant to be.'

Sir Walter Ralegh's name had been freely mentioned in the investigations, and the matter was not allowed to drop. He was watched, even his private conversation being retailed

---

[1] Harleian MSS. 6848, f. 218. Printed in full by C. F. Tucker Brooke, in *The Arden Marlowe, Dido*, p. 103. Dr. Boas, in his edition of Kyd's works, reproduces the letter in facsimile.

to the Lord Keeper. In the following year a special commission headed by Lord Thomas Howard was sent down to Ralegh's home at Cerne Abbas in Dorsetshire.[1] Ralegh and his friends were charged with 'impious opinions concerning God and Providence.' However, although the commissioners found much that was suspicious of heresy, no further action was taken. Soon afterwards Ralegh went on his Guiana voyage. When he returned, the affair had blown over and the Council had other and more serious problems to occupy their attention.

Kyd seems to have been released soon after, as nothing could be proved against him. He died in the late autumn of 1594.

So died Greene and Marlowe, the first two great English dramatists, to the great triumph of the godly, who saw in their fearful ends the manifest signs of divine retribution on naughty play-makers. With the passing of Greene and Marlowe the dominating influence of the University wits came to an end.

The year 1593 marks the end of an era with a distinctiveness unusual in literary history. The plague continued all through the autumn, and regular playing was not resumed in London until the summer of 1594. When the playhouses again opened the only writer of any standing was the new playwright, William Shakespeare.

Progress in the last six or seven years had been rapid. Playwrights had been learning and solving the problems of drama; and each of the three—Kyd, Marlowe and Greene —had added much to the store of common knowledge. They owed most to Kyd; for he had the greatest sense of drama. By instinct or good luck he had stumbled on the principles of plot construction, the artistic truth that a

[1] The examinations then taken are reproduced in full in my edition of *Willobie His Avisa*, in *Bodley Head Quartos*, xv.

play must move to an end and there finish. It was not enough to provide a succession of scenes however witty or thrilling, unless the complete pattern was itself a unity. Apart from plot, Kyd has some inkling of how to create a character. His Kings and Dukes are stately mouthpieces, but Lorenzo, the Machiavellian, and old Hieronomo (for all his rantings) are real people.

Marlowe had certainly perfected the mighty line. At its best it was never surpassed; though it was something too gorgeous for everyday use, and Marlowe's verse, when it fell, was not far from bathos. He had invented great personalities, bombastic and furious, sometimes sublime, sometimes verging on the ridiculous; but always unforgettable. Moreover those characters had a psychological interest, because their minds and emotions were at times as interesting as their actions. Tamburlaine's ambitions were crude, a lust for conquest and bloodshed, but yet a Titan's lust. Barrabas was not merely a stage bogey, born bold and bad, but a human being made so by the treatment of Christians. Faustus was the most human of all; for his temptation and fall is a universal and perennial problem. The soliloquies that reveal the working of his mind before his temptation and at the last were unsurpassed by any dramatist until Shakespeare wrote *Hamlet*.

Greene's contribution was less impressive, but not less valuable, for he learnt how to instil into comedy that atmosphere which is best called romantic, and he knew not a little of the art of the theatre, including that first principle, too often forgotten, which is that the chief business of a playwright is to entertain.

Chapter VIII

EDWARD ALLEYN AND THE ADMIRAL'S MEN

ALLEYN and Lord Strange's Men came back at Christmastide, and on the 29th December 1593, they started again at the Rose. They played throughout January, and produced two new plays, *The Jealous Comedy* on the 5th, and on the 30th *The Tragedy of the Guise*, written by Marlowe, which was later printed as *The Massacre at Paris*. But the season was very short. Plague again appeared and the playhouses were closed. The plague continued all through the early spring. At last Edward Alleyn and a select band of Lord Strange's players decided to go on tour. They were accorded a special licence by the Privy Council on the 6th May :

'Whereas it was thought meet that during the time of the infection and continuance of the sickness in the city of London there should no plays or interludes be used, for the avoiding of the assemblies and concourse of people in any usual place appointed near the said city, and though the bearers hereof, Edward Alleyn, servant to the Right Honourable the Lord High Admiral, William Kemp, Thomas Pope, John Hemmings, Augustine Phillips and George Brian, being all one company, servants to our very good Lord the Lord Strange, are restrained their exercise of playing within the said city and liberties thereof, yet it is not thereby meant but that they shall and may, in regard of the service by them done and to be done at the Court, exercise their quality of playing comedies, tragedies and such like in any other cities, towns and corporations where the infection is not, so it be not within seven miles of London or of the Court, that they may be in the better readiness hereafter for her Majesty's service whensoever they shall be thereunto called. This, therefore, shall be to will and require you that they may without their let or contradiction use their said exercise at their most convenient times and places (the accustomed times of divine prayers excepted).'[1]

The tour, however, had already started, for Alleyn wrote to his wife from Chelmsford on the 2nd May. This and several other letters which passed between Alleyn in the country and his family in London survive in the Dulwich Collection. It was an anxious time, for as the summer came on the plague developed into one of the worst visitations for years. On the 1st August, Alleyn being then at Bristol, wrote home to his wife :

'EMMANUEL,

'MY GOOD SWEET MOUSE,

'I commend me heartily to you and to my father, my mother, and my sister Bess, hoping in God though the sickness be round about you yet, by His mercy, it may escape your house, which, by the grace of God, it shall. Therefore use this course ; keep your house fair and clean, which I know you will, and every evening throw water before your door, and in your backside, and have in your windows good store of rue and herb of grace, and with all the grace of God, which must be obtained by prayers ; and so doing, no doubt but the Lord will mercifully defend you.

'Now, good mouse, I have no news to send you but this, that we have all our health, for which the Lord be

[1] *Acts of the Privy Council*, xxiv, 212 ; *Elizabethan Stage*, ii, 123.

praised. I received your letter at Bristow, by Richard Cowley, for the which I thank you.

'I have sent you by this bearer, Thomas Pope's kinsman, my white waistcoat, because it is a trouble to me to carry it. Receive it with this letter, and lay it up for me till I come.

'If you send any more letters, send to me by the carriers of Shrewsbury or to West Chester or to York, to be kept till my Lord Strange's players come.

'And thus, sweetheart, with my hearty commendations to all our friends, I cease from Bristow this Wednesday after Saint James his day, being ready to begin the play of *Harry of Cornwall*.

'Mouse, do my hearty commends to Mr. Grigs' wife and all his household, and to my sister Phillips.

Your loving husband,
E. ALLEYN.'

'Mouse, you send me no news of any things you should send of your domestical matters; such things as happen at home, as how your distilled water proves, or this, or that, or any thing what you will.

'And Jug, I pray you let my orange tawny stockings of woollen be dyed a very good black against I come home to wear in the winter.

'You sent me not word of my garden, but next time you will. But remember this, in any case, that all that bed which was parsley in the month of September, you sow it with spinach, for then is the time. I would do it myself but we shall not come home till Allholland tide. And so, sweet mouse, farewell, and brook our long journey with patience.'[1]

[1] *Henslowe Papers*, p. 35.

In reply to this letter Henslowe and Joan Alleyn wrote back to him :

'WELLBELOVED SON EDWARD ALLEYN,

'After our hearty commendations, both I and your mother and sister Bess all in general doth heartily commend us unto you ; and as for your mouse, her commendations comes by itself, which as she says comes from her heart and her soul, praying to God day and night for your good health, which truly to be plain we do so all, hoping in the Lord Jesus that we shall have again a merry meeting ; for I thank God we have been flitted with fear of the sickness, but thanks be unto God we are all this time in good health in our house ; but round about us it hath been almost in every house about us, and whole households died ; and yet my friend the bailly doth scape, but he smells monstrously for fear, and dares stay nowhere ; for there hath died this last week in general 1,603, of the which number there hath died of them of the plague 1,130–5, which has been the greatest that came yet. And as for other news of this and that, I can tell you none, but that Robert Brown's wife in Shoreditch and all her children and household be dead, and her doors shut up.

' As for your joiner, he hath brought you a court cupboard and hath set up your portowel [1] in the chamber, and says you shall have a good bedstead.

' And as for your garden, it is well, and your spinach bed not forgotten.

' Your orange coloured stockings dyed ; but no market in Smithfield, neither to buy your cloth nor yet to sell your horse, for no man would offer me above four pounds for him, therefore I would not sell him, but have sent him into the country till you return back again.

---

[1] 'portowle' in the original ; presumably a towel-rail.

'Thus like poor people rejoicing that the Lord hath encompassed us round and keepeth us all in health, we end praying to God to send you all good health, that it may please God to send that we may all merrily meet. And I pray you do our commendations unto them all, and I would gladly hear the like from them.

'And thanks be to God, your poor mouse hath not been sick since you went.

'Your loving wife till death,
JOAN ALLEYN.

Your poor and assured friend till death,
PHILLIP HENSLOWE.'[1]

On the 14th they wrote again:

'JESUS,

'WELLBELOVED SON EDWARD ALLEYN,

'I and your mother and your sister Bess have all in general our hearty commendations unto you, and very glad to hear of your good health, which we pray God to continue long to His Will and Pleasure, for we heard that you were very sick at Bath, and that one of your fellows were fain to play your part for you, which was no little grief unto us to hear. But thanks be to God for a mendment, for we feared it much because we had no letter from you when the other wives had letters sent, which made your mouse not to weep a little, but took it very grievously, thinking that you had conceived some unkindness of her, because you were ever wont to write with the first, and I pray you do so still, for we would all be sorry but to hear as often from you as others do from their friends. For we would write oftener to you than we do but we know not whither to send to you. Therefore I pray you forget not your mouse and us, for you sent in one letter that we returned not answer whether we received them or no, for we

[1] *Henslowe Papers*, p. 36.

received one which you made at Saint James's tide, wherein makes mention of your white waistcoat and your lute books and other things which we have received, and now lastly a letter which Peter brought with your horse, which I will be as careful as I can in it.

'Now, son, although long at the last I remember a hundred commendations from your mouse which is very glad to hear of your health and prayeth day and night to the Lord to continue the same, and likewise prayeth unto the Lord to cease His hand from punishing us with His Cross that she might have you at home with her, hoping then that you should be eased of this heavy labour and toil.

'And you said in your letter that she sent you not word how your garden and all your things doth prosper—very well, thanks be to God, for your beans are grown to high hedge and well codded, and all other things doth very well. But your tenants wax very poor, for they can pay no rent, nor will pay no rent while [1] Michelmas next, and then we shall have it if we can get it. And likewise your joiner commends him unto you, and says he will make you such good stuff and such good pennyworths as he hopeth shall well like you and content you, which I hope he will do, because he says he will prove himself an honest man.

'And for your good counsel which you gave us in your letter we all thank you, which was for keeping of our house clean and watering of our doors and strewing our windows with wormwood and rue, which I hope all this we do and more, for we strew it with hearty prayers unto the Lord which unto us is more available than all things else in the world, for I praise the Lord God for it, we are all in very good health, and I pray ye, son, commend me heartily to all the rest of your fellows in general, for I grow poor for lack of them, therefore have no gifts to send, but as good

[1] while = until.

and faithful a heart as they shall desire to have comen amongst them.

'Now, son, we thank you all for your tokens you sent us, and as for news of the sickness I cannot send you no just note of it because there is commandment to the contrary, but as I think doth die within the city and without of all sicknesses to the number of seventeen or eighteen hundred in one week.

'And this praying to God for your health, I end from London the 14th of August 1593.

'Your loving wife to command till death, JOAN ALLEYN.

Your loving father and mother to our powers, PH. A.

'To my well beloved husband, Mr. Edward Alleyn, one of My Lord Strange's Players, this to be delivered with speed.'[1]

On the 28th September, Henslowe and Joan Alleyn wrote grumbling 'because we cannot hear from you as we would do, that is when others do.' The plague was still all round them, almost all their neighbours were dead, and even their own household had not escaped, 'for my two wenches have had the plague and yet, thanks be to God, liveth and are well.'

As for My Lord of Pembroke's players, about whom Alleyn had enquired: 'They are all at home, and have been this five or six weeks, for they cannot save their charges with travel, as I hear, and were fain to pawn their parel for their charge.'

Lord Strange's Men changed their name in the autumn, for the old Earl of Derby died on the 25th September, and their master, Ferdinando Stanley, Lord Strange, succeeded to the title as fifth Earl of Derby. The company thus became Derby's Men; but not for long, for Ferdinando

[1] *Henslowe Papers*, p. 38.

EDWARD ALLEYN AND THE ADMIRAL'S MEN

Stanley died in strange circumstances on the 16th April 1594. He was succeeded by his brother William Stanley. The players for a while claimed the patronage of the Dowager Countess of Derby.

The plague still continued; during the year over ten thousand had died of it. It was not until the early summer that the players returned to London. Alleyn then reorganized his players and once more formed a separate Lord Admiral's company. They played for three days only—14th to 16th May—at the Rose, and then ceased; Henslowe's receipts were 48*s.*, 32*s.* and 42*s.*

On the 3rd June Henslowe began a new series of entries in the ledger. ' In the name of God, Amen. Beginning at Newington, my Lord Admiral's Men and my Lord Chamberlain's Men as followeth, 1594.'

Very little is known of the playhouse at Newington Butts; it was about a mile from London Bridge, and apparently a failure, for theatre-goers would not come so far out of London. The plays then acted were *Esther and Ahazuerus*, *The Jew of Malta* (twice), *Andronicus* (twice), *Cutlack*, *Bellendon*, *Hamlet*, *The Taming of the Shrew*. There is no indication of how the arrangement worked; whether the companies combined or acted on different days. Of these plays *Andronicus*, *Hamlet* and *The Taming of the Shrew* belonged to the Chamberlain's Men, and do not reappear in the *Diary*.

It was not a satisfactory arrangement, and the takings at Newington were poor; for the ten performances Henslowe only received £5. On the 13th June he drew a line under the account. In the next ten days, Henslowe took £21 11*s.* : the Admiral's Men had returned to the Rose and the receipts were increasing accordingly. The chief members of the new company were: Edward Alleyn, John Singer, Richard Jones, Thomas Towne, Martin Slaughter, Edward Juby,

Thomas Dutton and James Dunstan. In addition there were the boys and hired men.

Meanwhile a new Lord Chamberlain's company had been formed from the old members of the Strange Company and others. Their new patron was Henry Carey, Lord Hunsdon, who had been Lord Chamberlain since 1585. This new company included Richard Burbage, Will Kemp, and William Shakespeare.

Richard Burbage was the younger son of James Burbage. It is not known when he was born, but it was probably about 1568. He was already making a name for himself as a tragic actor. In later years his reputation far surpassed that of Alleyn.

Kemp in his own way was almost as famous as Alleyn. He was a low comedian, and particularly famous for his jigs.

Shakespeare by this time was well known. His Talbot Scenes in the *First Part of Henry the Sixth* had been most popular. Nashe indeed said that 10,000 people had witnessed them on various occasions. Moreover his two poems *Venus and Adonis*, published in the spring of 1593, and the *Rape of Lucrece*, published in the early summer of 1594, had both been the success of the year. Greene's words in the *Groatsworth of Wit* suggested that he had only recently turned playwright in 1592.

The Chamberlain's Men were not so fortunate as the Admiral's in their repertory, but when they opened at the Theatre they were beginning to accumulate. On the other hand, they had certain advantages which more than compensated for any inferiority in programme. James Burbage was always so harassed by his debts and law-suits that he could never have had the same power over the actors as Henslowe at the Rose. And indeed there is plenty of evidence that the Chamberlain's Men were a company of friends closely united. When Augustine Phillips died in 1605, he left 30*s*. in gold to Shakespeare and Condell, and 20*s*. in gold to five other members of the company. Similarly Shakespeare himself left 26*s*. 8*d*. apiece 'to buy them rings' to his fellows John Hemming, Richard Burbage and Henry Condell.

Thus both the Admiral's and Chamberlain's Men soon recovered from the effects of the lean years and began to outstrip rival companies.

Of the methods and economics of the Theatre little is known. Thanks to Henslowe's *Diary*, the name of every play produced during a decade at the Rose and the Fortune, its successor, is known, but without this evidence the usual sources of information, such as the Stationers' Register, and occasional references in books and letters would give a very inaccurate idea of the output of the Rose.

During this period, June 1594 to March 1603, the Admiral's Men acted in about 215 plays. Of these only fifteen were printed. Of the plays acted by the Chamberlain's Men during the same period eighteen were printed, of which ten were written by Shakespeare. It is probable that at least 80 per cent. of the plays acted by Shakespeare's company have perished, including not a few of his own. But these facts cannot be known until—if ever—Burbage's *Diary* comes to light!

The Admiral's Men were a hard-working company, and their time must have been fully occupied with rehearsals and playing. This can be seen from the list of first performances of plays, new and old, put on between June 1594 and the closing of the theatres on 28 July 1597.

Plays put on by the Admiral's Men at the Rose Theatre between 15 June 1594 and 28 July 1597

(The dates are those given in the *Diary*, which are sometimes a couple of days out; for all details Dr. Greg's edition of the *Diary*

ELIZABETHAN PLAYS AND PLAYERS

should be consulted. Henslowe noted the first performance of plays which were new or revised. The Company opened on the 15th with *Bellendon*, followed by *Cutlack* and *The Rangers' Comedy*, which were already in production at Newington Butts. Thereafter they added to their repertory by producing new or reviving old plays, as follows.)

Date	Play	New or Old	No. of Performances	Remarks
1594				
19 June	The Guise	old	10	By Marlowe—printed as *The Massacre of Paris*, n.d.
26 June	Galiaso	new	9	lost
9 July	Philipo and Hippolito	new	12	lost
19 July	Godfrey of Bulloigne	new	12	lost
30 July	The Merchant of Emden	old	1	lost
11 Aug.	Tasso's Melancholy	new	12	lost
14 Aug.	Mahomet	old	8	lost, unless it is *Alphonsus of Aragon*
25 Aug.	The Venetian Comedy	new	12	lost
28 Aug.	Tamberlaine, part I	old	15	By Marlowe—printed in 1590
17 Sept.	Palamon and Arcyte	new	4	lost
24 Sept.	The Love of an English Lady	new	2	lost
30 Sept.	Doctor Faustus	old	25	By Marlowe—entered 1601, earliest surviving text, 1604
4 Oct.	The Grecian Comedy	old	12	lost
18 Oct.	The French Doctor	old	14	lost
22 Oct.	A Knack to know an Honest Man	new	21	Printed 1596
8 Nov.	Caesar and Pompey	new	8	lost
16 Nov.	Dioclesian	new	2	lost
28 Nov.	Warlamchester	old	7	lost

Date	Play	New or Old	No. of Performances	Remarks
1594				
2 Dec.	*The Wise Man of West Chester*	new	32	By Munday—survives in MS. as *John a Kent and John a Cumber*: reprinted by the Malone Society
14 Dec.	*The Set at Maw*	new	4	lost
19 Dec.	*Tamberlaine*, part II	old	7	By Marlowe—printed 1590
26 Dec.	*The Siege of London*	old	12	lost
1595				
4 Jan.	*Antony and Valia*	old	4	lost
11 Feb.	*The French Comedy*	new	6	lost
14 Feb.	*Long Meg of Westminster*	new	16	lost
21 Feb.	*The Mack*	new	1	lost
5 Mar.	*Selio and Olimpo*	new	10	lost

(No playing between the 14th March and the 22nd April during Lent.)

7 May	*I Hercules*	new	11	By Heywood—printed as *The Silver Age*, 1613
23 May	*II Hercules*	new	8	By Heywood—printed as *The Brazen Age*, 1613
3 June	*The Seven Days of the Week*	new	22	lost
18 June	*II Caesar and Pompey*	new	2	lost

(No playing between the 26th June and the 25th August, because of riots in Southwark: see *II Elizabethan Journal*, p. 30.)

29 Aug.	*Longshanks*	new	14	lost
5 Sept.	*Crack me this Nut*	new	16	lost

Date	Play	New or Old	No. of Performances	Remarks
1595				
17 Sept.	*The New World's Tragedy*	new	11	lost
2 Oct.	*The Disguises*	new	6	lost
15 Oct.	*The Wonder of a Woman*	new	9	lost
28 Oct.	*Barnardo and Fiammetta*	new	7	lost
14 Nov.	*A Toy to please Chaste Ladies*	new	9	lost
28 Nov.	*Henry the Fifth*	new	13	lost; probably *not The famous Victories of Henry V*
29 Nov.	*The Welshman*	old	1	lost
1596				
3 Jan.	*Chinon of England*	new	14	lost
16 Jan.	*Pythagoras*	new	12	lost
22 Jan.	*II Seven Days of the Week*	new	2	lost
3 Feb.	*I Fortunatus*	old	6	An earlier version of the play rewritten by Dekker in Nov. 1599
12 Feb.	*The Blind Beggar of Alexandria*	new	22	By Chapman—printed in 1598

(No playing between the 27th Feb. and the 12th April during Lent.)

29 April	*Julian the Apostata*	new	3	lost
6 May	*I Tamar Cam*	new	10	lost—noted by Henslowe as new but a revision of an older play first acted at the Rose in 1592
19 May	*Phocas*	new	7	lost
11 June	*II Tamar Cam*	new	4	lost

Date	Play	New or Old	No. of Performances	Remarks
1596				
22 June	*Troy*	new	4	lost
1 July	*The Paradox*	new	1	lost
18 July	*The Tinker of Totnes*	new	1	lost

(No playing between the 15th July and the 26th October owing to fear of plague. See *II Elizabethan Journal*, p. 111.)

4 Dec.	*Volteger*	new	12	lost
11 Dec.	*Stukeley*	new	10	Anonymous—entered 11 Aug. 1600. Earliest text dated 1605
19 Dec.	*Nabuchodonozor*	new	8	lost
30 Dec.	*That will be shall be*	new	12	lost
1597				
7 Jan.	*Jeronimo* (i.e. *The Spanish Tragedy*)	new	13	By Kyd—entered 6 Oct. 1592. Earliest text dated 1596 —a revised version of the old favourite
14 Jan.	*Alexander and Lodovick*	new	15	lost
27 Jan.	*Woman hard to Please*	old	11	lost
3 Feb.	*Osric*	old	2	lost

(No playing between the 12th Feb. and the 3rd March during Lent.)

19 Mar.	*Guido*	new	5	lost
7 April	*Five plays in one*	new	10	lost
13 April	*Time's Triumph*	old	13	lost
15 April	*A French Comedy*	new	11	lost
29 April	*Uther Pendragon*	new	7	lost
11 May	*The Comedy of Humours*	new		i.e. Chapman's *Humorous Day's Mirth*. Printed 1599, see page 158

Date	Play	New or Old	No. of Performances	Remarks
1597				
26 May	*The Life and Death of Henry I*	new	6	lost
3 June	*Frederick and Basilia*	new	4	lost
22 June	*Hengist*	old	1	lost; but perhaps the same as *Volteger* (above)
30 June	*The Life and Death of Martin Smart*	new	3	lost
14 July	*The Witch of Islington*	old	2	lost

(On the 28th July the playhouses were closed by order of the Privy Council, see page 161.)

Chapter IX

THE CHAMBERLAIN'S MEN

ONCE settled in their own playhouse, the Chamberlain's men soon began to overtake the Admiral's. Shakespeare was their chief playwright, and as yet without any rival. He had, by this time, written the three parts of *Henry the Sixth*, *The Taming of the Shrew* and *Titus Andronicus*, which, in spite of the appalling bloodiness of its story, contained touches of poetry of a quality that no one else had reached. In a very different kind, he had written *Love's Labour's Lost*, a comedy for a select audience, sparkling with quips and private jokes, bubbling over with wit, poetry, and—if one paused to take the play seriously for a moment— a common-sense philosophy of life which showed up the essential insincerity of the amorist sonneteer and the book-learned sage. It owed much to Lyly. There had recently been a boom in Lyly's plays. *Campaspe* and *Sapho and Phao* had first been printed in 1584; but in 1591 the Widow Broome printed *Endimion*; new editions of *Campaspe* and *Sapho and Phao* followed; and in 1592 *Gallathea* and *Midas* were also printed. Shakespeare thus had Lyly in print, and learnt much from him. Moth, Armado, and Costard, the sallies of wit between the young noblemen and the ladies of France would never have been written but for Lyly's example; but not in a hundred years could Lyly have achieved the resilient exuberance of the language or the cleverness of the characterization.

Shakespeare's versatility in the early years was amazing. At the same time it was not—as critics usually forget—the exuberance of youth. Shakespeare was now thirty. If 'the Young Shakespeare' ever wrote anything, it has disappeared!

One of Shakespeare's first successes with the Chamberlain's Men was *Richard the Third*. In this play he ended the story of the Wars of the Roses, which he had begun in the first part of *Henry the Sixth*. He owed much to Marlowe in the language and general pattern of the play. It was another Machiavellian drama, and, like the *Jew of Malta*, it began with an opening soliloquy by the villain. The play has its symbolism. The aged Queen Margaret broods over all as an avenging fury. She was the nearest approach to the personified Revenges, Destinies and Murders of earlier drama which persisted to the end of the sixteenth century but which offended Shakespeare's sense of realism. It gave another villainous and astounding character to the English stage, and Richard Burbage his first good part. Burbage made his name in *Richard the Third*, and his acting in the final scene when Richard dies, furious and despairing, on Bosworth field, was much admired. Indeed there was a story current a generation or two later that when a Bosworth inn-keeper used to show visitors over the battlefield, he would point out to them the place where Burbage cried: ' A horse! A horse! My kingdom for a horse!'

Another play in the repertory of the Chamberlain's Men at this time was *A Comedy of Errors*. It was performed on Innocents' Day (the 28th December 1594) in the hall of Gray's Inn. That winter the young gentlemen of Gray's Inn had decided to hold revels on a grand scale. They turned themselves into a mock kingdom, elected a Prince of Purpool—a certain gentleman from Norfolk called

Henry Helmes—and set about the most elaborate parody of the ceremonials of state used by great Princes. The first night of their revels was attended by the junior members of the Temple in state, who entered into the spirit of the game and despatched an ambassador from the neighbouring kingdom of Templaria. The first night was so successful and caused so much excitement that the ambitious revellers were encouraged to overreach themselves.

'The next grand night'—so the official chronicle reads— 'was intended to be upon Innocents' Day at night; at which time there was a great presence of lords, ladies and worshipful personages, that did expect some notable performance at that time; which, indeed, had been effected, if the multitude of beholders had not been so exceeding great that thereby there was no convenient room for those that were actors; by reason whereof, very good inventions and conceipts could not have opportunity to be applauded, which otherwise would have been great contentation to the beholders.'

The ambassador of the Templarians appeared and was duly welcomed, but when the time came for the show to be presented '... there arose such a disordered tumult and crowd upon the stage that there was no opportunity to effect that which was intended. There came so great a number of worshipful personages upon the stage that might not be displaced; and gentlewomen, whose sex did privilege them from violence, that when the Prince and his officers had in vain a good while expected and endeavoured a reformation, at length there was no hope of redress for that present. The Lord Ambassador and his train thought that they were not so kindly entertained as was before expected, and thereupon would not stay any longer at that time, but, in a sort, discontented and displeased. After their departure the throngs and tumults did somewhat cease, although so much of them continued as was able to disorder and confound any good inventions whatsoever. In regard whereof, as also for that the sports intended were especially for the gracing of the Templarians, it was thought good not to offer any thing of account, saving dancing and revelling with gentlewomen ; and after such sports, *A Comedy of Errors* (like to Plautus his *Menechmus*) was played by the players. So that night was begun and continued to the end in nothing but confusions and errors ; whereupon, it was afterwards called The Night of Errors.' [1]

Apparently it was the second performance that the Chamberlain's Men gave that day. In the Chamber Accounts there is recorded a payment ' to William Kemp, William Shakespeare, and Richard Burbage, servants to the Lord Chamberlain, upon the Council's warrant, dated at Whitehall xv^{to} Martii, 1594 [–5] for two several comedies or interludes showed by them before her Majesty in Christmas time last past, viz. : upon Saint Stephen's Day and Innocents' Day, £13 6s. 8d. And by way of her Majesty's reward, £6 13s. 4d.' The Admiral's Men also were recorded as playing on Innocents' Day.[2]

The entry in the Court Accounts is the first actual mention of Shakespeare by name amongst the Chamberlain's players, or indeed any company. Shakespeare wrote several other plays in the months following. *A Midsummer Night's Dream* is usually assigned to the spring of 1595, and was apparently composed for a wedding. About the same time he wrote *Romeo and Juliet* which was immediately and permanently popular. It was by far the best tragedy that

---

[1] *Gesta Grayorum*, Malone Society Reprints, pp. 20, 22.

[2] *Elizabethan Stage*, iv, 164. Chambers believes that the Clerk made an error and that the actual date was the 27th December. It was not common for two plays to be given at Court on one day, though there were other instances recorded.

had yet appeared on the English stage. The plotting was magnificent, using every device of the theatre, and the poetry something quite new.

Richard the Second followed soon afterwards. Here Shakespeare ventured to rival Marlowe. Marlowe's *Edward the Second* was also the story of a weak king deposed by rough and indignant subjects. Audiences still liked listening to poetry, and Shakespeare gave them full measure in Richard's many soliloquies. Again he showed his sense of the theatre. In Marlowe's play history was hustled too quickly; he attempted more than a two hours' drama would allow. Shakespeare constructed a plot that surmounted the many difficulties of a chronicle play. It began with an exciting opening scene, reaching a first climax in the quarrel between Bolingbroke and Norfolk, and followed with fine episodes, all telling on the stage; the lists at Coventry; the death of old Gaunt; the deposition of the King: his murder; and the solemn mournful ending. The characterization, however, in *Richard the Second* was much weaker than in *Romeo and Juliet*. If *Richard* is the later play, then Shakespeare sacrificed realistic dramatization for the sake of poetic speech. There was a good deal of the same weakness in parts of *King John*; which seems to have followed soon after; but the likeliest explanation here is that the play was written by two hands.

Shakespeare's next play was *The Merchant of Venice*. By this time his stagecraft had matured. He had learned how to open a play with a scene which not only set the plot moving, but created a mood as well as stated a fact. In the trial scene he gave one of the most exciting reversals of the situation in all comedy, and in the final scene he created, by the sheer music of words, the atmosphere of romance and moonlight. During these months (1594–6) Shakespeare was without any serious rival.

As a result, the Chamberlain's Men soon ousted their rivals from popular favour. This can be seen from the records of Court performances. In the Christmas season of 1594–5, the Chamberlain's Men acted twice, the Admiral's three times. The following Christmas they acted four times at Court, the Admiral's twice, though the Admiral's played two plays at Shrovetide 1596 to the Chamberlain's one. In the Christmas holidays of 1596–7, the Chamberlain's Men again played four times at Court and twice at Shrovetide; but for neither holiday season were the Admiral's Men invited.

By this time new troubles were threatening at the Theatre. The lease between James Burbage and Giles Alleyn would expire in 1597. In the original contract it had been agreed that Burbage should have the option of renewing it upon agreed terms, but the landlord was propounding certain new and disagreeable conditions. He proposed to raise the rent from £14 to £24 a year, and further, that Burbage should only continue to use the Theatre as a playhouse for five years. This was impossible. It was clear to him that Giles Alleyn would not be reasonable.

Burbage therefore began to look around for another site. He remembered the former competition of the boys in the Blackfriars Theatre.[1] In the storey below that formerly occupied by Farrant's playhouse the old monks' parlour still existed. Beyond was the old hall. After Lyly's day these rooms had been used as a fencing school for noblemen and gentlemen where Rocco Bonnetti, a famous Italian fencing master, had established himself. The school had since ceased, and partitions had been erected, dividing it up into rooms. Burbage acquired the parlour and hall, removed all

---

[1] For the facts and records concerning the second playhouse in the Blackfriars, see Adams, Chapter XI and *Elizabethan Stage*, vol. ii, chapter xvii.

partitions, and restored the parlour to its former shape: further, by taking in the hall he made available a room 46 feet wide by 66 feet long. This was smaller than the open-air public playhouse, but had certain advantages. In the public playhouse plays were acted by daylight and there was no roof to the yard. On a wet day, therefore, the public playhouse was uncomfortable; and every day the company in the audience was very mixed.

In Burbage's private playhouse plays would be acted under cover, and by candlelight. There would be many advantages in this arrangement. Higher prices could be charged, and the playhouse would cater, as formerly in Lyly's day, solely for well-to-do spectators; and, as Burbage realized, the future of the business lay in further attracting the gentleman spectator, and not with the apprentices in the yard.

Burbage spent much money on his new playhouse. The original buildings cost him £600, and the cost of the alterations and decorations was considerable. In the autumn of 1596, when the playhouse was almost ready to be occupied, the inhabitants protested. They sent a petition to the Privy Council:

'Humbly showing and beseeching your Honours, the inhabitants of the precinct of the Blackfriars, London, that whereas one Burbage hath lately bought certain rooms in the same precinct near adjoining unto the dwelling houses of the Right Honourable the Lord Chamberlain and the Lord of Hunsdon, which rooms the said Burbage is now altering, and meaneth very shortly to convert and turn the same into a common playhouse, which will grow to be a very great annoyance and trouble, not only to all the noblemen and gentlemen thereabout inhabiting, but also a general inconvenience to all the inhabitants of the same precinct, both by reason of the great resort and gathering together of all manner of vagrant and lewd persons, that, under colour of resorting to the plays, will come thither and work all manner of mischief, and also to the great pestering and filling up of the same precinct, if it should please God to send any visitation of sickness as heretofore hath been, for that the same precinct is already grown very populous ; and besides, that the same playhouse is so near the Church that the noise of the drums and trumpets will greatly disturb and hinder both the ministers and parishioners in time of divine service and sermons : in tender consideration whereof, as also for that there hath not at any time heretofore been used any common playhouse within the same precinct, but that now all players being banished by the Lord Mayor from playing within the City by reason of the great inconveniences and ill rule that followeth them, they now think to plant themselves in liberties. That therefore it would please your Honours to take order that the same rooms may be converted to some other use, and that no playhouse may be used or kept there ; and your suppliants as most bounden shall and will daily pray for your Lordships in all honour and happiness long to live. Elizabeth Russell, dowager ; G. Hunsdon ; Henry Bowes ; Thomas Browne ; John Crooke ; William Meredith ; Stephen Egerton ; Richard Lee ; — Smith ; William Paddy ; William de Lavine ; Francis Hinson ; John Edwards ; Andrew Lyons ; Thomas Nayle ; Owen Lochard ; John Robbinson ; Thomas Homes ; Richard Feild ; William Watts ; Henry Boice ; Edward Ley ; John Clarke ; William Bispham ; Robert Baheire ; Ezechiell Major ; Harman Buckholt ; John Le Mere ; John Dollin ; Ascanio de Renialmire ; John Wharton.'[1]

Of the signatories, two are remarkable. The first, Elizabeth Russell, dowager, was a shrill-voiced lady whose grievances appear in every collection of Elizabethan documents. She was for ever complaining. She had married

[1] *Elizabethan Stage*, iv, 319.

the heir of the Earl of Bedford, but to her everlasting grief her husband died before succeeding to the title. She had ever afterwards insisted on regarding herself as a dowager countess. Some years later—in King James's reign—she greatly distinguished herself by conducting her own case against the Lord Admiral before the Star Chamber ; and she had her say to the bitter and voluble end, in spite of every attempt to stop the flow of her eloquence. It was natural to expect this lady's signature to any petition. It is, however, the more surprising to find Lord George Hunsdon among the petitioners, for he was the patron of Richard Burbage's company.

The Council accepted the petition, and issued an order that the house should not be used for plays. Burbage was thus completely thwarted. His plans had come to nothing and he had wasted £800 to £900. He did not survive these troubles long, but died in February 1597, leaving the Theatre property to his son Cuthbert, and the Blackfriars to Richard.

Chapter X

THE HUMOURS

Of the new plays put on by the Admiral's Men during these months at the Rose, two were especially remarkable: *The Blind Beggar of Alexandria*, and *An Humorous Day's Mirth*. Both were written by George Chapman. Hitherto Chapman had been known principally for certain long, obscure and rather pretentious poems. He was a learned poet.

As the theatres had prospered in recent years, and the standard of play-writing and acting had so vastly improved, so gentlemen of intelligence felt that they could, without demeaning themselves, patronize the players. This change in the social standing of the audience is increasingly obvious in the type of play produced.

Intellectuals at this time were becoming obsessed with the possibilities of the medical theory of 'humours.' Medieval scientists, basing their theory of medicine upon Aristotle, recognized four elements of matter: earth, air, fire and water. Into these elements, so they believed, all matter could ultimately be resolved. The theory was not to be taken too literally, for the four elements were rather principles or theoretical conceptions. It followed that the human body, being itself matter, must also be compounded of four elements. This was accepted as a basic principle of physiology. Physicians treated their patients with drugs to correct their particular humours and prescribed appropriate diets.

THE HUMOURS

Towards the end of the sixteenth century anatomy was much studied. Enlightened princes presented the local College of Surgeons with the corpse of a criminal for dissection. The word anatomy itself became popular in literary jargon. Thus *Euphues* was the 'anatomy of wit.' When they came to ponder over the human body, men of learning were impressed with the fact that it was damp all through : it possessed all-pervading *humor*, that is, the quality of wetness. But the 'humours' of the body were obviously of different kinds, and on the theory of the four elements, the body also had its four different kinds of 'humour.' So :

Earth—was represented by black bile, which was heavy and produced the *melancholic humour*.

Air—was represented by blood and produced a *sanguine humour*.

Fire—was represented by bile and produced a *choleric humour*.

Water—represented by phlegm—producing a *phlegmatic humour*.

In a healthy body all the 'humours' were accurately balanced one against the other, but if one 'humour' was predominant or deficient, then the individual became mentally and physically unbalanced. His body and his mind functioned irregularly. His bodily state was also reflected in his appearance. Too much blood produced an airy or sanguine temperament. Too much fire produced a choleric peppery temper and showed itself in a red, fiery face. Too much phlegm made a man heavy, dull and waterish. Too much black bile produced melancholic men. Hence, when a man suffered from the dumps, he was said to have a 'melancholic humour.' The word 'humour' was extended to include every kind of oddity of behaviour.

Though its use in this way can be traced back much earlier, yet about this time it suddenly became popular, as words sometimes will, and every intelligent person began to talk of his humours. Indeed it became the mark of an intellectual to have a humour, preferably melancholic; forty years later melancholy was still the mark of Il Penseroso, the serious student. Thus ' humour ' in the late 1590's and for the next few years had almost the meaning of the modern word ' complex,' and lack of humour is almost the same as ' inhibition.'[1]

Psychologists have progressed the full circle, and many modern theories have almost come back to Elizabethan notions. An excess or deficiency of glandular activity is nowadays regarded in much the same way as an excess or deficiency of humour by an Elizabethan. Moreover, just as Freudian psychology at fourth hand has furnished the critic and the biographer with technical jargon, so at the end of the sixteenth-century fashionable intellectuals suddenly took up the word ' humour ' and worked it to death.

Its first prominent appearance on the stage was in Chapman's play of *The Blind Beggar of Alexandria*. The play exists only in an unsatisfactory quarto of some sixteen hundred lines, and is therefore probably mutilated. The more serious speeches have disappeared and the comedy has survived. It was one of the most popular plays of the season at the Rose. The principal character was Irus, the blind beggar, a Protean person who affected many disguises. As Irus he had the reputation of being a profound soothsayer. As Leon, the rich usurer, he grasped into his own hands much of the wealth of Alexandria. As Count Hermes, the madbrained swashbuckler, he swaggered around. As Duke Cleanthes, he was the Queen's lover and hoped to become King.

[1] Some of the symptoms and causes of this notable outburst of melancholy are discussed in an *Essay on Elizabethan Melancholy*, appended to my edition of Nicholas Breton's *Melancholic Humours*.

Count Hermes was a man with a humour, as he carefully explained to the audience when before their eyes he was transformed from beggar to Count.

> ... Now to my wardrobe for my velvet gown;
> Now doth the sport begin.
> Come, gird this pistol closely to my side,
> By which I make men fear my humour still,
> And have slain two or three, as 'twere my mood,
> When I have done it most advisedly,
> To rid them, as they were my heavy foes.
> Now am I known to be the mad-brain Count,
> Whose humours twice five summers I have held,
> And said at first I came from stately Rome,
> Calling myself Count Hermes, and assuming
> The humour of a wild and frantic man,
> Careless of what I say or what I do;
> And so such faults as I of purpose do
> Is buried in my humour; and this gown I wear
> In rain, or snow, or in the hottest summer,
> And never go nor ride without a gown;
> Which humour does not fit my frenzy well,
> But hides my person's form from being known,
> When I Cleanthes am to be descried.

The new notion of the humours soon became satirical. Scientists unemotionally observing the behaviour of *homo sapiens*, can remain objective, but artists who study psychology are usually disgusted with humanity and erupt into satire. At this time of great national anxiety there was a ready public for satire of all kinds. The taste had been fostered by the Martin Marprelate flytings. Neither Nashe nor Dr. Gabriel Harvey could claim to be persons of any general importance, yet their quarrel had become a public and exciting event. The reading public was therefore ready for a new attempt at English verse satire on the Latin model. On the 31st March 1597 there was entered the first part of

Virgidemiarum, written by Joseph Hall, at that time a young, earnest, puritanical, Cambridge don. He claimed to be a pioneer :

> I first adventure with foolhardy might,
> To tread the steps of perilous despite :
> I first adventure ; follow me who list,
> And be the second English Satirist.

It was not entirely a just claim, for Lodge had already published verse satire in couplets some years before, but he was before his time. Hall very naturally reread his *Juvenal*, though his satires were sufficiently English in tone and matter. Satire at once became a literary fashion, and in the next two years new volumes of satire were appearing from the Press every few weeks. Since the reading public was also to a large extent the playgoing public, it was likely that some enterprising playwright would try to transfer the spirit of satire to the stage. Chapman was the first.

On the 11th May 1597 the Admiral's Men produced his play *An Humorous Day's Mirth* for the first time. It was very well received. A month later John Chamberlain remarked in a letter to Dudley Carleton : ' We have here a new play of humours in very great request, and I was drawn along to it by the common applause, but my opinion of it is (as the fellow said of the shearing of hogs) that there was a great cry for so little wool.' [1]

An Humorous Day's Mirth was the first true comedy of humours, and although the names are foreign, it is a play of contemporary life.

Count Labervele, an elderly nobleman, has married Florilla, a young Puritan girl. He is a jealous husband, and torments himself incessantly. The gallants are much

---

[1] *Letters written by John Chamberlain*, edited by Sarah Williams, Camden Society, p. 4.

interested in the lady, whose puritanism at first is excessive. When she comes in, she is tormented in conscience at her new clothes : ' What have I done ? ' she cries. ' Put on too many clothes ; the day is hot, and I am hotter clad than might suffice health ; my conscience tells me that I have offended, and I'll put them off. That will ask time that might be better spent ; one sin will draw another quickly so ; see how the devil tempts. But what's here ? jewels ? how should these come here ? '

She takes up the jewels which her husband has left, fearing that it is a sin to stoop to take them up ' bowing my body to an idle work ; the strength that I have had to this very deed might have been used to take a poor soul up in the highway.' She is full of pretty and priggish Puritan sentiments.

Labervele is a perfect Burtonian type. To torment himself, as such unbalanced persons are prone to do, he proposes that his wife shall put herself to the test and enter fast society. She takes very kindly to her temptation, to Labervele's increasing distrust. She is quite keen to experiment further into the ways of gallants, especially when led on by Lemot. Lemot takes her to Court and publicly shames her, pretending to be her adorer. He makes as if to kiss her hand, and bites it. Lemot is one of the earlier stage specimens of plain blunt man. Florilla returns disillusioned to her puritanism and all is well with her husband. She takes off her fine clothing and ends with the same sentiments that she began.

' Surely the world is full of vanity ; a woman must take heed she do not hear a lewd man speak ; for every woman cannot, when she is tempted, when the wicked fiend gets her into his snares, escape like me ; for grace's measure is not so filled up, nor so pressed down, in every one as me, but yet I promise you a little more. Well, I'll go seek my head, who shall take me in the gates of his kind arms, untouched of any.'

There were other types in the comedy; Monsieur Blanuel, the foolish gentleman who has the humour of compliment and can only echo the last words said to him. Most important was Dowsecer. He was the first of the many melancholics who, for the next few years, cumbered the English stage, half hidden in a large black cloak and a wide-brimmed hat, standing conspicuously apart, glowering on humanity, uttering harsh and embarrassing croaks. He comes in reading his Cicero, and scorning the world. He was not, however, the truest of melancholics, for he fell in love and changed his mind.

In *An Humorous Day's Mirth* there was not that excess of character drawing that mars some later specimens. Indeed the play was rather a comedy of situation, but it was essentially written for the upper classes—a sure indication of the change of audience. Henceforward the notion of the humours rapidly became popular, particularly in plays and poems written by and for young gentlemen.

Shortly after this John Marston wrote his *Scourge of Villainy*, the most popular of the books of satire. It is full of humours; type after type is sketched and lashed. Marston added a tenth satire: he called it '*Humours*,' and gave his little list of those who irritated him most: the gallant whose head was full of nothing but dancing; the inordinate playgoer; the young man who could think of nothing but fencing; the jester in season and out; the sour critic; the lecher; the fashion monger; they are all specimens of the humours who might well be missed.[1]

Early in the spring of 1597 some of the actors, apparently from the major companies, had banded together to form a new company under the patronage of the Earl of Pembroke.

[1] For a specimen see quotation on page 55.

The chief members of this new company were: Robert Shaw (his name is sometimes spelt Shaa), Richard Jones, Gabriel Spencer (who was apparently a Chamberlain's Man, and a good actor), William Bird (or Borne) and Thomas Downton. They agreed with Francis Langley, who owned the Swan Theatre on the Bankside, to play at his house for a year. In return Langley put up the capital to set them going and refurbished the playhouse.[1]

The new Pembroke's company acted at the Swan Theatre for some months quite successfully, but then, unhappily for themselves and for all other theatres, they chose to put on a play called *The Isle of Dogs*. This was written by Thomas Nashe, and a member of the company who now first comes into prominence—Benjamin Jonson.

For the last few years Nashe had been much in the public eye by reason of his quarrel with Gabriel Harvey. After Greene's death in September 1592, Harvey foolishly and vindictively published his obnoxious *Four Letters*. In the course of them Harvey had something to say to Nashe as a bright young man led astray by Greene. He had rebuked him as a don might rebuke a clever undergraduate who was wasting his time and his talents. Nashe was annoyed and always ready to squirt ink at anyone. Harvey's *Four Letters* were entered on the 4th December 1592. Nashe had quickly retorted with a pungent, witty, bitter reply called *Strange News of the Intercepting of a convoy of Verses as they were going privily to victual the Low Countries*. This was entered on the 12th January 1593. Harvey was rashly stung into answering it. He replied with *Pierce's Supererogation*. He also published *A New Letter of Notable Contents*. In 1596 Nashe hit back with *Have with you to Saffron Walden*, which is one of the finest pieces of scurrilous abuse in the English language.

[1] *Elizabethan Stage*, ii, 131.

Nashe was one who dipped his pen in vitriol. The fashion for abusing one's contemporaries was quickly gaining ground. Hall's *Satires* were finding many readers and imitators. Moreover, now that the theatres attracted a quick-witted public, dramatists were encouraged to risk prosecution and to become openly critical of society and its rulers. A satiric comedy by Nashe was likely therefore to have been bitter. *The Isle of Dogs* has unfortunately perished, but it caused no small noise at the time.

Either because of the scandal caused by this play, or because of their perennial dislike of players, the Lord Mayor directed one of the periodical letters from the City to the Council, asking for the playhouses to be suppressed. The letter was dated the 28th July :

'Our humble duties remembered to your good Lordships and the rest. We have signified to your Honours many times heretofore the great inconvenience which we find to grow by the common exercise of stage plays. We presumed to do as well in respect of the duty we bear towards Her Highness for the good government of this her City, as for conscience' sake, being persuaded (under correction of your Honours' judgment) that neither in polity nor in religion they are to be suffered in a Christian commonwealth, specially being of that frame and matter as usually they are, containing nothing but profane fables, lascivious matters, cozening devices and scurrilous behaviours, which are so set forth as that they move wholly to imitation, and not to the avoiding of those faults and vices which they represent. Among other inconveniences it is not the least that they give opportunity to the refuse sort of evil disposed and ungodly people that are within and about this City to assemble themselves and to make their matches for all their lewd and ungodly practices ; being as heretofore we have found by the examination of **divers** apprentices and other servants who have confessed unto us that the said stage plays were the very places of their rendezvous appointed by them to meet with such others as were to join with them in their designs and mutinous attempts, being also the ordinary places for masterless men to come together and to recreate themselves. For avoiding whereof we are now again most humble and earnest suitors to your Honours to direct your letters as well to ourselves as to the Justices of Peace of Surrey and Middlesex for the present stay and final suppressing of the said stage plays, as well at the Theatre, Curtain and Bankside as in all other places in and about the City. Whereby we doubt not but the opportunity and the very cause of many disorders being taken away, we shall be more able to keep the worse sort of such evil and disordered people in better order than heretofore we have been. And so most humbly we take our leaves. From London the 28th of July 1597.

' The Inconveniences that grow by Stage Plays about the City of London :

' 1. They are a special cause of corrupting their youth, containing nothing but unchaste matters, lascivious devices, shifts of cozenage and other lewd and ungodly practices, being so as that they impress the very quality and corruption of manners which they represent, contrary to the rules and art prescribed for the making of comedies even among the heathen, who used them seldom and at certain set times, and not all the year long as our manner is. Whereby such as frequent them, being of the base and refuse sort of people or such young gentlemen as have small regard of credit or conscience, draw the same into imitation and not to the avoiding the like vices which they represent.

' 2. They are the ordinary places for vagrant persons, masterless men, thieves, horse stealers, whoremongers, cozeners, connycatchers, contrivers of treason and other idle and dangerous persons to meet together and to make their matches to the great displeasure of Almighty God and the hurt and annoyance of Her Majesty's people, which cannot be prevented nor discovered by the Governors of the City for that they are out of the City's jurisdiction.

'3. They maintain idleness in such persons as have no vocation and draw apprentices and other servants from their ordinary works and all sorts of people from the resort unto sermons and other Christian exercises, to the great hindrance of trades and profanation of religion established by Her Highness within this Realm.

'4. In the time of sickness it is found by experience that many having sores and yet not heart-sick take occasion hereby to walk abroad and to recreate themselves by hearing a play. Whereby others are infected and themselves also many things miscarry.'[1]

There was nothing new in the Lord Mayor's complaint (except the interesting observation about the artistic deficiencies of comedy, which showed that someone had been reading critical theory). The Council were moved to immediate action. They were becoming seriously alarmed at the increasing levity of writers and the criticism of society (which reflected on the Government) now everywhere apparent. The same day letters were sent out to the magistrates of Middlesex and Surrey. 'Her Majesty,' they said, 'being informed that there are very great disorders committed in the common playhouses both by lewd matters that are handled on the stages and by resort and confluence of bad people, hath given direction that not only no plays shall be used within London or about the City or in any public place during this time of summer, but that also those playhouses that are erected and built only for such purposes shall be plucked down.' The magistrates were therefore

[1] *Malone Society Collections*, i, 78, reprinted in *Elizabethan Stage*, iv, 321.

ordered to send for the owners of the playhouses and to enjoin them 'forthwith to pluck down quite the stages, galleries and rooms that are made for people to stand in ; and so to deface the same that they may not be employed again to such use.'

The Lords of the Council were indeed very angry, which makes it more regrettable that Nashe's play has not survived. They took their revenge on the players ; Gabriel Spencer, Robert Shaw and Benjamin Jonson were sent to prison in the Marshalsea. Nashe escaped. He took to his heels. For some weeks his whereabouts were unknown, but in the early autumn he turned up at his native town of Yarmouth. On the 15th August the Council directed :

'A letter to Richard Topcliffe, Thomas Fowler and Richard Skevington, esquires, Doctor Fletcher and Mr. Wilbraham. Upon the information given us of a lewd play that was played in one of the playhouses on the Bankside, containing very seditious and slanderous matter, we caused some of the players to be apprehended and committed to prison, whereof one of them was not only an actor but a maker of part of the said play. For as much as it is thought meet that the rest of the players or actors in that matter shall be apprehended to receive such punishment as their lewd and mutinous behaviour doth deserve, these shall be therefore to require you to examine those of the players that are committed, whose names are known to you, Mr. Topcliffe, what is become of the rest of their fellows that either had their parts in the devising of that seditious matter or that were actors or players in the same ; what copies they have given forth of the said play, and to whom ; and such other points as you shall think meet to be demanded of them ; wherein you shall require them to deal truly as they will look to receive any favour. We pray you also to peruse such papers as were found in Nashe his lodgings, which Ferrys, a messenger of the Chamber, shall deliver unto you, and to certify us the examinations you take. So, etc.'[1]

It was most unfortunate for the players of the other companies who were not implicated. The season, as Henslowe's *Diary* shows, was promising. And now, after an almost uninterrupted run for three years, chaos had come again.

Now that disaster had fallen upon them, Pembroke's Men realized that their venture had been a failure. Henslowe saw his chance. He reorganized his own company and attracted the best players from Pembroke's. One by one they came over to the Rose and there agreed that henceforward they would play for him. Ben Jonson was one of the first; indeed he compacted with the Admiral's on the day that he went to jail. There are two entries in the *Diary*, dated the 28th July 1597.[2] One is a record that Henslowe received 3s. 9d. 'of Benjamin Jonson's share.' The other was recorded at the end of the book:

'Lent unto Benjamin Jonson player the 28th of July 1597 in ready money the sum of four pounds, to be paid it again whensoever either I or any for me shall demand it. I say . . . . £4.
'Witness, E. Alleyn and J. Singer.'

Jones arrived nine days later, and again the book was taken down:

'Memorandum that the 6th of August 1597 I bound Richard Jones by an assumpsit of 2d. to continue and play with the company of My Lord Admiral's players from Michælmas next after the day above written until the end and term of 3 years immediately following, and to play in my house only known by the name of the Rose, and in no other house about London public, and if restraint be granted then to go for the time into the country, and after to return

---

[1] *Elizabethan Stage*, iv, 323. [2] i, 47, 200.

again to London. If he break this assumpsit then to forfeit unto me for the same a hundred marks of lawful money of England. Witness to this, E. Alleyn and John Middleton.

'Moreover Richard Jones at that time hath taken one other 2*d.* of me upon an assumpsit to forfeit unto me one hundred marks if one Robert Shaw do not play with My Lord Admiral's Men as he hath covenanted before in every thing and time to the uttermost. Witness, E. Alleyn, John Middleton.' [1]

Borne (alias Bird) signed a similar agreement on the 10th August, and Downton on the 6th October. When playing did start again, the Rose would be in a strong position.

[1] Henslowe's *Diary*, i, 202.

Chapter XI

BEN JONSON

THE restraint on playing continued all through the summer, but the Council relented earlier than might have been expected. On the 3rd October, a warrant was directed to the Keeper of the Marshalsea to release Spencer, Shaw and Jonson. On the 11th playing began again at the Rose. Henslowe started a new series of entries in his ledger:

'October, 1597

'In the name of God, Amen.

'The 11th October began my Lord Admiral's and my Lord Pembroke's Men to play at my house, 1597.'[1]

Their first three plays were: *The Spanish Tragedy*, *The Comedy of Humours* and *Doctor Faustus*.

After a few days Henslowe ceased to record the daily plays and takings. With the new combination of companies the relations between company and owner were altered. Henceforward Henslowe acted as banker for the players. He paid out money on their behalf to their clients, and from time to time recorded their repayments to him. From this point the *Diary* changes, and as a revelation of theatrical economics is even more illuminating. For the next four and a half years Henslowe reveals minutely the affairs of the players. He headed this new account:[2]

[1] Henslowe's *Diary*, i, 54.
[2] Henslowe's *Diary*, i, 82. These extracts have been left in their original spelling as a specimen of Henslowe's orthography.

BEN JONSON

A Juste a cownt of all suche money as J haue
layd owt for my lord admeralles players begynyng
the xj of october whose names ar as foloweth
borne gabrell shaw Jonnes dowten Jube towne
synger & the ij geffes 1597

---

layd owt vnto Robarte shawe to by a boocke for the
companey the 21 of october 1597 the some of . . } xxxx^s
called the cobler   wittnes E. Alleyn

---

lent vnto Robarte shaw to by a boocke of yonge harton
the 5 of novmber 1597 the some of . . . . } x^s
   wittnes E. Alleyn

---

lent vnto Robarte shaw for the companey to bye viij
y^{r}des of clothe of gowlde for the womones gowne in bran } iiij^{ll}
howlte the 26 of novmber 1597 the some of. . .

---

lent vnto Robarte shaw to geue the tayller to by tynssell
for bornes gowne the j of desember 1597 . . . } ix^s

---

layd owt for the companye to by tafetie & tynssell
for the bodeyes of a womones gowne to playe allce perce
wch j dd vnto the littell tayller the 8 of desember 1597 } xx^s
   wittnes E. Alleyn

---

layd owt for mackynge allce perces bodeyes & a payer
of yeare sleaues the some of . . . . } vj^s vij^d

---

lent vnto Bengemen Johnson the 3 of desember 1597
vpon a boocke wch he showed the plotte vnto the
company wch he promysed to dd vnto the company } xx^s
at cryssmas next the some of . . . .

---

lent vnto Robart shawe to by cop^r lace of sylver for
a payer of hosse in alls perce the 10 of desember 1597. } xvj^s
   wittnes w^m borne Jube & gabrell spenser

ELIZABETHAN PLAYS AND PLAYERS

The members of the reorganized company were thus: William Borne, Gabriel Spencer, Robert Shaw, Richard Jones, Thomas Dutton, Edward Juby, Thomas Towne, John Singer, Humphrey Jeffes, Anthony Jeffes. Alleyn, for the time, had retired from playing.

Meanwhile the Chamberlain's Men had lost some ground. Gabriel Spencer had left them, and the Admiral's, although they lacked the great Alleyn, had been strengthened by certain notable additions.

It was not long before the Chamberlain's Men reasserted their superiority and produced the play which was their greatest success of all. Its full title was '*The History of Henry the Fourth with the Battle at Shrewsbury between the King and Lord Henry Percy, surnamed Henry Hotspur of the North, with the humorous conceits of Sir John Falstaff.*'

During the restraint of the summer Andrew Wise, a printer of repute, had published Shakespeare's *Richard the Second*—but without the deposition scene. For various reasons contemporaries affected to see in the troubles and scandals of King Richard's Court certain likenesses to their own discontents. The play, therefore, had a peculiar topical significance.[1] It was immediately popular. Two new editions were printed in 1598. The *History of Henry the Fourth* was, in the circumstances, an obvious sequel to *Richard the Second*.

The madcap prince had for many years been a stage favourite. In an old play (called *The Famous Victories of Henry the Fifth*), Prince Hal's companion in mischief was Sir John Oldcastle. Shakespeare first named the fat knight Oldcastle. This caused trouble. Sir John Oldcastle was an honoured rebel in the days of Henry V who was burned

[1] The significances of *Richard the Second* are detailed in *Shakespeare at Work*.

at the stake, and had accordingly found his place in John Foxe's *Book of Martyrs*. Sir John's descendants were represented by Lord Cobham, a petulant young man who had newly succeeded to the title. The family was much offended to find its illustrious ancestor parodied in so debauched a disguise on the common stage. Shakespeare had therefore hurriedly to alter the name to Falstaff; whereby, as it happened, he committed an equal wrong upon the memory of an illustrious soldier of King Henry VI's time.

Fuller puts it thus, in recording the Worthies of Norfolk... 'John Fastolfe, Knight, was a native of this Country, as I have just cause to believe, though some have made him a Frenchman, merely because he was Baron of Sineginle in France, on which account they may rob England of many other Worthies. He was a ward (and that the last) to John, Duke of Bedford, a sufficient evidence, to such who understand time and place, to prove him of English extraction. To avouch him by many arguments valiant, is to maintain that the Sun is bright, though since the stage hath been overbold with his memory, making him a thrasonical puff, and emblem of mock valour.

'True it is, Sir John Oldcastle did first bear the brunt of the one, being made the make-sport in all plays for a coward. It is easily known out of what purse this black penny came; the Papists railing on him for a heretic, and therefore he must also be a coward, though indeed he was a man of arms, every inch of him, and as valiant as any in his age.

'Now as I am glad that Sir John Oldcastle is put out, so I am sorry that Sir John Fastolfe is put in, to relieve his memory in this base service, to be the anvil for every dull wit to strike upon. Nor is our comedian excusable, by some alteration of his name, writing him Sir John

Falstafe (and making him the property of pleasure for King Henry the Fifth to abuse), seeing the vicinity of sounds intrench on the memory of that worthy knight, and few do heed the inconsiderable difference in spelling of their name. He was made Knight of the Garter by King Henry the Sixth; and died about the second year of his reign.'

The play of *Henry the Fourth* as Shakespeare developed it also gave him an unexpected opportunity for attacking his rivals at the Rose. When Falstaff proposes to act a play in which he shall take the part of the indignant King rebuking his prodigal son, he begins in the Marlowe vein:

> Weep not, sweet queen, for trickling tears are vain.

'O, the father! how he holds his countenance,' gasps Mistress Quickly admiringly. And Falstaff continues in the same heroic strain,

> For God's sake, lords, convey my tristful queen,
> For tears do stop the flood-gates of her eyes.

'Oh Jesu!' says Mistress Quickly, 'He doth it as like one of these harlotry players as ever I see!'[1]

As the Admiral's Men were the only other company of players, harlotry or otherwise, then playing, it is likely that Falstaff affected not a little of the mannerisms of the great Ned Alleyn. The play was a great success, and thenceforward Falstaff was Shakespeare's most popular character.[2]

The success of the play led Shakespeare to write a sequel, *The Second Part of Henry the Fourth, continuing to his death and the Coronation of Henry the Fifth: with the humours of Sir John Falstaff and swaggering Pistol.* In writing the second part of the play, Shakespeare developed the parodies.

---

[1] *King Henry the Fourth*, Act II, sc. IV.

[2] The evidence will be found in *The Shakespeare Allusion Book*, edited by John Munro; see index, *Falstaff*.

Pistol's whole vocabulary was made up of play scraps; misquotations from *Tamburlaine*, from *The Blind Beggar*, from Greene's *Alphonsus*, and other Rose plays. He was a kind of walking parody of Alleyn and the ranting style, which hitherto had been so popular at the Rose, but was now beginning to appear as ridiculous to the younger generation of playgoers as the stiff artificialities of Lyly's *Euphues*.

Compared with the success of Falstaff, the Admiral's Men had little to offer, but for the next year they continued to put on a new play every few days. Between the 11th October 1597 and the following September, they produced thirty-eight new plays. Most of them were written by syndicates of three or more writers, of whom Dekker, Chettle and Drayton were most prolific. Chapman wrote one play, called *The Fount of New Fashions*, which was not printed. Jonson was supposed to be writing for them. He produced the plot of a play on the 3rd December, and drew 20*s*. on the promise to complete it by Christmas, but he failed to deliver the manuscript. In August he was paid for writing his share in a play called *Hot Anger soon Cold*. His partners were Chettle and Henry Porter. Of all the plays produced by the Admiral's in this year only four have survived in print.

In later years, when he had become famous, Ben Jonson did not care to remember his early plays, but he had evidently some reputation as a writer. On the 7th September 1598, Francis Meres' book, *Palladis Tamia*, was entered. Meres has secured a quite undeserved place in fame principally because he happened to mention twelve of Shakespeare's plays, but also because he made lists of those Englishmen who had distinguished themselves in different kinds of writing. Jonson came last in his catalogue of the English tragic poets. None of his early tragedies remain, even as a name.

More is known of Ben Jonson than of any of his contemporaries. Apart from the usual sources of information, there are many references to him in the works of his admirers, and he was 'father' to most of the young poets of the next generation. He died as late as 1637, and therefore there were several who knew him still surviving when Bishop Fuller (who died in 1661) compiled his *Worthies of England*, and John Aubrey was collecting his gossip towards the end of the seventeenth century. At that time Ben was still regarded as one of the greatest of English writers; he was one of the few whose reputation survived the Commonwealth, and remained acceptable to the wits of Charles the Second's time.

Fuller included Jonson under the Worthies of Westminster:

'Benjamin Jonson was born in this City. Though I cannot with all my industrious inquiry *find him* in his *cradle*, I can *fetch him* from his *long coats*. When a *little child* he lived in Harts-horn Lane, near Charing Cross, where his mother married a bricklayer for her second husband.

'He was first bred in a private school in Saint Martin's Church; then in Westminster School, witness his own epigram:

> *Camden*, most reverend Head, to whom I owe
> All that I am in Arts, all that I know;
> How nothing's that to whom my Country owes
> The great renown and *Name* wherewith she goes, etc.

'He was *statutably* admitted into Saint John's College in Cambridge (as many years after incorporated an honorary Member of Christ Church in Oxford) where he continued but *few weeks* for want of further maintenance, being fain to return to the trade of his father-in-law. And let not them blush that have, but those that have not, a lawful calling. He helped in the building of the new structure of

Lincoln's Inn, when, having a *trowel* in his hand, he had a *book* in his pocket.

' Some gentlemen, pitying that his parts should be buried under the rubbish of so mean a calling, did by their bounty manumise him freely to follow his own ingenious inclinations. Indeed his parts were not so *ready* to *run of themselves*, as *able to answer the spur* ; so that it may be truly said of him that he had an *elaborate wit* wrought out by his own industry. He would sit silent in learned company, and suck in (besides *wine*) their several humours into his observation. What was *ore* in others, he was able to refine to himself.

' He was paramount in the Dramatic part of Poetry, and taught the Stage an exact conformity to the laws of Comedians. His Comedies were above the *Volge* (which are only tickled with downright obscenity), and took not so well at the *first stroke* as at the *rebound*, when beheld the second time ; yea, they will endure reading, and that with due commendation, so long as either *ingenuity* or *learning* are fashionable in our Nation. If his *later* be not so spriteful and vigorous as his *first pieces*, all that are old will, and all that desire to be old should, excuse him therein.

' He was not very happy in his children, and most happy with those which died first, though none lived to survive him. This he bestowed as part of an Epitaph on his eldest son, dying in infancy :

> Rest in soft peace ; and, ask'd, say here doth lie,
> *Ben Jonson* his best piece of *Poetry*.

' He died Anno Domini 1638 ; and was buried, about the Belfry, in the Abbey Church at Westminster.'

Aubrey picked up many scraps from sources of differing values : [1]

---

[1] Aubrey's *Brief Lives*, edited by Andrew Clark, ii, 11.

' Mr. Benjamin Johnson, Poet Laureat :—I remember when I was a scholar at Trin. Coll. Oxon, 1646, I heard Dr. Ralph Bathurst (now Dean of Wells) say that Ben Jonson was a Warwickshire man—*sed quaere*. 'Tis agreed that his father was a minister; and by his epistle dedicat. of " Every Man . . ." to Mr. William Camden that he was a Westminster scholar, and that Mr. W. Camden was his school-master.'

' His mother, after his father's death, married a bricklayer; and 'tis generally said that he wrought sometime with his father-in-law (and particularly on the garden wall of Lincoln's Inn next to Chancery Lane—from old parson (Richard) Hill, of Stretton, Hereff., 1646), and that . . . a knight, a bencher, walking through and hearing him repeat some Greek verses out of Homer, discoursing with him, and finding him to have a wit extraordinary, gave him some exhibition to maintain him at Trinity College in Cambridge, where he was . . . (*quaere*).'

' Then he went into the Low Countries, and spent some time (not very long) in the army, not to the disgrace of . . . as you may find in his *Epigrams*.

' Then he came over into England, and acted and wrote, but both ill, at the Green Curtain, a kind of nursery or obscure playhouse, somewhere in the suburbs (I think towards Shoreditch or Clerkenwell)—from J. Greenhill.

' Then he undertook again to write a play, and did hit it admirably well, viz. " Every Man . . ." which was his first good one.'

' Sergeant John Hoskins, of Herefordshire, was his *father*. I remember his son (Sir Bennet Hoskins, baronet, who was something poetical in his youth) told me, that when he desired to be adopted his son : " No," said he, " 'tis honour enough for me to be your brother ; I am your father's son, 'twas he that polished me, I do acknowledge it." '

' He was (or rather had been) of a clear and fair skin ; his habit was very plain. I have heard Mr. Lacy, the player, say that he was wont to wear a coat like a coachman's coat, with slits under the armpits. He would many times exceed in drink (Canary was his beloved liquour) : then he would tumble home to bed, and, when he had thoroughly perspired, then to study. I have seen his studying chair which was of straw, such as old women used, and as Aulus Gellius is drawn in.

' When I was in Oxon, Bishop Skinner (of Oxford), who lay at our College, was wont to say that he understood an author as well as any man in England.'

' He mentions in his Epigrams a son that he had, and his epitaph.'

' Long since, in King James' time, I have heard my uncle Danvers say (who knew him), that he lived without Temple Bar, at a comb-maker's shop, about the Elephant and Castle. In his later time he lived in Westminster, in the house under which you pass as you go out of the churchyard into the old palace ; where he died.'

' He lies buried in the north aisle in the path of square stone (the rest is lozenge), opposite to the scutcheon of Robertus de Ros, with this inscription only on him, in a pavement square, of blue marble, about 14 inches square,

O RARE BENN IOHNSON

which was done at the charge of Jack Young (afterwards

knighted) who, walking there when the grave was covering, gave the fellow eighteen pence to cut it.

'His motto before his (bought) books was, *Tanquam Explorator*. I remember 'tis in Seneca's Epistles.

'He was a favourite of the Lord Chancellor Egerton, as appears by several verses to him. In one he begs his lordship to do a friend of his a favour.

''Twas an ingenious remark of my Lady Hoskins that B. J. never writes of love, or if he does, does it not naturally.

'He killed Mr. . . . Marlow, the poet;[1] on Bunhill, coming from the Green Curtain playhouse.—From Sir Edward Shirburn.'

'Ben Jonson had one eye lower than t'other, and bigger, like Clun, the player: perhaps he begot Clun. He took a catalogue from Mr. Lacy (the player) of the Yorkshire dialect. 'Twas his hint for clownery to his comedy called *The Tale of a Tub*. This I had from Mr. Lacy.

'King James made him write against the Puritans, who began to be troublesome in his time.'

'A Grace by Ben Johnson, extempore, before King James.

> Our King and Queen, the Lord God bless,
> The Palzgrave and the Lady Bess,
> And God bless every living thing
> That lives and breathes and loves the King.
> God bless the Council of Estate,
> And Buckingham, the fortunate.
> God bless them all, and keep them safe,
> And God bless me, and God bless Raph.

[1] An interesting example of the merging of two traditions: Marlowe's death at the hands of Frizer, and the death of Spencer (player not poet) at the hands of Jonson, which did occur near the Curtain. See later, p. 188.

'The King was mighty inquisitive to know who this Raph was. Ben told him 'twas the drawer at the Swan Tavern by Charing Cross, who drew him good canary. For this drollery His Majesty gave him an hundred pounds.'

'This account I received from Mr. Isaac Walton (who wrote Dr. John Donne's &c. Life), December 2nd 1680, he being then eighty-seven years of age. This is his own handwriting.

" ' For your friend's query this :

'I only knew Ben Johnson : but my Lord of Winton knew him very well, and says he was in the 6°, that is the uppermost form in Westminster School. At which time his father died, and his mother married a bricklayer, who made him (much against his will) to help him in his trade. But in a short time, his school master, Mr. Camden, got him a better employment, which was to attend or accompany a son of Sir Walter Ralegh's in his travels.[1] Within a short time after their return they parted (I think not in cold blood), and with a love suitable to what they had in their travels (not to be commended) ; and then, Ben began to set up for himself in the trade by which he got his subsistence and fame. Of which I need not give any account. He got in time to have a £100 a year from the King, also a pension from the City, and the like from many of the nobility and some of the gentry, which was well paid for love or fear of his railing in verse or prose, or both. My Lord of Winton told me, he told him he was (in his long retirement and sickness, when he saw him, which was often) much afflicted that he had profaned the scripture in his plays ; and lamented it with horror ; yet, that at that time of his long retirement, his pensions (so much as came in)

---

[1] As Ralegh did not marry till 1592, Walton's memory must have telescoped events considerably. See later, p. 182.

was given to a woman that governed him, with whom he lived and died near the Abbey in Westminster; and that neither he nor she took much care for next week, and would be sure not to want wine; of which he usually took too much before he went to bed, if not oftner and sooner. My Lord tells me, he knows not, but thinks he was born in Westminster. The question may be put to Mr. Wood very easily upon what grounds he is positive as to his being born there.' "[1]

Above all there are the notes of Jonson's own conversations made by the Scottish poet, William Drummond of Hawthornden, whom Jonson visited in the winter of 1618–19. Jonson stayed with Drummond for three or four weeks, and Drummond appears to have kept notes from day to day of what he said. When his guest had departed he summed up Jonson's character. The original manuscript has been lost, but a transcript was made by Sir Robert Sibbald of Edinburgh, a physician and antiquary of great learning. Sibbald died in 1722 at the age of 81.[2]

The notes which Drummond made are grouped into nineteen sections, and give Jonson's opinions on various matters. The longest section (13) is an account of his own life, education, birth and actions.

---

[1] Aubrey's *Brief Lives*, edited by A. C. Clark, ii, 11–15.

[2] The best edition of the *Conversations* is that included in the Oxford Edition of *The Works of Ben Jonson*, edited by C. H. Herford and Percy Simpson, vol. i, Appendix 1. Some years ago the authenticity of the *Conversations* was challenged by Mr. C. L. Stainer (in *The Conversations of Jonson and Drummond*), who roundly asserted that Sibbald had forged them. Mr. Stainer was severely chastized by the official guardians of Jonson's fame. If Sibbald was a forger he showed great skill, but as Mr. Stainer pointed out, there are curious errors in the *Conversations*, notable discrepancies with the English traditions recorded by Fuller and Aubrey, and very little which a clever practical joker with a good knowledge of the period could not have made up from Jonson's own works, including the Epigrams, and Dekker's *Satiro-mastix*.

'His grandfather came from Carlisle, and he thought from Anandale to it. He served King Henry VIII and was a gentleman. His father lost all his estate under Queen Mary, having been cast in prison and forfeited, at last turned minister. So he was a minister's son. He himself was posthumous born a month after his father's decease, brought up poorly, put to school by a friend (his master Camden), after taken from it, and put to another craft (I think was to be a wright or bricklayer), which he could not endure. Then went he to the Low Countries, but returning, soon he betook himself to his wonted studies. In his service in the Low Countries he had in the face of both the camps killed an enemy and taken opima spolia from him. And since his coming to England being appealed to the fields he had killed his adversary, which had hurt him in the arm and whose sword was ten inches longer than his, for the which he was imprisoned and almost at the gallows. Then took he his religion by trust of a priest who visited him in prison. Thereafter he was twelve years a papist.

' He was Master of Arts in both the Universities by their favour, not his study.

' He married a wife who was a shrew yet honest. Five years he had not bedded with her, but remained with my Lord Albany.

' In the time of his close imprisonment under Queen Elizabeth his judges could get nothing of him to all their demands but Ay and No. They placed two damned villains to catch advantage of him with him, but he was advertised by his keeper. Of the spies he hath an Epigram.

' When the King came in England, at that time the pest was in London, he being in the country at Sir Robert Cotton's house with old Camden, he saw in a vision his eldest son (then a child and at London) appear unto him with the mark of a bloody cross on his forehead, as if it had been cutted with a sword, at which, amazed, he prayed unto God; and in the morning he came to Mr. Camden's chamber to tell him, who persuaded him that it was but an apprehension of his fantasy at which he should not be dejected. In the mean time comes these letters from his wife of the death of the boy in the plague. He appeared to him, he said, of a manly shape and of that growth that he thinks he shall be at the Resurrection.

'He was delated by Sir James Murray to the King for writing something against the Scots in a play *Eastward Ho!* and voluntarily imprisoned himself with Chapman and Marston, who had written it amongst them. The report was that they should then have their ears cut and noses. After their delivery he banqueted all his friends; there was Camden, Selden and others. At the midst of the feast his old mother drank to him, and show him a paper which she had (if the sentence had taken execution) to have mixed in the prison among his drink, which was full of lusty strong poison, and that she was no churl she told she minded first to have drunk of it herself.

'He had many quarrels with Marston, beat him, and took his pistol from him. Wrote his *Poetaster* on him the beginning of which were that Marston represented him in the stage.

'In his youth given to venery. He thought the use of a maid nothing in comparison to the wantonness of a wife, and would never have another mistress. He said two accidents strange befell him; one that a man made his own wife to court him, whom he enjoyed two years ere he knew of it, and one day finding them by chance was passingly delighted with it. One other, lay divers times with a woman, who showed him all that he wished except the last act, which she would never agree unto.

'Sir W. Ralegh sent him Governor with his son, anno

1613, to France. This youth being knavishly inclined, among other pastimes (as the setting of the favour of damosels on a codpiece) caused him to be drunken and dead drunk, so that he knew not where he was. Thereafter laid him on a car which he made to be drawn by pioners through the streets, at every corner showing his Governor stretched out, and telling them that was a more lively image of the Crucifix than any they had. At which sport young Ralegh's mother delighted much (saying his father young was so inclined) though the father abhorred it.

' He can set horoscopes, but trusts not in them. He, with the consent of a friend, cozened a lady, with whom he had made an appointment to meet an old astrologer in the suburbs, which she kept; and it was himself disguised in a long gown and a white beard at the light of a dim burning candle up in a little cabinet reached unto by a ladder.

' Every first day of the New Year he had £20 sent to him from the Earl of Pembroke to buy books.

' After he was reconciled with the Church, and left off to be a recusant, at his first communion in token of true reconciliation, he drank out all the full cup of wine.

' Being at the end of my Lord Salisbury's table with Inigo Jones, and demanded by my Lord why he was not glad, " My Lord," said he, " you promised I should dine with you, but I do not," for he had none of his meat; he esteemed only his meat which was of his own dish.

' He hath consumed a whole night in lying looking to his great toe, about which he hath seen Tartars and Turks, Romans and Carthaginians fight in his imagination.

' Northampton was his mortal enemy, for brawling on a St. George's Day one of his atteneders. He was called before the Council for his *Sejanus* and accused both of popery and treason by him. Sundry times he hath devoured his books, i.e. sold them all for necessity.

'He hath a mind to be a churchman, and so he might have favour to make one sermon to the King, he careth not what thereafter should befall him, for he would not flatter though he saw death. At his hither coming Sir Francis Bacon said to him he loved not to see poesy go on other feet than poetical dactyl and spondee.'

Drummond's account of Ben Jonson dates from twenty years after his first connection with the Admiral's Men, and therefore refers principally to later incidents in his life. So far as it goes, it is a true outline of his early life, but there are several events which he was not pleased to remember. Other sources of information—the entries in Henslowe's *Diary*, for instance, and the unkind words of Dekker in *Satiromastix*—show that between his service in the Low Countries and his first efforts as a playwright, Jonson had tried acting with poor success.

According to Nashe, Jonson wrote the greater part of the *Isle of Dogs*. If so, it is probable that he was developing the notion of the comedy of humours already tried out by Chapman. Jonson from the first had theories about the drama. Comedy, as he stressed later, had a moral purpose to display the follies of the time ; but the distinction between holding a mirror up to folly and holding it up to contemporary fools was very fine, and Jonson had paid for not observing it. He had now, however, written a comedy which achieved perfect balance and was just what the public were wanting. He called it *Every Man in his Humour* ; but for some reason now not discoverable, it was sold, not to the Admiral's but to the Chamberlain's Men, who brought it out in September 1598. The date is accidentally known because Toby Matthew (the flighty son of the Archbishop of York) in writing a gossipy letter to his friend Dudley Carleton, mentions that there was a Frenchman who had been welcomed at Court : '... there were with him divers Almans, whereof one lost out of his purse at a play 300 crowns. A new play called *Every Man's Humour*.'[1] The letter is dated the 20th September.

The play of *Every Man in his Humour*, in the version best known to modern readers, is not the same as that which was first played in 1598. In 1616 Jonson published a collection of his own plays. He rewrote *Every Man in his Humour* and revised it throughout. Moreover, in the first version, the scene was set, not in England, but in a dramatist's Florence, which had all the physical features of London. The names of the characters too were Italian. The Knowells were called Lorenzo ; Masters Matthew and Stephen were Signors Matheo and Stephano ; Wellbred was Prospero ; Squire Downright, Guillano ; and Bobadil's name appeared in the Spanish form of Bobadilla. Chapman's *Humorous Day's Mirth* had shown how contemporaries might be treated on the English stage, and Jonson brought the picture closer. He presented a mixed collection of London characters, all the types present or very familiar amongst the audience. The heroes of the piece, in so far as social comedy has heroes, were the two young gentlemen Lorenzo and Prospero. They were typical specimens of the best kind of gentleman produced at the Inns of Court, and from whom, in later years were recruited ' the Tribe of Ben.' Jonson had always an acute eye and ear for everything going on around him ; and his plays are accurate reflections of the interests, scandals and catch-phrases of the moment.

Every Man in his Humour remains one of the best of Jonson's plays, and was as good a comedy as any that had yet appeared on an English stage. Jonson wrote the play

[1] State Papers Domestic, 268 f. 61.

as a man of the theatre and not as a moralist. It remains still most excellent fun.[1]

He satirized many things in *Every Man in his Humour* without bad temper and with considerable skill—the pose of melancholy affected by the intellectuals, for instance. Stephano and Matheo, the gulls, were the counterparts to Prospero and young Lorenzo, poor imitators, apeing their intellectual superiors. To be in the fashion they must be melancholy. Bobadilla and Matheo also represented what in Jonson's eyes was perfect bad taste. They were still so far behind the fashion that they regarded the *Spanish Tragedy* as the top of dramatic accomplishment. The gulls, however, personified general and contemporary follies.

Jonson kept closer still to his originals. Some of the incidents were dramatization of current gossip. Thus Bobadilla was made to reveal his essential cowardice when Guilliano challenged him to fight and he could only make the tame excuse that he had been bound over to observe the peace. As it happened, in June 1598, when Jonson was still working on the play such an incident was the latest piece of gossip. Sir Melchior Leven, a German gentleman whom Essex had knighted a year before at Cadiz, fell foul of Sir Charles Blount in Paris, but when challenged to fight refused on the grounds that the French king had forbidden duels. Similarly he makes Cob talk of Bobadilla as ' that rogue, that foist, that fencing Burgullian.' The ' Burgullian ' was a certain Burgonian fencer who had come over to challenge all English fencers, but was hanged on the 11th July for killing an officer of the city.[2] The

---

[1] This was amply demonstrated in the excellent production at the Memorial Theatre, Stratford-upon-Avon, in 1937. On the stage it is still a sparkling, quick, witty comedy.

[2] II *Elizabethan Journals*, p. 286 and note, and p. 291.

play, to contemporaries, had thus a very strong spice of immediate malice.

In the revised edition Jonson printed a prologue. It was a challenge, a statement of his own literary creed.

> Though need make many poets, and some such
> As art and nature have not bettered much,
> Yes ours, for want, hath not so loved the stage
> As he dare serve th'ill customs of the age,
> Or purchase your delight at such a rate
> As, for it, he himself must justly hate.
> To make a child, now swaddled, to proceed
> Man, and then shoot up, in one beard and weed
> Past threescore years; or, with three rusty swords,
> And help of some few foot-and-half-foot words,
> Fight over York and Lancaster's long jars:
> And in the tiring-house bring wounds to scars.
> He rather prays, you will be pleased to see
> One such, to-day, as other plays should be.
> Where neither Chorus wafts you o'er the seas;
> Nor creaking throne comes down, the boys to please;
> Nor nimble squibble is seen, to make afear'd
> The gentlewomen; nor rolled bullet heard
> To say, it thunders; nor tempestuous drum
> Rumbles, to tell you when the storm doth come;
> But deeds, and language, such as men do use:
> And persons, such as Comedy would choose,
> When she would show an image of the times,
> And sport with human follies, not with crimes.
> Except we make 'em such by loving still
> Our popular errors, when we know they're ill.
> I mean such errors, as you'll all confess
> By laughing at them, they deserve no less:
> Which when you heartily do, there's hope left, then,
> You, that have so graced monsters may like men.

This prologue does not appear in the quarto of *Every Man in his Humour* printed in 1600, and in its present form could hardly have been allowed at the Curtain, for it was a manifest criticism of the methods of the Chamberlain's players. It does, however, reflect those theories which, from the first, Ben Jonson expressed loudly and incessantly.

In the revised version also Jonson printed a list of the principal comedians. They were :

' Will. Shakespeare.	Ric. Burbage.
Avg. Philips.	Joh. Hemings.
Hen. Condel.	Tho. Pope.
Will Slye.	Chr. Beeston.
Will. Kempe.	Joh. Duke.'

Jonson's success had an immediate and unfortunate sequel. Gabriel Spencer, now prospering with Henslowe, had formerly been a Chamberlain's Man. As one of Pembroke's Men, he and Jonson together had shared misfortune in the Marshalsea over the *Isle of Dogs*. Spencer, like most of his contemporaries, was ready with his knife. Two years before, he also slew his man, not in the sight of both camps, but in a barber's shop, when his adversary was armed with a brass candlestick.

On the 22nd September Gabriel and Ben met in Shoreditch and fought in the fields. This time Jonson was the survivor. He was arraigned at the Old Bailey in October and the Jail Delivery Roll records that a true bill was found against him.

'*He confesses the indictment, asks for the book, reads like a clerk, is marked with the letter T, and is delivered according to the statute, etc.*'

' Middlesex :—The jurors for the Lady the Queen present, that Benjamin Johnson, late of London, yeoman, on the 22nd day of September, in the fortieth year of the reign of our Lady Elizabeth by God's grace Queen of

England, France and Ireland, Defender of the Faith, etc. with force and arms, etc., made an attack against and upon a certain Gabriel Spencer, being in God's and the said Lady the Queen's peace, at Shoreditch in the aforesaid county of Middlesex, in the Fields there, and with a certain sword of iron and steel called a rapier, of the price of three shillings, which he then and there had and held drawn in his right hand, feloniously and wilfully beat and struck the same Gabriel, giving then and there to the same Gabriel Spencer with the aforesaid sword a mortal wound of the depth of six inches and of the breadth of one inch, in and upon the right side of the same Gabriel, of which mortal blow the same Gabriel Spencer at Shoreditch aforesaid, in the aforesaid county, in the aforesaid Fields, then and there died instantly. And thus the aforesaid jurors say upon their oath, that the aforesaid Benjamin Johnson, at Shoreditch aforesaid, in the aforesaid county of Middlesex, and in the aforesaid Fields, in the year and day aforesaid, feloniously and wilfully killed and slew the aforesaid Gabriel Spencer, against the peace of the said Lady the Queen, etc.'[1]

Jonson was then able to plead benefit of clergy. He was branded on the thumb and released with the forfeiture of his goods.

Henslowe thus suffered a double loss. Jonson, hitherto a promising playwright, had gone over to the rival company; Spencer, one of his best actors, was dead. Edward Alleyn was away in the country at the time. Henslowe took pen and very sorrowfully wrote him a letter:

'SON EDWARD ALLEYN,

'I have received your letter, the which you sent unto me by the carrier, wherein I understand of both of your good

[1] Original Latin and translation are printed in *A Biographical Chronicle of the English Drama, 1559–1642*, by F. G. Fleay, i. 343.

healths, which I pray to God to continue. And further I understand you have considered of the words which you and I had between us concerning the Bear garden, and according to your words, you and I and all our friends shall have as much as we can do to bring it unto a good end. Therefore I would willingly that you were at the banquet, for then with our loss, I should be the merrier. Therefore if you think as I think, it were fit that we were both here to do what we mought and not as two friends, but as two joined in one. Therefore, Ned, I love not to make many great glosses and protestations to you as others do, but as a poor friend you shall command me, as I hope I shall do you. Therefore I desire rather to have your company and your wife's than your letters. For our last talk which we had about Mr. Pascal, assure you I do not forget.

'Now to let you understand news, I will tell you some, but it is for me hard and heavy. Since you were with me I have lost one of my company, which hurteth me greatly, that is Gabriel, for he is slain in Hogsden Fields by the hands of Benjamin Jonson, bricklayer. Therefore I would fain have a little of your counsel if I could.

'Thus with hearty commendations to you and my daughter, and likewise to all the rest of our friends, I end from London, the 26th of September 1598.

'Yours assured friend to my power,
'PHILLIP HENSLOWE.'[1]

[1] *Henslowe Papers,* p. 47.

Chapter XII

THE GLOBE

The Chamberlain's Men still had their problems. The dispute with their landlord continued. After the restraint of July 1597, they had gone to play at the Curtain, leaving the Theatre empty. Master Giles Alleyn did not live in London, but he came up at the four quarters to collect his rents. Then Cuthbert Burbage would go to him, pay his dues, and plead with his landlord to settle the matter. Alleyn, however, could never be persuaded to anything definite. He only made vague promises.

Cuthbert Burbage was uneasy. By the original terms of the old lease of 1576, the tenant was obliged to take down the playhouse and to remove its timber or else to forfeit it to the landlord. Cuthbert was in a quandary. If the lease could be renewed, then all would be well ; but if not there was considerable danger lest at any time Alleyn would demand that the Theatre property should be surrendered. Matters reached a climax on the 29th September 1598. At last Alleyn produced a lease ; but the terms which he proposed were quite impossible. When Burbage refused to sign, Alleyn retorted that all rights in the Theatre were now vested in himself ; it was his intention to tear it down and to put the material to some better use.

The Burbages were not men of meekness. They were quite used to acting resolutely, and regardless of what the Law might say afterwards. The company was now prosperous. Accordingly the chief members compacted together to form a syndicate and to put up the money to build a new playhouse. It was agreed between them that Cuthbert Burbage and his brother Richard should pay half the expenses of a new playhouse, and that Shakespeare, Hemmings, Phillips, Pope and Kemp should pay for the other half; that is, the five players each held one share in the new venture, while the two Burbages held two and a half shares apiece. They decided also to leave the Shoreditch neighbourhood. On the 25th December 1598, they leased a piece of ground on the Bankside, not far from the Rose Theatre. Three days later they set to work, when as Alleyn bitterly complained to the courts:

'The said Cuthbert Burbage, having intelligence of your subject's purpose herein, and unlawfully combining and confederating himself with the said Richard Burbage and one Peter Street, William Smith, and diverse other persons to the number of twelve, to your subject unknown, did about the eight and twentieth day of December, in the one and fortieth year of your Highness' reign, and sithence your Highness' last and general pardon, by the confederacy aforesaid, riotously assembled themselves together, and then and there armed themselves with diverse and many unlawful and offensive weapons, as namely swords, daggers, bills, axes, and such like, and so armed did then repair unto the said Theatre, and then and there armed as aforesaid, in very riotous, outrageous, and forcible manner, and contrary to the laws of your Highness' realm, attempted to pull down the said Theatre. Whereupon, diverse of your subjects, servants and farmers, then going about in peaceable manner to procure them to desist from that unlawful enterprise, they, the said riotous persons aforesaid, notwithstanding procured then therein with great violence, not only then and there forcibly and riotously resisting your subjects, servants and farmers, but also then and there pulling, breaking, and throwing down the said Theatre in very outrageous, violent, and riotous sort.'[1]

The timber and fittings were thereupon carried over to the south bank of the Thames and dumped on the new site. Thus the old Theatre died, and from its dead bones the more famous Globe was born.

In the early spring the Chamberlain's Men produced Shakespeare's *Henry the Fifth* at the Curtain. About a year had passed since the *Second Part of Henry the Fourth*, and much had happened in the theatres. The promise to repeat Falstaff was not carried out. Instead Falstaff died off stage. Ancient Pistol, however, reappeared, with a new worthy as his colleague, Corporal Nym, who is for ever prating of his humours. In some ways the play was a reversion to earlier methods of historical writing. It was full of trumpetry, and Shakespeare indulged in rhetoric of a kind, though certainly of finer quality, which he had not attempted for some years. He also made an unmistakable reference to contemporary events. In the chorus before Act V he offered an obvious, but—as the sequel showed—unfortunate compliment to the Earl of Essex, who had just departed for Ireland in great triumph, an event which occurred on the 24th March 1599, when all London turned out to wish him luck.[2]

During the summer Shakespeare wrote *As you Like It*,

[1] Quoted in Adams' *Shakespearean Playhouses*, p. 63.
[2] In the first chorus Shakespeare makes his well-known apology to the audience for the short-comings of the theatre :

> '... May we cram
> Within this wooden O the very casques
> That did afright the air at Agincourt.'

It is often stated that these words refer to the Globe. They do not. The Globe was not yet built, and anyhow a man who has put his money into building a theatre does not go out of his way to condemn its insufficiencies !

which contained, in the character of the melancholy Jaques, his first and only contribution to the Comedy of Humours. About the same time the Chamberlain's Men put on Ben Jonson's *Every Man out of his Humour.*

Apparently the Globe was finished and ready for occupation in July, and thither the Chamberlain's Men transported themselves and their plays. Amongst their repertory at this time was a play called : *A Warning for Fair Women*, which was published in 1599 ' as it hath been lately divers times acted by the Right Honourable the Lord Chamberlain his servants.' It was one of a number of plays which dramatized sensational crimes and murders. The *Warning* presented a murder committed in 1573, when Mr. George Sanders, a worthy merchant, and John Beane, his man, were stabbed to death by Captain George Browne. Browne loved Sanders's wife, and was encouraged to commit the murder by a Mistress Anne Drury, who promised to arrange the match. When arraigned for the murder, Browne tried to clear his mistress ; but she, Mistress Drury, and her man, Roger, who was go-between, were all condemned to death as accessories to the crime. The most sensational part of the business—to an Elizabethan expert in crime—was that Mistress Sanders persistently declared her innocence almost to the end. This was clean contrary to normal behaviour ; for, as every decent-minded man felt, even a criminal would be horrified at the thought of leaping down to hell with a lie still on his lips. And indeed it was very rare for condemned persons to die without the most abject confession of guilt. At the last moment, when Mistress Sanders found that Mistress Drury would not corroborate her innocence, she too repented, confessed the truth and made an edifying end.

Of its kind the play was a good mixture of tragedy, horror, pathos and edification. Though the verse never rose to any height, it seldom descended to the utter doggerel of some of the murder plays. Its most permanent interest is in the Induction. These Inductions in which Revenge, Murder, the Three Furies and the rest of the brood open a tragedy, were common in the 1580's; *The Spanish Tragedy* is a good example. But here the author introduced History, Tragedy and Comedy, who discuss their functions, and incidentally, give some interesting side-lights on the customs of the theatre. Tragedy comes in as a scold, with a whip and a knife, and would drive Comedy away.

TRAGEDY. I must have passions that must move the soul;
Make the heart heavy and throb within the bosom,
Extorting tears out of the strictest eyes—
To rack a thought, and strain it to his form,
Until I rap the senses from their course.
This is my office.
 COMEDY. How some damn'd tyrant to obtain a crown
Stabs, hangs, impoisons, smothers, cutteth throats:
And then a Chorus, too, comes howling in
And tells us of the worrying of a cat:
Then, too, a filthy whining ghost,
Lapt in some foul sheet, or a leather pilch,
Comes screaming like a pig half stick'd,
And cries, *Vindicta!*—Revenge, Revenge!
With that a little rosin flasheth forth,
Like smoke out of a tobacco pipe, or a boy's squib.
Then comes in two or three like to drovers,
With tailor's bodkins, stabbing one another—
Is not this trim? Is not here goodly things,
That you should be so much accounted of?
I would not else.
 HISTORY. Now, before God, thou'lt make her mad anon;
Thy jests are like a whisp unto a scold.
 COMEDY. Why, say I could, what care I, History?
Then shall we have a Tragedy indeed;
Pure purple buskin, blood and murther right.

TRAGEDY. Thus, with your loose and idle similies,
You have abused me; but I'll whip you hence:
I'll scourge and lash you both from off the stage.
Tis you have kept the Theatres so long,
Painted in play-bills upon every post,
That I am scorned of the multitude,
My name profan'd.

Shakespeare's *Julius Cæsar* followed soon after. A German traveller named Platter, who kept a diary of his travels, noted that he saw it acted.

'After dinner on the 21st of September, at about two o'clock, I went with my companions over the water, and in the strewn roof-house saw the tragedy of the first Emperor Julius with at least fifteen characters very well acted. At the end of the comedy they danced according to their custom with extreme elegance. Two in men's clothes and two in women's gave this performance, in wonderful combination with each other.' [1]

On another occasion Platter saw a comedy played, apparently, at the Curtain: 'Here they represented various nations, with whom on each occasion an Englishman fought for his daughter, and overcame them all except the German, who won the daughter in fight. He then sat down with him, and gave him and his servant strong drink, so that they both got drunk, and the servant threw his shoe at his master's head and they both fell asleep. Meanwhile the Englishman went into the tent, robbed the German of his gains, and thus he outwitted the German also. At the end they danced very elegantly, both in English and in Irish fashion.

'And thus every day at two o'clock in the afternoon in the city of London two and sometimes three comedies are performed, at separate places, wherewith folk make merry together, and whichever does best gets the greatest audience.

[1] Translated in *Elizabethan Stage*, ii, 364-5.

THE GLOBE

The places are so built, that they play on a raised platform, and every one can well see it all. There are, however, separate galleries and there one stands more comfortably and moreover can sit, but one pays more for it. Thus anyone who remains on the level standing pays only one English penny : but if he wants to sit, he is let in at a further door, and there he gives another penny. If he desires to sit on a cushion in the most comfortable place of all, where he not only sees everything well, but can also be seen, then he gives yet another English penny at another door. And in the pauses of the comedy food and drink are carried round amongst the people, and one can thus refresh himself at his own cost.

'The comedians are most expensively and elegantly apparelled, since it is customary in England, when distinguished gentlemen or knights die, for nearly the finest of their clothes to be made over and given to their servants, and as it is not proper for them to wear such clothes but only to imitate them, they give them to the comedians to purchase for a small sum.'

On October 24th the Chamberlain's Men produced another new play on recent history.[1] It told the story of the Battle of Turnholt, and the victory won by a combined force of Dutch and English on the 14th January 1597. The English were under the command of Sir Francis Vere, who had greatly distinguished himself. The original protagonists were introduced by name on the stage ; the player representing Sir Francis wore a beard resembling his ; Sir Robert Sidney (Sir Philip's younger brother) was also represented killing and overthrowing Spaniards ; and the play was full of quips. Hamlet's argument that the players were ' the abstracts and brief chronicles of the time ' was exact. During these months both companies often staged events within a short time of their happening.

[1] III *Elizabethan Journals*, 47 and note.

Not long afterwards the company acted another of Ben Jonson's comedies. It was called *Every Man out of his Humour* and it was a failure. Jonson unfortunately was more intent on drawing humours than in writing a good comedy. The success of *Every Man in his Humour* had gone to his head, and he showed a mighty fine opinion of himself. He began his play with an Induction. He modernized the old-fashioned personifications of the Arts, and instead, after the second sounding of the trumpets, which announced that the play was about to begin, he sent on to the stage three characters who looked like spectators : Cordatus, Asper and Mitis. Asper is a severe censor of manners. He takes notice of the audience—but not to fawn on their applause like other poets ; he prefers their censure if he deserves it.

> Only vouchsafe me your attentions,
> And I will give you music worth your ears.
> O, how I hate the monstrousness of time,
> Where every servile imitating spirit,
> Plagued with an itching leprosy of wit,
> In a mere halting fury, strives to fling
> His ulcerous body in the Thespian spring,
> And straight leaps forth a poet !

It was Jonson's first fling at Marston : ' In faith,' Mitis answers, ' this humour will come ill to some,'

> You will be thought to be peremptory.

Asper takes him up sharply : ' Why this " humour ? " '
And then he launches out into a long lecture on the proper use of the word ' humour.'

> Why, humour, as 'tis *ens*, we thus define it,
> To be a quality of air, or water,
> And in itself holds these two properties,
> Moisture and fluxure : as, for demonstration,
> Pour water on this floor, 'twill wet and run :

> Likewise the air, forced through a horn or trumpet,
> Flows instantly away, and leaves behind
> A kind of dew; and hence we do conclude,
> That whatsoe'er hath fluxure and humidity,
> As wanting power to contain itself,
> Is humour. So in every human body,
> The choler, melancholy, phlegm, and blood,
> By reason that they flow continually
> In some one part, and are not continent,
> Receive the name of humours. Now thus far
> It may, by metaphor, apply itself
> Unto the general disposition:
> As when some one peculiar quality
> Doth so possess a man, that it doth draw
> All his effects, his spirits, and his powers,
> In their confluctions, all to run one way,
> This may be truly said to be a humour.
> But that a rook, by wearing a pied feather,
> The cable hatband, or the three-piled ruff,
> A yard of shoe-tie, or the Switzer's knot
> On his French garters, should affect a humour!
> O, it is more than most ridiculous.

Once more Marston was put in his place for misusing the word in *The Scourge of Villainy*. Then Asper turns to threaten the audience. He rises as if to go in to take his place in the play. He asks Mitis to watch how the spectators behave.

> ... If in all this front
> You can espy a gallant of this mark,
> Who, to be thought one of the judicious,
> Sits with his arms thus wreathed, his hat pulled here,
> Cries mew and nods, then shakes his empty head,
> Will shew more several motions in his face
> Than the new London, Rome, or Nineveh,
> And now and then, breaks a dry biscuit jest,
> Which, that it may more easily be chewed,
> He steeps in his own laughter ...

> . . . O, I would know 'em; for in such assemblies
> They are more infectious than the pestilence:
> And therefore I would give them pills to purge
> And make them fit for fair societies.
> How monstrous and detested is't to see
> A fellow, that has neither art nor brain,
> Sit like an Aristarchus, or stark ass,
> Taking men's lines, with a tobacco face,
> In snuff, still spitting, using his wry'd looks,
> In nature of a vice, to wrest and turn
> The good aspect of those that shall sit near him,
> From what they do behold! O, 'tis most vile.

When Asper has left the stage, Cordatus and Mitis discuss most learnedly the history of comedy, old and new; and at long last the play starts.

The play itself falls far short of *Every Man in his Humour*, though the individual characters and some of the episodes are amusing enough in themselves, and must have been more amusing when the follies which Jonson portrays were fresh, and probably the individuals were recognizable. But Jonson came too near to his victims. They lack the universality, both of character and circumstance, to be perennially amusing. Jonson parodied some of the types that he disliked himself. Sogliardo, the yeoman who will buy gentility at any price; Sordido, his brother, the grasping farmer who profiteers out of the dearth; Puntarvolo, the gentleman who must indulge his whimsical humours in such strange pranks as going a journey to Constantinople with his cat; Fastidious Brisk, the fashionmonger, closely and admiringly imitated by Fungoso, Sordido's son, who, however is always one new suit behind.

There is a plot of sorts for those who can follow the play through patiently to the end; but it is not surprising that the play failed on its own faults. Jonson also committed a lapse in taste which caused offence. He introduced Queen

Elizabeth as a character (probably idealized as Cynthia or Astraea) to restore sanity at the end of the play.

Meanwhile at the Rose Henslowe's Men had continued active. Since October 1598 they had produced a number of plays, some of which were printed. They included *The Two Angry Women of Abingdon*, by Henry Porter; a play by Chapman called *All Fools*, which he seems afterwards to have revised for the Children of Blackfriars; and *The Shoemaker's Holiday*, Dekker's most successful play, and indeed one of the jolliest of all Elizabethan comedies. In all, in eight months they had added about twenty-five plays to their repertory.

In August Jonson came back to them. After the failure of *Every Man out of his Humour* he seems to have quarrelled with the Chamberlain's Men. Indeed, with success Jonson became unbearable. It was bad enough for the actors and their audiences to be lectured on the art of comedy, but infinitely worse when the man mocked their own notions of dramatic fitness in a play which was itself a complete failure.

So Jonson returned to the Rose. And there, on the 10th August he and Dekker drew 40s. in earnest of a play which they undertook to write. It was another dramatization of a sordid murder, nine years old. The play was called *The Lamentable Tragedy of Page of Plymouth*. It is a pity that the play was never printed, for the case itself was sensational, and evoked a pamphlet and three ballads, one of them written by Thomas Deloney.[1]

The event was more than ordinarily sensational, and occurred in 1590. Eulalia Glanfield fell in love with her

---

[1] Printed in *Deloney's Works*, edited by F. O. Mann. A prose account is reprinted in vol. 2, p. 482, of the *Papers of the Shakespeare Society*, edited by J. Payne Collier. Other ballads are printed in the *Roxburgh Collection*.

father's manager, George Strangwidge, but her parents, on leaving Tavistock to live in Plymouth, were persuaded to sell the girl, in spite of her protestations, to a loathsome old widower called Page. Eulalia found life so unendurable that with the aid of her lover and two murderers she strangled Page in the night, and then went round to her neighbours to say that her husband had died suddenly. The neighbours were inquisitive, and noticed marks of violence on the corpse. All four conspirators were arrested and ultimately hanged. Public opinion, however, was greatly stirred by the case, and there was much sympathy with the unfortunate girl, who had been led into such desperate courses by the cruelty of her parents. It is likely that Jonson and Dekker between them would have made a good play of this unsavoury story.

By this time the Chamberlain's Men were well established at the Globe, a matter of no small anxiety to Henslowe and the Admiral's Men, for their rivals not only had an excellent repertory, but were producing these detestable Falstaff plays within shouting distance of their own house. The players at the Rose resolved to get even. The best way seemed to be by reviving the old ill-feeling cause by Shakespeare's Oldcastle *alias* Falstaff. They decided to produce a play dealing with the real Oldcastle. Its progress can be traced in the *Diary*.

'This 16 October 1599

'Received by me, Thomas Downton of Phillip Henslowe to pay Mr. Monday, Mr. Drayton and Mr. Wilson and Hathway for the First Part of the Life of Sir John Oldcastle, and in earnest of the Second Part for the use of the company Ten Pounds I say received . . . . . £10.'[1]

The play was hurried on, and produced in the first week

[1] Henslowe's *Diary*, i, 113.

of November. Apparently it was a great success, for the *Diary* records :

'Received of Mr. Hinchlow for Mr. Munday and the rest of the poets at the playing of Sir John Oldcastle the first time . . . . 10s.'

which Henslowe marked in the margin as 'a gift.' The occasion must have been regarded as momentous. The Second Part of the play has not survived, though both parts were entered for publication on the 11th August 1600. It came out as *The First Part of the True and Remarkable History of the Life of Sir John Oldcastle, the good Lord Cobham*. It was an open and admitted attempt to counter Shakespeare's Falstaff plays, by reviving the old ill-feeling, as was self-righteously asserted in the Prologue :

> The doubtful title, gentlemen, prefixed
> Upon the argument we have in hand,
> May breed suspense, and wrongfully disturb
> The peaceful quiet of your settled thoughts :
> To stop which scruple, let this brief suffice :
> It is no pamper'd glutton we present,
> Nor aged Councillor to youthful sin,
> But one, whose virtue shone above the rest,
> A valiant martyr and a virtuous peer ;
> In whose true faith and loyalty express'd
> Unto his Sovereign, and his country's weal,
> We strive to pay that tribute of our love,
> Your favours merit. Let fair Truth be grac'd
> Since forged invention former time defac'd.

It was a rousing, noisy, bawdy, heroic drama, which lifted a good deal from the original Falstaff. By the irony of fate or the villainy of booksellers, it was afterwards passed off as 'written by William Shakespeare.'

The war between the Admiral's and the Chamberlain's

Men thus reached its climax, but the struggle did not continue long. In the next months both companies had far too many troubles of their own. Moreover, both were threatened with outside competition, which, for a while, seemed likely to ruin them.

Chapter XIII

BOY PLAYERS

In the autumn of 1599, William Stanley, Earl of Derby, at great expense set up the Paul's Boys once more, and by November they were playing regularly. It had been noted by gossips in the previous June that the Earl was busy penning comedies for the common players. None of these plays was printed with his name.

The speculation succeeded. Soon John Marston was regularly writing for this company. Marston was a poet by choice and not of necessity. He was the only son and heir of John Marston of Coventry, a Bencher of the Middle Temple, and his wife Maria, daughter of Andrew Guarsi, an Italian surgeon who had settled in London. Marston was baptised on the 7th October 1576 at Wardington, in Oxfordshire. He was matriculated at Brazenose College, Oxford, on the 4th February 1592. He took his B.A. Degree in 1594, having already been admitted to the Middle Temple on the 2nd August 1592 by his Father, who was then Reader. He had attracted considerable notice by his Satires, but writing interfered with his progress at the Bar.

Just about the time when he was first writing for the Paul's Boys, his father made his will and soon afterwards died. By it he bequeathed most of his property to his wife for life, and then to his son, to whom also he left the furniture in his chambers in the Middle Temple, and his law books, adding the note ' whom I hoped would have profited by them in the study of the law, but man proposeth and God disposeth.' Marston ultimately was ordained in the Church of England, and in 1616 was presented to the living of Christchurch in Hampshire, which he resigned in 1631. He died on the 24th June 1634 in London, and was buried beside his father in the Temple Church, with the inscription : *Oblivioni Sacrum*. His will, which was drawn up only eight days before he died, was not that of a poor man.

So Marston turned dramatist. As a gentleman of some means, it would have been degrading for him to write for hire for the public stage, but there was no social stigma in writing for my Lord of Derby's boy players at a private house.

The new playhouse was very small and certain of its features can be gleaned from the stage directions and incidental comments in Marston's plays. In the Induction to *What You Will*, Atticus says to Doricus ' Let us place ourselves within the curtains, for, good faith, the stage is so very little we shall wrong the general eye else.'

The immediate success of the Boys is amply explained by a remark in *Jack Drum's Entertainment*. Sir Edward Fortune observes :

I saw the Children of Paul's last night,
And troth they pleased me pretty, pretty well.
The apes in time will do it handsomely.
 PLANET. I'faith, I like the audience that frequenteth there
With much applause. A man shall not be choked
With the stench of garlic ; nor be pasted
To the barmy jacket of a beer-brewer.
 BRABANT JUNIOR. 'Tis a good, gentle audience, and I hope the
  boys
Will come one day into the court of requests.[1]

One of Marston's first efforts as a dramatist was to furbish

[1] Act V.

up an old academic piece called *Histriomastix or the Player Whipped*; a very old-fashioned kind of entertainment, full of symbolical characters, in six acts, with a number of little scenes, and a vast range of small parts—in all about a hundred and twenty. It was part symbolical, part realistic and satirical, on the theme that Peace breeds parasites which thrive in times of plenty. Hence Pride has her chance to stir up trouble, which encourages War and his brood, Ambition, Fury, Horror and Ruin. Civil Strife follows, then Poverty enters with her friends Famine, Sickness, Bondage and Sluttishness. After a while Peace returns with Bacchus, Ceres and Plenty. Poverty and the rest vanish, and the play comes to an end with Astraea (that is, the personification of Queen Elizabeth), mounting her throne, supported by Fortitude, Religion, Virginity and the Arts, amidst general adoration and rejoicings.

The symbolical scenes were divided by a number of little sketches in which, after the manner of a *revue*, the lessons of the allegory were illustrated. Many of these scenes were concerned with the players of Sir Oliver Owlet, who were called Ingle,[1] Belch, Gut and their poet, Posthaste (whom some identify as Anthony Munday). The players wax prosperous and insolent in peace, but in the war are marched off as soldiers. From time to time appears the melancholy scholar Chrisoganus, to brood over the follies of mankind.

Marston, like other gentlemen of the Inns of Court, was a great admirer of Ben Jonson, and in two respects he imitated him closely. The introduction of Queen Elizabeth at the end of the play copied the original unhappy conclusion of *Every Man out of his Humour*, and the speeches and personality of Chrisoganus were a close and obvious imitation of Jonson's Asper-Macilente.

[1] i.e. hanger-on.

The play was not entered or published until 1610, and then without any details of its origin, so that it cannot certainly be assigned to the Paul's Boys : it might have been acted by some amateur company of the Inns of Court. The boys, however, could have mustered a sufficient caste.[1]

Marston's first surviving play which was definitely written for the children of Paul's was called *Antonio and Mellida,* an interesting piece with many subtle touches. He began with the now fashionable Induction. Nine of the small players enter ' *with parts in their hands, having cloaks cast over their apparel* ' and discuss their characters.

ALBERTO. Whom do you personate ?
PIERO. Piero, Duke of Venice.
ALBERTO. O ho ! then thus frame your exterior shape
To haughty form of elate majesty,
As if you held the palsy-shaking head
Of reeling chance under your fortune's belt
In strictest vassalage : grow big in thought,
As swoll'n with glory of successful arms.
PIERO. If that be all, fear not, I'll suit it right ;
Who cannot be proud, stroke up the hair, and strut ?

After the Induction and Prologue, ' *enter Antonio, disguised like an Amazon.*' Elizabethan audiences seemed never to tire of the odd mixtures of sex which occurred when boys played girls, and especially girls masquerading as boys.

In opening the play Marston reverted to Marlowe's favourite device of the introductory soliloquy by the hero, but with vastly increased subtlety, for he was master of a peculiarly vivid though often disgusting imagery. In this opening speech he had to give both mood and information. Antonio comes forward to the centre of the stage :

[1] See later, p. 218.

Heart, wilt not break ? and thou abhorred life,
Wilt thou still breathe in my enraged blood ?
Veins, sinews, arteries, why crack ye not,
Burst and divulst with anguish of my grief ?
Can man by no means creep out of himself,
And leave the slough of viperous grief behind ?
Antonio, hast thou seen a fight at sea,
As horrid as the hideous day of doom,
Betwixt thy father, Duke of Genoa,
And proud Piero, the Venetian Prince :
In which the sea hath swoln with Genoa's blood,
And made spring-tides with the warm reeking gore,
That gush'd from out our galleys' scupper-holes ?
In which thy father, poor Andrugio,
Lies sunk, or leap'd into the arms of chance,
Chok'd with the labouring ocean's brackish foam ;
Who, even despite Piero's canker'd hate,
Would with an armed hand have seiz'd thy love,
And link'd thee to the beauteous Mellida ?
Have I outliv'd the death of all these hopes ?
Have I felt anguish pour'd into my heart,
Burning like balsamum in tender wounds ?
And yet dost live ! Could not the fretting sea
Have roll'd me up in wrinkles of his brow ? [1]
Is death grown coy, or grim confusion nice,
That it will not accompany a wretch,
But I must needs be cast on Venice's shore?
And try new fortunes with this strange disguise
To purchase my adored Mellida?

Antonio withdraws into obscurity as the procession enters :
'*The cornets sound a senet. Enter Feliche and Alberto, Castilio and Forobosco, a page carrying a shield ; Piero in armour ; Catzo and Dildo and Balurdo. All these (saving Piero) armed with petronels. Being entered they make a stand in divided files.*'

---

[1] 'Wrinkles of his brow '—as Polonius would doubtless have agreed—is good, and certainly a modern kind of image.

Marston was so careful of his stage directions that it is often possible to recapture the action. He made much use of musical effects, particularly with flutes and cornets, which in the private theatres took the place of the more raucous trumpet, and whenever possible he arranged the action so that one or more of the boys might sing. His plays abound with symbolical pageantry.

The plot moves forward. Piero has proclaimed a huge price on the heads of Antonio and Andrugio. The two young princes of Milan and of Florence are announced. Piero goes out to meet his guests.

'*The cornets sound a senet. Enter above, Mellida, Rossaline and Flavia. Enter below, Galeatzo with attendants; Piero meeteth him, embraceth; at which the cornets sound a flourish; Piero and Galeatzo exeunt; the rest stand still.*

The ladies continue on the upper stage, commenting on the action below until all but Antonio have gone off. Then they notice the supposed Amazon, and decide to go down. Marston gives Antonio ten lines of soliloquy to cover the time taken for them to pass down to the lower stage. When Mellida and the two other ladies reappear below, Antonio does not reveal himself, but pretends to be a messenger; and as such, breaks into a bravura account of the sea fight and the imaginary death of himself. . . .

> Sailing some two months with inconstant winds,
> We view'd the glistering Venetian forts;
> To which we made: when lo! some three leagues off,
> We might descry a horrid spectacle;
> The issue of black fury strow'd the sea
> With tatter'd carcasses of splitted ships,
> Half sinking, burning, floating topsy-turvy.
> Not far from these sad ruins of fell rage,
> We might behold a creature press the waves;
> Senseless he sprawl'd, all notch'd with gaping wounds.

> To him we made, and, short, we took him up;
> The first thing he spake was, ' Mellida ';
> And then he swooned.

He ends with the description of Antonio casting himself into the sea. Finally he goes in with the ladies and the act ends.

As is clear from the stage directions, the acts into which the play is divided were not casual breaks, but clearly defined pauses. After each division the music plays, and within the act, there is a unity of action.[1]

The second act is concerned with the wooing of Mellida by the two princes, who are called Galeatzo and Matzagente, and Antonio's revelation to her that he is alive. Antonio and Mellida plan to run away together, and he leaves her a note directing her what to do. There is real passion and feeling in this scene.

The third act shifts to the marshy shore near Venice where old Andrugio and Lucio his faithful servant wander disconsolate. Andrugio is utterly cast down with grief for the supposed loss of Antonio, but he makes a brave show of it.

> Well, ere yon sun set, I'll show myself myself,
> Worthy my blood. I was a Duke; that's all.
> No matter whither, but from whence we fall.

The action then returns to the Court, and to Feliche, one of the courtiers, who, in utter contrast to his fellows, is an upright, truthful commentator. Feliche is another of the melancholics, though he differs from most of the brood in being entirely happy in his own self-security.

> I envy none; but hate, or pity all.
> For when I view, with an intentive thought,
> That creature fair but proud; him rich, but sot;
> Th' other witty, but unmeasured arrogant;

---

[1] See later, p. 244.

> Him great, yet boundless in ambition;
> Him high-born, but of base life; t'other fear'd,
> Yet feared fears, and fears most to be loved;
> Him wise, but made a fool for public use;
> The other learned, but self-opinionate:
> When I discourse all these, and see myself
> Nor fair, nor rich, nor witty, great nor fear'd,
> Yet amply suited with all full content;
> Lord, how I clap my hands, and smooth my brow,
> Rubbing my quiet bosom, tossing up
> A grateful spirit to Omnipotence!

Feliche is not merely a passive spectator. Humbugs annoy him, particularly effeminates such as Castilio, with his perfumes and pretended love letters from great ladies, whom Feliche beats with relish.

Piero enters, finds Antonio's note, which Mellida has dropped; and all is in confusion. Feliche quick wittedly saves Antonio, who is disposed to rant irresolutely, and tells him to hide himself in his chamber. A moment later Antonio emerges, shrouded in Feliche's sea gown, runs crying through the Court as if in hot pursuit of himself, and so escapes. Mellida, dressed as a page, follows close on his heels, but is pursued.

In the fourth act, Antonio, having fled to the seashore, there encounters Andrugio, so that father and son are unexpectedly reunited. Mellida joins them; and after the usual misunderstandings is once more in Antonio's arms; but she is terrified lest they shall be followed, and sends Antonio to scout over the marsh. Meantime Piero and his followers track her down and seize her. Piero is angry. He decrees that she shall marry Galeatzo that same night. Andrugio swears that he will follow her to the Court.

In the fifth act Marston staged a number of surprises. He began with the preparations and masquings for Mellida's wedding. Then Feliche appears at the Court, bringing with him an armed knight. It is Andrugio, his face concealed beneath his helmet. He stands forth to claim the tyrant's reward for Andrugio's head; and then reveals himself. Piero is overcome with astonishment at such magnanimity. His royal spirits are numbed. He clasps his former enemy with seeming submission :

> I joy my state ; him whom I loathed before
> That now I honour, love, nay more, adore.

But his protestations are interrupted. '*The still flutes sound a mournful senet.*' A coffin is brought in. Within lies Antonio. Mellida laments over the corpse. Piero protests :

> Oh that my life, her love, my dearest blood,
> Would but redeem one minute of his breath.

At this confession Antonio sits up in his coffin,[1] and everything, for the moment, ends happily, with Antonio betrothed to Mellida and general rejoicing.

There is movement and excitement in this play, and its story is not more extravagant or impossible than many which have won approval. Marston indeed has not received his due from critics. Elizabethan dramatists were put through a kind of Honours Examination by Victorian critics, and then classified in their respective places. Marston's merits were not of the kind then appreciated. His ideas and his language were condemned as extravagant and unsavoury, and he was therefore awarded a poor second class.[2] Nor has

---

[1] The coffin trick became popular.
[2] The late Sir Adolphus Ward, by his *History of English Dramatic Literature*, became a kind of Victorian Chief Examiner, and was largely responsible for the reputation of Elizabethan dramatists. He was upset by the low tone of Marston's *Insatiate Countess* : ' Such characters as Isabella have probably existed, and the type is familiar to readers of Tacitus and Gibbon. The age in which Marston wrote was unhappily signalized by the shamelessness of some of its women as well as of its

his reputation had much chance of revaluation in modern times, for few of his plays are readily accessible. Unlike Marlowe's and Ben Jonson's, they have not been reprinted in cheap and popular editions,[1] so that critics must perforce read them in the British Museum or some other library, where the atmosphere may be good for scholarship but does not induce æsthetic enthusiasm.

Yet Marston was the exact contemporary of John Donne; and they had much in common. Marston was not so damnably clever, but he had certain strength which Donne had not. Both belong to a generation which, like their fathers, loved to experiment with language and ideas. Lyly and his contemporaries played with assonances and cadences and rhythmic effects, that were often mightily soporific; there was nothing like the reading aloud of a euphuistic novel to send one to sleep on a hot summer's afternoon or a winter's evening by the fire.

Marston's generation sought the contrary effect. At all costs they must keep the hearer awake and alert with kicks, jerks, pricks, stabs and shocks of surprising notions, images and situations. This was well shown in the sequel to *Antonio and Mellida*. It was called *Antonio's Revenge* and was produced in the late autumn of 1599.

From the first Marston appreciated the peculiar advantages of the private playhouse. The public stages, open to the sky

men; but nothing can excuse the creation of such a figure in a work of the imagination. A moral monstrosity such as the Isabella of this play is a subject as unfitting for poetical treatment as is a physical monstrosity for treatment by the sculptor's or painter's art' (ii, 58). As a result Ward had a low opinion of Marston himself, and in his class list Marston hardly even secures a bare Pass. 'Thus altogether his merits seem less conspicuous than most of the great dramatists with whom it has been his fortune to be habitually ranked; and is doubtful whether he deserves to be remembered among those who have adorned our dramatic literature by creations of original genius' (ii, 67).

[1] Except *The Malcontent*, in the Temple Dramatists.

and weather, naturally demanded robust methods of presentation. It needed no small effort to persuade spectators that the bare stage of the Rose or the Curtain did indeed portray the field of Agincourt or the gardens of Belmont by moonlight. In the small private playhouse, which was lit by candlelight, there was a far greater sense of intimacy. Moreover, subtle and delicate lighting effects were now possible. Plays, especially tragedies, could be performed on a dim-lit stage, and the horror was vastly intensified by physical darkness. Much of *Antonio's Revenge* was acted by the light of solitary candles or flickering torches. It was the first specimen of a new type of tragedy which contemporaries labelled ' nocturnal,'[1] and might as justly have called ' charnel.'

The play opens with a remarkable prologue, in which the right mood for the tragedy is most dismally created :

> The rawish dank of clumsy winter ramps
> The fluent summer's vein ; and drizzling sleet
> Chilleth the wan bleak cheek of the numb'd earth,
> Whilst snarling gusts nibble the juiceless leaves
> From the nak'd shudd'ring branch ; and pills the skin
> From off the soft and delicate aspects.
> O now, methinks, a sullen tragic scene
> Would suit the time with pleasing congruence.

After thirty-three lines in this strain :

' *Enter Piero, unbraced, his arms bare, smeared in blood, a poniard in one hand bloody, and a torch in the other ; Strotzo following him with a cord.*'

Gasper Strotzo is a new character to the play. He is Piero's minion, prepared to do anything that will serve his

[1] Dekker, in *The Seven Deadly Sins of London*, describing how the shops were shut up to welcome Candlelight, says, " the Citty lookt like a priuate Playhouse, when the windows are clapt downe, as if some *Nocturnal*, or dismal *Tragedy* were presently to be acted before all the *Trades-men*."—Edited by H. F. B. Brett-Smith, Percy Reprints, p. 30.

master and himself. The scene is acted almost in the dark. The horrors accumulate. Piero speaks :

Ho, Gasper Strotzo, bind Feliche's trunk
Unto the panting side of Mellida !
              Exit Strotzo.

'Tis yet dead night, yet all the earth is clutch'd
In the dull leaden hand of snoring sleep ;
No breath disturbs the quiet of the air,
No spirit moves upon the breast of earth,
Save howling dogs, night-crows and screeching owls,
Save meagre ghosts, Piero, and black thoughts.
One, two. Lord, in two hours what a topless mount
Of unpeer'd mischief have these hands cast up !
             Enter Strotzo.
I can scarce coop triumphing vengeance up
From bursting forth in braggart passion.
    STROTZO. My lord, 'tis firmly said that—
    PIERO. Andrugio sleeps in peace : this brain hath chok'd
The organ of his breast. Feliche hangs,
But as a bait upon the line of death,
To tice on mischief. I am great in blood,
Unequall'd in revenge. You horrid scouts
That sentinel swart night, give loud applause
From your large palms. First, know, my heart was rais'd
Unto Andrugio's life upon this ground—
    STROTZO. Duke, 'tis reported—
    PIERO. We both were rivals in our May of blood,
Unto Maria, fair Ferrara's heir.
He won the lady, to my honour's death ;
And from her sweets cropp'd this Antonio ;
For which I burnt in inward swelt'ring hate,
And fester'd rankling malice in my breast,
Till I might belk revenge upon his eyes :
And now, O blessèd now ! 'tis done. Hell, night,
Give loud applause to my hypocrisy.
When his bright valour even dazzled sense,
In off'ring his own head, public reproach

Had blurr'd my name. Speak, Strotzo, had it not?
If then I had—
 Strotzo. It had, so please—
 Piero. What had, so please? Unseasoned sycophant,
Piero Sforza is no numbèd lord,
Senseless of all true touch; stroke not the head
Of infant speech, till it be fully born.
Go to!

And so in jerks and starts and interrupted sentences the full night's work is revealed: Feliche dead, Mellida shamed, Andrugio choked, and Maria, Andrugio's duchess, due to arrive in the court that very morning.

 Poison the father, butcher the son, and marry the mother!

Piero is a rare avenger. As he goes out to bed, the dawn comes, and with it Maria, eager to clasp husband and son. With clear daylight Antonio, the day's bridegroom, comes forth, but full of dread. Mother and son meet. Antonio goes to summon his bride, and then:
 '*The curtain's drawn, and the body of Feliche, stabb'd thick with wounds, appears hung up.*'
One by one the horrors of the night are discovered: Andrugio is dead in bed: Pandulfo, Feliche's father, learns of his son's death, but the father, like the son, looks on Fate with clear eyes:

> Would'st have me cry, run raving up and down,
> For my son's loss? Would'st have me turn rank mad,
> Or wring my face with mimic action:
> Stamp, curse, weep, rage, and then my bosom strike?
> Away, 'tis apish action, player-like.
> If he is guiltless, why should tears be spent?
> Thrice blessed soul that dieth innocent.

This speech ends the first act.

The second begins in funeral pageantry and a full stage.
The opening action requires twenty-one actors :

'*The cornets sound a sennet.*

'*Enter two mourners with torches, two with streamers; Castilio and Forobosco, with torches; a Herald bearing Andrugio's helm and sword; the coffin; Maria, supported by Lucio and Alberto; Antonio by himself; Piero and Strotzo, talking; Galeatzo and Matzagente, Balurdo and Pandulfo; the coffin set down; helm, sword, and streamers hung up, placed by the Herald, whilst Antonio and Maria wet their handkerchers with their tears, kiss them, and lay them on the hearse, kneeling : all go out but Piero. Cornets cease, and he speaks :*'

Piero's epitaph over his dead rival is typical :

Rot there, thou cerecloth that enfolds the flesh
Of my loath'd foe ; moulder to crumbling dust ;
Oblivion choke the passage of thy fame !
Trophies of honour'd birth drop quickly down :
Let nought of him, but what was vicious, live.
Though thou art dead, think not my hate is dead :
I have but newly twone my arm in the curl'd locks
Of snaky vengeance. Pale, beetle-brow'd hate
But newly bustles up. Sweet wrong, I clap thy thoughts !
O let me hug thy bosom, rub my breast,
In hope of what may hap. Andrugio rots :
Antonio lives : umh : how long ? ha, ha ! how long ?
Antonio pack'd hence, I'll his mother wed,
Then clear my daughter of supposed lust,
Wed her to Florence heir. O excellent !
Venice, Genoa, Florence at my beck,
At Piero's nod. Balurdo, O ho !—
O 'twill be rare, all unsuspected done.
I have been nursed in blood, and still have suck'd
The steam of reeking gore.

Directly following this, Marston commits an odd lapse

of taste. Balurdo, who is the comic figure among the courtiers, appears, with his beard half off, half on, ' because the tiring man hath not glued on my beard half fast enough.' The whole of this act, which is short, is taken up with the incitements to Antonio to vengeance.

In the third act, set in St. Mark's Church, Venice, preliminary dumb show presents Piero making love to Maria, apparently with success. Then, after the dumb show :

' *Enter two pages, the one with tapers, the other holding a chafing-dish ; a perfume in it ; Antonio, in his night-gown and a night-cap, unbraced, following after.*'

Antonio has come to pay reverence to the tomb of his father. Andrugio's ghost appears, cries for revenge, reveals the murder, and warns his son that Maria is yielding. Maria also comes down to the tomb, but finding Antonio distraught, she leaves him. He calls on the spirits of the dead, and they echo from above and beneath his word of ' murder.' Piero himself enters. He is following Maria, but finding that she has gone, he goes out, leaving his little son Julio with Antonio. Here is the chance for vengeance : exchange of a son for a father.

Antonio takes hold of the boy, cuts his throat, and lets the warm blood splash over the tomb of Andrugio. The scene then passes to Maria going to bed on the night before her wedding. When her pages and nurse have left her, she draws the curtain of the bed to find the ghost of Andrugio, sitting there. Antonio rushes in, his arms still bloody from the death of Julio. The ghost warns him to assume some disguise to escape from Piero's vengeance. And then as Maria, now joined with the avengers, gets into bed, the ghost draws the curtain.

The fourth act begins with Antonio disguised as a fool blowing bubbles. It is concerned principally with the trial of Mellida for inchastity. The chief witness is Strotzo, who, as has already been agreed between him and Piero, protests that he had given false testimony by the instigation of Antonio, and claims that he is unworthy to live. Piero strangles him quickly and effectively in grim earnest. Then, as part of the plot to deceive Piero, it is announced that Antonio is drowned. This is too much for Mellida, whose heart is broken. She is carried away, swooning, and a few moments after, dies. Antonio and the rest of Piero's enemies now plan final vengeance.

The fifth act opens with the wedding masque of Piero and Maria, a brave scene, full of dancing and torchlight. The masquers persuade Piero to dismiss the rest of his attendants, for they would banquet with him alone. Piero at last is at their mercy. Antonio, Pandulfo, Alberto and Balurdo bind him, pluck out his tongue, and triumph over him. The banquet is produced, and Piero is mockingly bidden to taste of it; when the cover is taken off, the dish reveals the limbs of little Julio. But still Piero must die slow:

'*They offer to run all at Piero, and on a sudden stop.*'

At last even their vengeance is surfeited, and they stab him in turn. The ghost of Andrugio, which has been watching these proceedings with approval, is satisfied. It goes out after a closing speech to the audience in favour of the author, and hoping that:

> when the closing Epilogue appears,
> Instead of claps, may it obtain but tears.

And so the play is wound up in general woe.[1]

Antonio's Revenge is a remarkable play which needs its original nocturnal setting to gain its full effects. Marston,

[1] It is obvious to anyone who reads the play closely that there are coincidences between *Antonio's Revenge* and Shakespeare's *Hamlet* too strong to be accidental. Whence it follows either that the greater part of *Hamlet* was written before the autumn of 1599, or that Shakespeare did not hesitate to borrow from Marston. Either is possible.

however, forgot the golden rule of μηδὲν ἄγαν. The horror in individual scenes is most skilfully created, but there is too much of it. In the first act the cumulation of crimes is admirable ; but long before Piero has been sent to rot in eternal silence, the feelings have become numbed and juiceless with these excessive stimulations.

About this time Edward Alleyn returned to the stage, perhaps because of the increasing competition of rival companies. Clearly it was quite hopeless for the Rose to attempt to compete with the new and fashionable Globe. There was nothing for it but a move. Accordingly Alleyn and Henslowe decided to try their fortunes elsewhere. They found a suitable piece of ground on the north of the City in the parish of St. Giles-without-Cripplegate, near the Fields. Alleyn paid £240 for the lease, which ran for forty-three years. The agreement was signed on the 22nd December 1599.

On the 8th January Henslowe and Alleyn signed a contract with Peter Street, who had built the Globe Theatre in the previous year, for the erection of a new playhouse. The agreement set out in great detail the construction and the material to be used. The theatre was to be ' made and contrived in and to the late erected playhouse on the Bank in the said parish of said St. Saviour's called the Globe.' It laid down the size of the playhouse, which was to be set square and ' to contain four-score foot of lawful assize every way square without, and fifty-five foot of like assize square every way within, with a good, sure and strong foundation of piles, brick, lime and sand.' There were to be three storeys, ' with four convenient divisions for gentlemen's rooms ' and other divisions for ' two-penny rooms ' with seats. The stage was to be forty-three feet long and in breadth extending to the middle of the yard (i.e. twenty-seven and a half feet). Unfortunately the original plan which went with the agreement has not survived, but the contract itself is the only full description of an Elizabethan playhouse that exists.[1]

As soon as it was known in the neighbourhood that Alleyn proposed to build a playhouse the usual objections were made. Alleyn therefore went to his patron, the Lord Admiral and sought his help. He came away with a warrant addressed:

'To all and every Her Majesty's Justices and other Ministers and Officers within the county of Middlesex and to every of them and to all others whom it shall concern.

'Whereas my servant Edward Alleyn, in respect of the dangerous decay of that house which he and his company have now on the Bank, and for that the same standeth very noisesome for resort of people in the winter time, hath therefore now of late taken a plot of ground near Redcross Street, London, very fit and convenient for the building of a new house there; and hath provided timber and other necessaries for the effecting thereof, to his great charge. Forasmuch as the place standeth very convenient for the ease of people, and that her Majesty (in respect of the acceptable service which my said servant and his company have done and presented before her Highness to her great liking and contentment, as well this last Christmas as at sundry other times) is graciously moved toward them with a special regard of favour in their proceeding; this shall be, therefore, to pray and require you and every of you to permit and suffer my said servant to proceed in the effecting and finishing of the said new house, without any your let or molestation towards him or any of his workmen. And so, not doubting of your observation in this behalf, I bid you right heartily farewell at the Court at Richmond, the 12th of January 1599 [-1600].[2]

'NOTTINGHAM.'

[1] *Henslowe Papers*, p. 4.   [2] *Ibid.*, p. 49.

In spite of this the nobility and gentry of the neighbourhood protested. So strong was the opposition that they petitioned the Council. Whereupon the Council caused a letter to be directed to the Justices of the Peace in the county of Middlesex :

'We are given to understand by our very good lord, the Lord Willoughby and other gentlemen and inhabitants in the parish of St. Giles-without-Cripplegate that there is a purpose and intent in some persons to erect a theatre in Whitecross Street, near unto the Bars in that part that is in the county of Middlesex, whereof there are too many already not far from that place ; and as you know not long since you received special direction to pluck down those and to see them defaced. Therefore if this new erection should be suffered it would not only be an offence and scandal to divers, but a thing that would greatly displease her Majesty. These are therefore to will and require you in any case to take order that no such theatre or playhouse be built there, or other house to serve for such use, both to avoid the many inconveniences that thereby are likely to ensue to all the inhabitants, and the offence that would be to Her Majesty, having heretofore given sufficient notice unto you of the great mislike Her Highness hath of those public and vain buildings for such occasions that breed increase of base and lewd people and divers other disorders. Therefore we require you not to fail forthwith to take order that the aforesaid intended building may be stayed, and if any be begun, to see the same quite defaced.'[1]

Meantime Street was collecting the material to be ready for building. Henslowe jotted down on the back of his copy of the contract the payments which he made : On the 19th January £10 ' in earnest of twenty and odd loads of

[1] *Acts of the Privy Council*, xxx, 146 ; reprinted in *Elizabethan Stage*, iv, 326.

timber unto Richard Deller, bargeman'; two days later, '£20 for forty loads of timber'; on the 24th, '£3 to pay the sawyers.'

Then, as counterblast to 'our very good Lord, the Lord Willoughby,' the local inhabitants of lesser standing were persuaded to petition the Council that the building of the playhouse might proceed. The petitioners put forward three reasons :

'First, because the place appointed out for that purpose standeth very tolerable near unto the Fields, and so far distant and remote from any person or place of account as that none can be annoyed thereby.

'Secondly, because the erectors of the said house are contented to give a very liberal portion of money weekly towards the relief of our poor, the number and necessity whereof is so great that the same will redound to the continual comfort of the said poor.

'Thirdly and lastly, we are the rather contented to accept this means of relief of our poor, because our parish is not able to relieve them, neither hath the Justices of the Shire taken any order for any supply out of the County as is enjoined by the late Act of Parliament.'[1]

Such as could sign appended their signatures ; the others made their mark. There were twenty-seven signatories including the constable, the churchwarden and two overseers ' for our poor.'

Again the Lords of the Privy Council were disposed to listen ; and another warrant to the Justices of the Peace of the county of Middlesex, especially of St. Giles-without-Cripplegate and ' to all others whom it may concern ' was signed by the Lord Admiral, Lord George Hunsdon, the Lord Chamberlain, and Sir Robert Cecil. These noblemen were quite prepared to use their official positions as

[1] *Henslowe Papers*, p. 50.

members of the Council to forward the affairs of their own servants.

So the building was begun at last, and its progress can be traced in the *Diary* where Henslowe recorded ' A note what I have laid out since we went about our new house as followeth 1600.' The entries are mostly for drink and dinners. The foundations were finished on the 8th May, but in June there seems to have been trouble, for the last entry made on the back of the contract was on the 10th ' To Street, to pacify him, 4s.'

Street's anger, however, seems soon to have cooled. Henslowe paid for his dinner on the 16th. Throughout July Street (who becomes Peter in the accounts on the 6th July), Gilbert East, Henslowe's bailiff, and Henslowe were dining together most days, and until the 8th August, by which time the house seems to have been finished. In all the cost of building came to £520. The new playhouse was called the Fortune.

Meanwhile in the early spring the Chamberlain's Men had provided a sensation. Playing was not allowed in Lent, but as with all Elizabethan regulations, the restriction was sometimes observed and sometimes neglected. As the list of plays printed on pages 140–4 shows, the Admiral's Men ceased playing for thirty-nine days in 1595; but in 1597 they shortened the period of abstention to nineteen days. Now, however, owing to the many troubles of the time, regulations were being more strictly observed. The Chamberlain's Men would thus be without employment. Will Kemp therefore accepted bets that he would dance all the way from London to Norwich.

The journey was well advertised. On the first Monday in Lent, the 10th February, attended by Thomas Sly, his taborer, William Bee, his servant, and George Spratt, appointed as referee, he started off from the house of the

Lord Mayor of London about seven o'clock in the morning. Great crowds were waiting to see him go, and many of them bestowed on him bent sixpences and groats with their blessings.

He danced as far as Stratford Bow, and there rested, staunchly refusing the many drinks that were proffered him. Then he went on as far as Ilford. Here he rested until night, when he continued the journey by moonlight as far as Romford. There he rested until the Thursday, when he got up early, went back to his stopping-place, and continued through Romford and on to Brentwood. That night he went on to Ingatestone, the crowds still following him.

Next day he reached Chelmsford, where great crowds had gathered to greet him; thence on the Monday to Braintree. There he rested for a day, and on the Wednesday he reached Sudbury. From Sudbury he danced to Melford, and there stayed till the Saturday. Thence he reached Clare, where a very bountiful widow called Everet entertained him royally. From Clare he danced to Bury St. Edmunds, which he reached on the Saturday afternoon at the same time as the Lord Chief Justice entered the town by another gate, to find the streets deserted, as everyone had gone to see the clown.

Kemp was now held up for six days because of a great fall of snow. On the Friday he left Bury at seven and reached Thetford, making good progress over the heath. Another hearty week-end followed at the house of Sir Edwin Rich. The eighth day's journey, on Monday, 2nd March, he danced to Rockland and thence to Hingham. On the ninth day's work he reached Barford Bridge and so came within sight of Norwich, where there were great crowds of people waiting for him. He was advised not to complete the last stage of his journey that day, but to wait until everyone should be ready to greet him. So he rode into the city, where the mayor sent for him and asked him to complete his dance on the following Saturday.

When Saturday afternoon came he went out of the city, and, continuing where he had left off, he danced through St. Stephen's Gate where one Thomas Gilbert, in the name of the citizens, presented him with a welcome in rhyme. He went on with the greatest of difficulty because of the crowds until he reached the cross in the market place. Here, as he arrived, the city waits struck up with voice, viol and violin. On he went towards the mayor, taking a short cut by leaping over the churchyard wall of St. John's, but this in the end proved a false move, because Spratt, having lost sight of him in the crowd, insisted on his going back on the Monday to finish the last few yards again, and besides, the people of Norwich had taken up a turnpike so that he might have free passage. At last he reached the Guildhall, where the mayor, ladies, knights and gentlewomen were waiting to welcome him. The mayor gave him £5 in Elizabeth angels, and a pension of 40s. during life, and as well he was made a freeman of the merchant venturers. For a memorial he left his dancing shoes which were nailed up in the Guildhall.

It was a most triumphant progress that was talked of for years.

Kemp came back to London to find that his prowess was being celebrated in ballads. He therefore wrote up his own account, which he called *Kemp's Nine Days' Wonder*.[1]

The dance had an important sequel. Kemp was so well satisfied with his success that he accepted bets to undertake the more ambitious venture of a dance over the Alps to Rome. Accordingly he parted with his share in the Globe Theatre, and left his old colleagues in the Chamberlain's company. It was the most important break since their partnership had been formed in the autumn of 1594.

In the early summer both professional companies had their anxieties. Complaints against Alleyn's new playhouse

[1] Reprinted in the *Bodley Head Quartos*, vol. iv.

continued, and it seemed necessary to the Council that they should at least make some show of doing something. On the 22nd June they sent down an order 'to restrain the excessive number of playhouses and the immoderate use of stage plays in and about the City.' The order began by setting out the complaints that had been made and granting 'that the multitude of the said houses and the misgovernment of them hath been made and is daily occasion of the idle, riotous and dissolute living of great numbers of people.

'... And yet nevertheless, it is considered that the use and exercise of such plays, not being evil in itself, may with a good order and moderation be suffered in a well governed estate, and that, her Majesty being pleased at some times to take delight and recreation in the sight and hearing of them, some order is fit to be taken for the allowance and maintainence of such persons as are thought meetest in that kind to yield her Majesty recreation and delight, and consequently of the houses that must serve for public playing to keep them in exercise.'[1]

The Council therefore laid down three regulations: the first that there should be about the City two houses, and no more, to serve for the use of common stage plays; one on the Bankside, the other in Middlesex. Alleyn's new house might be allowed as it was understood that the Curtain was either to be plucked down or put to some other use. This playhouse should serve for the Lord Admiral's players. The other house was for the Lord Chamberlain's servants, who had chosen the Globe. It was particularly forbidden that any stage plays should be played in common inns.

'Secondly, forasmuch as these stage plays, by the multitude of houses and company of players, have been too frequent, not serving for recreation but inviting and calling the people

[1] *Malone Society's Collections*, i, 80; reprinted in *Elizabethan Stage*, iv, 330.

daily from their trade and work to misspend their time. It is likewise ordered that the two several companies of players assigned unto the two houses allowed may play each of them in their several house twice a week and no oftener, and especially that they shall refrain to play on the Sabbath day, upon pain of imprisonment and further penalty ; and that they shall forbear altogether in the time of Lent, and likewise at such time and times as any extraordinary sickness or infection of disease shall appear to be in and about the City.'

To this the Council added a ' thirdly,' which suggested that they had no great hopes—perhaps even intentions— that their regulations would ever be obeyed. They ordered that copies of this order should be sent to the Lord Mayor and to the Justices of the Peace of Middlesex and Surrey, with special covering letters to see the orders carried out. The covering letter was mildly sarcastic in tone. After observing the complaints which had been made of the great abuses caused by stage plays, the Council note that they have made certain orders of which a copy is enclosed, but, their Lordships continued—

'. . . as we have done our parts in prescribing the orders, so unless you perform yours in looking to the due execution of them, we shall lose our labour, and the want of redress must be imputed unto you and others unto whom it appertaineth ; and therefore we do hereby authorize and require you to see the said orders to be put in execution, and to be continued, as you do wish the amendment of the aforesaid abuses and will remove the blame thereof from yourselves.' [1]

The dealings of the lords of the Council seem not always to have been single-hearted. In this instance they apparently

[1] *Acts of the Privy Council*, xxx, 411 ; reprinted in *Elizabethan Stage*, iv, 332.

issued an order knowing quite well that it would not be carried out. The order, however, seems to have had some effect. According to Henslowe's *Diary*, in 1599, the Admiral's Men produced eighteen new plays between the 1st July and the 31st December. They produced sixteen between the 1st January and the 30th June 1600, but between July and December only two.

On the whole the year 1600 was lean. Between the playing of *Sir John Oldcastle* in November 1599 and their departure from the Rose in the summer of 1600, the Admiral's Men acquired twenty new plays. Two of these were afterwards printed: *Patient Grissel*, of which the earliest edition is dated 1603; it was the work of Chettle, Dekker and Haughton; and *Old Fortunatus*, one of Dekker's plays. The list also included a play called *Thomas Merry, or Beech's Tragedy*, another play on a sensational murder which occurred on the 23rd August 1594, and at the time had evoked a pamphlet and four ballads.

The entries for *Old Fortunatus* throw considerable light on Dekker's methods as a dramatist. A play of Fortunatus in two parts had been in the repertory of the Admiral's Men in 1596. In November, 1599, Dekker undertook to rewrite it as a single play. On the 9th he received 40s. from Henslowe 'in earnest'; on the 24th he received £3 more, also 'in earnest'; on the 30th November he received 20s. 'in full payment of his book of *Fortunatus*'. On the 31st November [*sic*] he received 20s. for the 'altering of the book of the *Whole History of Fortunatus*.' The play went into production at once; between the 6th and the 12th December, the company spent £10 'for to buy things for Fortunatus,' and on the 12th Dekker drew a further 40s. 'for the end of Fortunatus for the Court'—presumably for the performance which the Admiral's Men gave at Court on the 28th December or the 6th January. It follows that

Dekker wrote the book between the 9th November and the 30th—a matter of three weeks. There is nothing improbable in this, for he was a rapid writer. In 1598 he had written two plays by himself and collaborated in fourteen. In 1599 he wrote four plays by himself and collaborated in six.

In the late spring (1600) the Paul's Boys put on another of Marston's plays—a comedy called *Jack Drum's Entertainment, or the Comedy of Pasquil and Katherine*.[1]

The play is a London comedy of contemporary manners, supposed to take place in Highate. The plot is vastly complex, for this is a story of domestic intrigues rather after the manner of *An Humorous Day's Mirth*, and belongs to the kind which later generations called ' French farce.' Sir Edward Fortune, a broad-minded gentleman, has two daughters, Camelia, who is fickle, and Katherine, who is constant. Camelia is wooed by Brabant junior, a gallant from the Court and a yeoman called John Ellis. She wavers between them, and then turns to Planet, Brabant's friend. Katherine is wooed by Pasquil, another young gentleman, and Mammon, a usurer. When Mammon finds himself turned down, he hires a comic Frenchman called John Fo-de-King to murder Pasquil. But he tells Pasquil about it. Pasquil pretends to be dead. Katherine, thinking he is indeed dead, goes mad and runs away. Pasquil is so angry with Mammon that he takes away from him his bonds and tears them up ; so the usurer also goes mad, as does Pasquil. Both lovers are ultimately cured when they meet again.

---

[1] Entered in the Stationers' Register, the 8th September. Editions of 1601, 1616, and 1618 are known. There is no author's name, but the style is unmistakable. The play can be dated within a few weeks by reference to Kemp's ' Morris.' Sir John Fortune in the play says :

' 'Tis Whitsuntide and we must frolic it.'

As the comedy was meant to be exactly contemporary is seems likely that it was acted at Whitsun.

Camelia is suitably punished for her inconstancies when all the suitors refuse her.

Mingled with these two stories are the adventures of Jack Drum, Sir Edward's man. He is in love with Winifred, Katherine's maid. Monsieur John, who is always looking for a wench, makes love to her. She tells him that if he will carry her away in a sack, she will let him have what he wants, but Jack gets into the sack, and when Monsieur John opens it, leaps out and beats him. At the end of the play Brabant senior, who fancies himself as a wit, plays a great joke on Monsieur John. He pretends that his own wife is a courtesan, and sends Monsieur John to her, supposing that he would quickly be sent about his business. But Brabant senior miscalculates. The Frenchman comes back highly delighted and the plays ends with Brabant crowned with horns.

It is not one of Marston's more successful efforts. The comedy was meant to be contemporary, and the illusion was kept up by a sprinkling of quite natural topicalities, including a gird at the new poet Mellidus (author of *Antonio and Mellida*)—Marston was always ready to laugh at himself—and a few lines of retort to Ben Jonson. It was typical of the comedies provided for the boys' companies and their audiences, and quite possibly there was some foundation in fact for the story.[1]

As soon as the Fortune was ready, the Admiral's Men moved in. On the 14th August 1600, Henslowe began a new series of accounts. About the same time a rival project was gathering head. Henry Evans, who had at one time been a sharer in the profits of Lyly's company of boys at the Blackfriars playhouse,[2] took notice of the revival of the Paul's

---

[1] Jonson's quarrel with Marston is more fully discussed in Chapter 15. See also page 292, *The Old Joiner of Aldgate*.

[2] See page 25.

Boys. He noticed further that the indoor playhouse which James Burbage had created at such cost was still available. The boys as before could be recruited from the Royal Chapel, and the opposition in the Blackfriars precinct to common stage plays did not apply to private performances by choirboys.

There had also been a change in the Mastership of the Chapel. Hunnis had died in 1597. He was succeeded by Nathaniel Giles. When Giles's patent had been granted it included the usual clause authorizing him to take up such children as he should think meet ' in all cathedral, collegiate parish churches, chapels or any other place.'

Evans and Giles put their heads together. The patent might be stretched to include other ventures. Giles could therefore recruit a company of boy players without trouble. Here, then, were some very interesting possibilities.

On the 22nd September 1600 Evans agreed with Richard Burbage to rent the Blackfriars playhouse for £40 a year. Then he and Giles set about collecting the company, and soon they had gathered some very bright boys ; including Nathan Field, one of Mulcaster's boys who became famous in a later generation as an actor and dramatist ; and Salmon (or Salathiel) Pavy, who died not long after at the age of twelve, and received a verse epitaph from Ben Jonson, which shows that he was expert at acting old men.

The Children of the Chapel were soon the vogue. Playwrights of the best class were attracted. Ben Jonson, who seems at this time to have quarrelled both with the Admiral's and with the Chamberlain's Men, was one of the first who turned to them ; and this winter he wrote *Cynthia's Revels.*

Jonson fully realized that he was writing for a special and select audience of gentlemen. He revelled in it. But he took a good look at Lyly first. He began *Cynthia's Revels* with another Induction. Three of the children enter quarrelling. One of them tries to give the audience an outline of the plot—which was very desirable for they would otherwise have had much difficulty in following it. They then imitate the offensive behaviour of gentlemen spectators in their playhouse, and at last allow the prologue to have his say.

Seemingly Jonson had intended this play for the Court. It is part satire, part masque. Cupid and Mercury meet. Cupid is intending to disguise himself as a page to follow some of Diana's maids in the Court. Mercury promises to help him. So they call on Echo, and find that they are near the fountain where Niobe died; the Fountain of Self-love, whose waters are cursed. Amorphus, a foolish gentleman, drinks the water and meets Asotus (yet another of the up-starts turned courtier). They introduce themselves and their clothes and chatter, to the unfeigned contempt of the scholar Crites.

Cupid and Mercury find their way to Court, disguise themselves as pages, and take service. Scene after scene follows with the various foolish courtiers and ladies displaying their clothes, their faces, and their follies. They are shown playing their parlour games; and reveal themselves as a complete set of nit-wits. Amorphus gives Asotus instruction in accosting a mistress, and they rehearse the scene. At last Crites, at Mercury's command, agrees to devise a suitable punishment for the foolish courtiers, but he is afraid that the Court itself may take it ill. Mercury answers his objections:

> You are deceived. The better race in Court
> That have the true nobility called virtue
> Will apprehend it, as a grateful right
> Done to their separate merit; and approve
> The fit rebuke of so ridiculous heads,
> Who with their apish customs and forced garbs
> Would bring the name of courtier in contempt,
> Did it not live unblemished in some few,
> Whom equal Jove hath loved, and Phœbus formed
> Of better metal, and in better mould.

The courtiers and ladies continue their foolish ways. Asotus comes out as a champion to challenge all comers at Court compliment in four rounds : The Bare Accost, the Better Regard, the Solemn Address, and the Perfect Close. Crites joins in the game, and puts the others to shame. When he has suitably rebuked the triflers, Arete appears and commands him to prepare a masque for Cynthia. Cynthia nerself comes down to watch the entertainment. At this point Jonson provided several masques of the elaborate kind which he afterwards produced in great numbers for the Court of King James I. Cynthia is delighted. With grave dignity she congratulates him :

> Not without wonder, nor without delight,
> Mine eyes have viewed, in contemplation's depth,
> This work of wit, divine and excellent.

The masques continue ; Crites adding suitable and lengthy comment, and condemning the victims of the waters of Self-love to visit the Well of Knowledge.

By this time Jonson's head was swollen to bursting. His prologue was saucy enough. His Muse, said he, was not one to hunt after popular applause—

> Or foamy praise, that drops from common jaws ;
> The garland that she wears, their hands must twine,
> Who can both censure, understand, define
> What merit is : then cast those piercing rays,
> Round as a crown, instead of honoured bays,
> About his poesy ; which, he knows, affords
> Words, above action ; matter, above words.

The epilogue was even more conceited. He'll make no epilogue ; not he. Nor will he praise the play ; that might tax the maker of Self-love.

> I'll only speak what I have heard him say,
> ' By God, 'tis good, and if you like't, you may.'

Jonson was mistaken. It is not good. *Cynthia's Revels* is too long and too diffuse. The fools are tedious and their follies not worth chastising. Nor was the ex-bricklayer well equipped for the business. Moreover, he had fallen from the higher levels of the true satire. He had ceased whipping manners and was now pillorying men. Henceforth no one felt himself safe from this universal condemnation. It did not make matters easier in the Blackfriars playhouse, although it might raise the laughter of those who were not themselves victims.

From the first the Children of the Chapel were a boisterous set of imps, and encouraged to be as impudent as possible by their patrons, managers and playwrights. Evans himself was quite ready to act high-handedly. In December, under colour of Giles's commission, he and his partner, called James Robinson, kidnapped a boy, by name Thomas Clifton, as he was coming home from school. The boy's father was a gentleman. When he heard what had happened he went to the playhouse, interviewed Evans and Robinson, and asked them to release his son. They refused. Master Clifton threatened that he would complain to the Council. They replied insolently that he could complain to whom he would. The angry father retorted that it was not seemly for a gentleman of his standing to have his only son and heir so basely used. They replied that they had authority sufficient to take any nobleman's son; further, to annoy the father more, they gave the boy a scroll containing a part, and told him to learn it by heart or he would be beaten. Master Clifton went straight off to Sir John Fortescue, one of the Privy Council, and complained. Twenty-four hours later the boy was released, but the father swore vengeance. Evans had not heard the last of the matter.

Chapter XIV

ESSEX'S REBELLION

THE year 1601 started badly. The times were full of anxiety and rising temper, for as every thinking man realized, the affairs of the Earl of Essex were reaching a climax. Since his failure in Ireland, and his ignominious return home in September 1599, Essex had lived in disgrace. In October 1600 the patent which granted him the tax on sweet wines expired. It was Essex's only valuable source of income. When the Queen refused to renew the grant it was clear that she did not intend to restore him to favour. Essex grew desperate, and by Christmas it was obvious that he and his discontented friends were planning some *coup d'état*. Essex House was closely watched by the Council and the reports which reached the Court at Whitehall became more and more alarming.

Shakespeare's play *Richard the Second* had become curiously involved with Essex's fortunes. So early as 1597, when the play was first published, it had sold well because of the topical significance which some readers affected to see in it. In January 1599, just before Essex set out for Ireland, a young doctor of the law named John Hayward had foolishly published a prose history of the desposition of Richard the Second. It was called *The First Part of the Life and Reign of King Henry the Fourth, extending to the End of the First Year of his Reign*. He dedicated it to Essex in a curious and equivocal Latin epistle. At once it was suspected of being a work of deep and sinister import.[1]

In the following July Hayward was committed to the Tower, and all who had been implicated in the publication were closely examined; including the Chaplain of the Bishop of London, who had carelessly passed the book for the press without troubling himself to read it, and John Wolfe, the printer who had printed it. Again in January 1601, Hayward was closely questioned about the sources which he had used. The Queen herself was very suspicious.

On Friday the 6th February, a party of Essex's friends went over the river from Essex House to the Globe Theatre, and there spoke to some of the players. They asked them to play *Richard the Second* on the Saturday. The players were not enthusiastic. It was an old play, they said, long out of use, and they would have little or no audience. The gentlemen urged them, and promised to give them 40s. extra as well as their takings; the bribe was meagre, but the season was very poor. The players foolishly agreed, and *Richard the Second* was accordingly acted on the afternoon of Saturday, the 7th February, before an audience of Essex's friends.

The next day, Sunday, the 8th February, Essex was forced to make his mad and precipitate attempt to raise the City against the Queen. It was a complete and utter fiasco, and before midnight he and all his friends were prisoners.

The Council took a very serious view of the episode at the Globe. In the trial of the conspirators and of Essex himself, the matter of *Richard the Second* was stressed. Coke, the Attorney-General, made much of it in his speech for the prosecution against Sir Gilly Meyricke, Essex's

---

[1] For the story of this book see my *Life and Death of Robert Devereux, Earl of Essex*.

steward, and those who were arraigned with him. He spoke of ' the story of *Henry IV* being set forth in a play, and in that play there being set forth the killing of the King upon a stage ; the Friday before, Sir Gilly Meyricke and some others of the Earl's train having an humour to see a play, they must needs have the play of *Henry IV*. The players told them that was stale, they should get nothing by playing of that, but no play else would serve ; and Sir Gilly Meyricke gives forty shillings to Phillips the player to play this, besides whatsoever he could get.'

The incident was again stressed by Francis Bacon in his official account of the rebellion.

' The afternoon before the rebellion, Meyricke, with a great company of others, that afterwards were all in the action, had procured to be played before them the play of deposing King Richard the Second. Neither was it casual, but a play bespoken by Meyricke. And not so only, but when it was told him by one of the players that the play was old and they should have loss in playing it because few would come to it, there was forty shillings extraordinary given to play it ; and so thereupon played it was. So earnest he was to satisfy his eyes with the sight of that tragedy which he thought soon after his lord should bring from the stage to the state, but that God turned it upon their own heads.' [1]

There is no evidence that the Chamberlain's players were zealous partisans of the Earl of Essex or in any way wished to support his rebellion. Their patron was one of Essex's enemies and took a considerable part in hunting down the conspirators. But certainly they had acted very foolishly. Probably, the theatres were closed during the fortnight between the rebellion and Essex's execution. Hamlet, in his often quoted remarks to Rozencrantz and Guildenstern

[1] Both passages are reproduced in Sir Edmund Chambers's *William Shakespeare*, ii, 325–6.

when they announce the coming of the players, asks : ' How chance it they travel ? Their residence, both in reputation and profit, was better both ways.' To which Rozencrantz answers : ' I think their inhibition comes by means of the late innovation.' The remark was topical. It appeared only in the quarto of 1604. At this time the normal meaning of the word ' innovation ' was revolution, and there was no other event during these years which could be called an innovation. There is, however, no record of formal prohibition of playing ; but this is not surprising, because apart from such official documents as the Acts of the Privy Council or the City Records, the survival of any fact about plays or playhouses is entirely a matter of luck. If the playhouses were closed because of the Essex affair, it would only have been for an extra fortnight, for Lent began on the 25th February, and then playing would automatically cease.

The Chamberlain's players were not punished for their action, and on Shrove Tuesday, the 24th February, the night before Essex was beheaded, they played at Court : the name of the play chosen for that grim evening is not known. The next day was Ash Wednesday and the beginning of Lent, when the public playhouses were shut, and lest the private houses should be under any misapprehension, a letter was sent from the Privy Council to the Lord Mayor on the 11th March, requiring him :

'. . . not to fail to take order the plays within the City and the liberties, especially at Paul's and in the Blackfriars, may be suppressed during this time of Lent.' [1]

When they reopened, the playhouses were carefully watched. In the general uneasiness of the times plays could too easily be used for seditious propaganda. There was trouble at the Curtain almost at once. On the 11th May

[1] *Acts of the Privy Council*, xxxi, 218 ; reprinted in *Elizabethan Stage*, iv, 332.

ESSEX'S REBELLION

certain justices of the County of Middlesex received a letter from the Privy Council:

'... We do understand that certain players that use to recite their plays at the Curtain in Moorfields do represent upon the stage in their interludes the persons of some gentlemen of good desert and quality that are yet alive under obscure manner, but yet in such sort as all the hearers may take notice both of the matter and the persons that are meant thereby. This being a thing very unfit, offensive and contrary to such direction as have been heretofore taken that no plays should be openly showed but such as were first perused and allowed, and that might minister no occasion of offence or scandal, we do hereby require you that you do forthwith forbid those players to whomsoever they appertain that do play at the Curtain in Moorfields to represent any such play, and that you will examine them who made that play, and to show the same unto you. And as you in your discretions shall think the same unfit to be publicly showed, to forbid them from henceforth to play the same either privately or publicly, and if upon view of the said play you shall find the subject so odious and inconvenient as is informed, we require you to take bond of the chiefest of them to answer their rash and indiscreet dealing before us.'[1]

In the early spring Marston wrote another comedy for the Paul's Boys. It was called *What You Will*:[2]

[1] *Acts of the Privy Council*, xxxi, 346; reprinted in *Elizabethan Stage*, iv, 332.

[2] The time of the play's first production is apparently fixed by Jacomo's words:

'The wanton spring lies dallying with the earth
And pours fresh blood in her decayed limbs.'

With another dramatist these indications of season would not be important, but Marston seems to have added such touches to give verisimilitude to the first production. Compare the prologue to *Antonio's Revenge*, page 215, and page 231 note.

Once more there is an Induction.

'*Before the music sounds for the Act, enter Atticus, Doricus, and Philomuse; they sit a good while on the stage before the candles are lighted, talking together, and on a sudden Doricus speaks.*'

As the tireman enters with lights Doricus bursts out with indignation at the 'knights of the mew,' who kill plays with their cat-calls. Philomuse answers indignantly and in the Jonsonian strain, but Doricus pulls him up short, and they fall to talking of the play, which is *What You Will*,

'—a slight toy, lightly composed, too swiftly finished, ill plotted, worse written, I fear me worst acted, and indeed *What You Will*.'

They give way to the Prologue, who is as modest, and claims the play merely as 'a silly subject, too too simply clad.' After this, except for an occasional gibe, Marston forgets Jonson.

What You Will is a lively comedy, neatly written. It belongs to the Comedies of Humour, but the humours are not excessive, and the plot is amusing. Quadratus, the scholar, a plump epicurean, meets his friend Jacomo, who is utterly love-sick for Celia. The lady is the supposed widow of Albano, a wealthy merchant, whose death at sea has but recently been reported, and whose widow is already thronged with would-be successors to his bed and hoard. Quadratus has no use for forlorn lovers, for he is no illusioned idealist. Meanwhile Albano's brothers, Randolfo and Andrea, are vehemently opposed to Celia's new chosen bridegroom, Sir Laverdure, a Frenchman. They plot with Jacomo to stop the marriage. First they would petition the Duke, but he is a frivolous sybarite and merely uses their petition as a pipe-lighter. So they introduce Francisco, a perfumer, to pose as the dead Albano. It is an excellent first act, very neatly constructed.

In the second act, Laverdure is visited by Quadratus, Lampatho Doria, and Simplicius Faber. After a good deal of talk which was doubtless more amusing to contemporaries than it is now, Quadratus (who, in this company, is the counterpart of Shakespeare's Berowne) most eloquently defends fantasticality against the railing of the conventional.

> A man can scarce put on a tuck'd-up cap,
> A button'd frizado suit, scarce eat good meat,
> Anchovies, caviare, but he's satired
> And term'd fantastical by the muddy spawn
> Of slimy newts, when, troth, fantasticness—
> That which the natural sophisters term
> *Phantasia incomplexa*—is a function
> Even of the bright immortal part of man,
> It is the common pass, the sacred door,
> Unto the privy chamber of the soul;
> That barr'd, nought passeth past the baser court
> Of outward sense; by it th' inamorate
> Most lively thinks he sees the absent beauties
> Of his loved mistress;
> By it we shape a new creation
> Of things as yet unborn; by it we feed
> Our ravenous memory, our intention feast;
> 'Slid he that's not fantastical's a beast.

All three men then go on to visit a school where the little boys are at their Latin lesson. Simplicius carries off one of them to be his page. Then follows a remarkable dialogue between Lampatho Doria and Quadratus. Lampatho Doria is suffering from the scholar's melancholy. After seven useful springs, deflowered in making notes of 'crossed opinons 'bout the soul of man' he is left with his intellectual doubts worse than before, knowing nothing except that he knows nothing. Quadratus listens to him with amusement, and gives him the cynical advice to turn a temporist and row with the tide. The whole act is digression, but this outburst is remarkable and reveals the real sensitiveness of Marston's nature.

In the third act Francisco, the fake Albano, dresses up, with the assistance of Jacomo, Andrea and Randolfo. The opening stage direction of this act is worth noting :

'*Enter Francisco, half-dressed, in his black doublet and round cap, the rest rich ; Jacomo bearing his hat and feather ; Andrea his doublet and band ; Randolfo his cloak and staff. They clothe Francisco whilst Bidet creeps in and observes them. Most of this done whilst the act is playing.*' [1]

Bidet, who is Laverdure's page, perceives what is happening and slips away to tell his master. Albano, when excited, was apt to stutter, and this characteristic Francisco now imitates. In the next scene the real Albano turns up, learns what is going on in his house and is disgusted at this revelation of the rottenness of love which can die so soon. It is another remarkable outburst, far too serious for its context. Albano watches Laverdure and his friends as they pass on their way, and hears Bidet tell his master of the trick. Albano himself steps forward and threatens the Frenchman, who is amused at what he supposes to be brilliant imitation.

'Hark you, perfumer,' says he, 'tell Jacomo, Randolfo and Andrea 'twill not do.'

He passes on, leaving the merchant furious. Even his two brothers take him for a clever impostor, to his wild indignation.

Up to this point Marston had kept his women characters out of the plot. He now introduces Celia, her sister, and her friends, discussing their menfolk. Laverdure comes in with Quadratus, Lampatho Doria, and Simplicius. Lampatho Doria is attracted by Meletza, Celia's sister, and she by him ; but he is a clumsy wooer and she soon sheers off.

---

[1] i.e. during the orchestral overture. See page 211.

Then both true and false Albanos clamour for entry, and abuse each other, stuttering with rage.

The final scene Marston set in bright light. '*Enter as many pages with torches as you can ; the Duke with attendants.*' The Duke is now ready to begin his day. He calls for his evening's entertainment. Lampatho would offer him a comedy entitled *Temperance*, but Quadratus promises him better sport, more fitting to a prince of intellect. He waxes eloquent on his own theme, but the true and false Albanos break in. The real Albano draws Celia aside, quickly convinces her of his identity and all ends in riotous merriment.

It is an amusing play with some excellent moments of first-class comedy, which deserves to be better known.

Meanwhile the Admiral's Men, at the new Fortune playhouse, had been slack. In September 1600 they had paid Dekker for a new play called *Fortune's Tennis*, but no more new plays were bought until January 1601, when Haughton was paid for *Robin Hoods Pen'orths*. Between January and April five other plays were commissioned : *Hannibal and Scipio*, *Scogan and Skelton*, *The Conquest of Spain by John of Gaunt*, *All is not Gold that Glisters*, *The Conquest of the West Indies*.

In May Chettle and Dekker were paid in full for *King Sebastian of Portingal*, which dealt with a very recent sensation. Sebastian, King of Portugal, was slain in the battle of Alcazar in 1578. Amongst others who fell in the engagement was a famous English soldier of fortune, Captain Thomas Stukeley, whose exploits had given much matter for ballad-makers. At least two plays had dramatized the event : *The Battle of Alcazar*, and *The Famous History of the Life and Death of Captain Tom Stukeley*. Interest in the matter was suddenly revived early in 1599 when news reached England that Sebastian had not in fact been killed, but had escaped from the battle, and after many adventures, had reached Venice, where many people believed him to be genuine. The interest in his case continued for several years.[1]

On the 30th March 1601 a book was entered in the Stationer's Register which set out his story. It was called *The Strangest Adventure that ever happened either in Ages Past or Present*. The Admiral's Men were therefore quick off the mark to take advantage of the new sensation.

The season improved somewhat, and in the next five months five plays were commissioned. They were : *The Six Yeomen of the West, Cardinal Wolsey (Life and Rising, Parts I and II), The Honourable Life of the Humorous Earl of Gloucester with his Conquest of Portugal, Friar Rush and the Proud Woman of Antwerp, Tom Dough, Part II*. None of them has survived.

Little is known of the output of the Chamberlain's Men during these years. Portions of *Hamlet* were certainly written during 1601, and *Twelfth Night* also reflects some contemporary events.[2]

On the whole for the professional companies this year was the worst since the plague years of '92, '93 and '94. Apart from the political troubles at home and the ever-increasing charges and losses of the wars abroad in the Low Countries, in Ireland and at sea, the boys were drawing away the best part of the audiences from the public playhouses. It was small consolation for the Chamberlain's Men that at the end of August Kemp should have returned from his Morris dance over the Alps, having failed to repeat the success of 1600. His return was noted by a certain Richard Smith of Abingdon in his little Latin Diary under the date 2nd September 1601 : '*Kemp, mimus quidam, qui peregrinationem quandam in Germaniam et Italiam instituerat,*

---

[1] See III *Elizabethan Journal*, pp. 4, 10, 125, 175.
[2] See *Shakespeare at Work*, pp. 260, 283.

post multos errores et infortunia sua, reversus, multa refert de Antonio Sherley equite aurato quem Romae, Legatum Persicum agentem, convenerat.' [1]

To add to their troubles, in the early autumn the quarrel between Ben Jonson and Marston came to a head when Jonson wrote *Poetaster* for the Children of Blackfriars. It was the first of two pitched battles, which brought the Stage War to an end.

[1] *MSS. Sloan*, 414, f. 56.

Chapter XV

THE STAGE WAR

The Stage War was an important event which caused much dust and heat in the world of the playhouses in 1600 and 1601. In more recent times scholars have resumed the controversy. Since, however, the main facts have sometimes been misunderstood, it is as well to consider the Stage War by itself, and apart from the general history of the theatre.[1]

Certain *caveats* usually disregarded are necessary. Our knowledge of the past, and especially of intimate social events and personalities, more often than not is utterly distorted. Events survive only when recorded, and the written records of any age present but a tiny fragment of what is said, thought and done. Most men have no memorial.

Writers, from the literary genius to the casual letter writer, have their peculiar reward in that they, and they only, confer perpetuity. Unless a man's life and person-

[1] The best discussions of the Stage War are by J. H. Penniman, *The War of the Theatres*; and R. A. Small, *The Stage Quarrel between Ben Jonson and the so-called Poetasters*. *Poetaster* and *Satiromastix* were afterwards edited by Professor Penniman in one volume for the Belles Lettres Series: his introduction to this volume is particularly valuable. I disagree on many points with both these studies, and have therefore thought it best to interpret the facts as I see them without pausing every few paragraphs to wrangle, like some Hyde Park orator, with those whose views are different.

ality happen to be preserved in writing, they are utterly lost, and he survives at most as a name in a list. In a controversy which occurred at a time whence personal letters or diaries are rare, a host of little details will have disappeared irrecoverably ; all that was once conveyed by a gesture, a tone or a make-up is utterly lost. The modern scholar can therefore only hope to understand a small fragment of the controversy.

Naturally, but wrongly, scholars often make the mistake of assuming that many of the personalities of the Stage War are still identifiable; and they endeavour to label individuals and interpret references from such scanty facts as survive.

Occasionally the evidence exists for complete and satisfactory identification. Professor C. J. Sisson discovered in the Public Record Office the records of lawsuits concerning two plays which actually dramatized contemporary scandals—*The Old Joiner of Aldgate*, written by Chapman, and *Keep the Widow Waking*, written years later by Dekker. As it happens, neither play has survived, though the nature of the play and the details are clear enough. *The Old Joiner of Aldgate* was played by the Paul's Boys, in 1603.[1] If, as is probable, *The Old Joiner of Aldgate* is a typical comedy performed by the Boys, it follows that many of these plays of the scandals of the social life were directly founded on incidents which the original audiences would have quickly recognized. Without knowledge of the full facts—and these only will exist in those rare cases where the injured parties went to law—nothing can now be rediscovered.

There was, indeed, a very large undercurrent of scurrility in the plays of the 1590's and 1600's. The comedies, especially those written for the Boys, were as full of personalities as Pope's *Dunciad* ; unfortunately no one at the time supplied a detailed commentary.

[1] See later, page 292.

The history of the Stage War is, in the main, simpler than has always been realized. Except for *Poetaster* and *Satiromastix*, there was very little personal attack on each other in the plays written either by Marston or by Jonson during these years ; and a reader who was not aware of the controversy might quite easily overlook even those passages which were intended to be personal. At first it was simply a matter of gags and sly hits—no more. Neither Marston nor Jonson created characters as a whole to satirize the other.

This fact has not always been realized. Sir Edmund Chambers, for instance, accepting too readily the conclusions of earlier scholars,[1] states that ' Marston's representation of Jonson as Chrysoganus was complimentary, that as Brabant senior in *Jack Drum's Entertainment*, offensive ; and it was doubtless the latter that stirred Jonson to retaliate on Marston, perhaps as Hedon in *Cynthia's Revels*, certainly as Crispinus in the *Poetaster*. Marston's final blow was with Lampatho Doria in *What You Will*.'

From this one would assume that Brabant senior and Lampatho Doria have some recognizable likeness to Ben Jonson, as contemporaries knew him in 1600. In fact they have none. Brabant senior is a gentleman and a man of means ; and Jonson was not. He has a conspicuous young brother ; and Jonson had not. His only possible resemblance is a contempt for living poets, and this quality he shared with many other conceited young gentlemen of all generations. It would be as sensible to identify young Ovid in *Poetaster* with Marston, because he was a poet and his father a lawyer. Similarly Lampatho Doria was a scholar who had spent seven years at the University ; and Jonson had not. He suffered from genuine intellectual doubts, and Jonson did not. Lampatho had a sensitive mind, which Jonson had not. And, finally, Lampatho is

[1] See *Elizabethan Stage*, iii, 428.

most sympathetically presented, and the character is in no sense an attack on anyone. There is thus no resemblance whatever between Lampatho Doria and Ben Jonson; but both Brabant and Lampatho Doria do make remarks about Ben Jonson and his unpleasant hectoring ways, as in a contemporary comedy of manners they could with complete propriety.

A chronological table will help to make clear the progress of the affair:

1597   28th July. Jonson agrees to play at the Rose and draws £4 from Henslowe. He is imprisoned in the Marshalsea for his share in the *Isle of Dogs*.

3rd October. Jonson, Spencer and Shaw released from the Marshalsea.

3rd December. Jonson proposes a plot to the Admiral's Men.

1598   27th May. Marston's *Pygmalion's Image and Certain Satires* entered.

Spring and Summer. Jonson writing *Every Man in his Humour*.

8th September. Marston's *Scourge of Villainy* entered.

c. 15th September. Jonson's *Every Man in his Humour* staged at The Curtain.

22nd September. Jonson kills Gabriel Spencer and is imprisoned.

c. October. Jonson released from jail.

28th December. The Theatre demolished.

1599   *c.* April. Shakespeare's *Henry the Fifth* staged at The Curtain.

Spring and Summer. Jonson writing *Every Man out of his Humour*.

c. July. The Globe Theatre occupied by the Chamberlain's Men.

As You Like It staged.

Every Man out of his Humour staged at the Globe and a failure; coolness between Jonson and the Chamberlain's Men.

ELIZABETHAN PLAYS AND PLAYERS

1599   10th August. Jonson goes back to the Rose and draws money from Henslowe.

3rd–27th September. Jonson draws money from Henslowe.

November. The Paul's Boys again begin to present plays. Marston's *Histriomastix Antonio and Mellida*, *Antonio's Revenge* acted by the Paul's Boys.

1600   8th. April. Jonson's *Every Man out of his Humour* entered for publication. Three editions published during the year.

c. June. Marston's *Jack Drum's Entertainment* played by the Paul's Boys.

4th August. Jonson's *Every Man in his Humour* stayed from printing by the Chamberlain's Men.

14th August. Jonson's *Every Man in his Humour* entered to Burby and Burr.

September. The Children of the Chapel begin to act plays in the Blackfriars.

c. December. Jonson's *Cynthia's Revels* acted by the Children of the Chapel at Blackfriars.

1601   Early Spring. Marston's *What you Will* played by the Paul's Boys.

23rd May. Jonson's *Cynthia's Revels* entered.

c. end of May. Jonson begins to write *Poetaster*.

c. 10th September. Jonson's *Poetaster* first played by the Children of the Chapel at Blackfriars.

25th September. Jonson leaves the Blackfriars and goes back to Henslowe.

c. 15th October. Dekker's *Satiromastix* played by the Chamberlain's Men and the Paul's Boys.

11th November. *Satiromastix* entered.

21st December. *Poetaster* entered.

1602   22nd June. Jonson draws money from Henslowe in earnest of *Crookback*.

1603   12th February. Jonson living in retirement and scorning the world.

The Stage War began with *Every Man out of his Humour* and probably with the *printed* version. As a result of the success of *Every Man in his Humour*, Jonson became insufferably conceited. He always had held strong notions about dramatic propriety and his own cleverness; and he suffered in these earlier years from an acute sense of social inferiority. His insistence on his own superior education and ability was thus a kind of compensation for his sensitiveness in other directions.

Marston first annoyed Ben Jonson by misusing the word 'humour.' Jonson had come almost to regard himself as having some kind of monopoly in the word; its misuse made him livid. In *Every Man out of his Humour* he set out his notion of the humours at great length and severely snubbed those who took it lightly. Genuine humour, on the other hand, he was ready to approve, and even to praise. In 1600 Nicholas Breton published a volume of verse called *Melancholic Humours*. Jonson honoured the volume with a prefatory sonnet *In Authorem* to certify that this was the real thing.

> Thou, that wouldst find the habit of true passion,
>   And see a mind attir'd in perfect strains;
> Not wearing moods, as gallants do a fashion,
>   In these pied times, only to show their brains,
>
> Look here on Breton's work, the master print:
>   Where such perfections to the life do rise.
> If they seem wry, to such as look asquint,
>   The fault's not in the object, but their eyes.
>
> For, as one coming with a lateral view,
>   Unto a cunning piece wrought perspective,
> Wants faculty to make a censure true:
>   So with this Author's Readers will it thrive:
>
> Which being eyed directly, I divine,
> His proof their praise, will meet, as in this line.

The failure of *Every Man out of his Humour* embittered Jonson; he was angry with the Chamberlain's Men and their audiences. He relieved some of his spleen when he published the play eight months or so later; for *Every Man out of his Humour* as acted and as printed, differed in several particulars, as Jonson himself admitted on the title page of the first quarto: 'The comical satire of *Every Man out of his Humour* as it was first composed by the Author, B. J. *Containing more than hath been publicly spoken or acted.*'

It is not possible to say what was omitted from stage performances or what was added afterwards, though certain gibes seem obvious additions. Sogliardo's motto, which he chooses to go with his coat-of-arms—' Not without Mustard '—is as clear a hit as may be at the motto chosen by the Shakespeares for their new coat-of-arms—' *Non sans droit* '—Not without Right; the issue of a coat-of-arms to a player had excited much bitter comment. Jonson again mocked the coat-of-arms in *Poetaster*. The Chamberlain's Men would hardly have tolerated so nasty a hit in one of their own plays. There is also a remark about Kemp's old shoes, presumably a reference to the dance to Norwich, which, in April 1600—when the play was sent to the press—was the latest gossip.

In the same way, Jonson made his first direct hit at Marston individually through Messrs. Clove and Orange, who were dragged into *Every Man out of his Humour* solely that they might talk fustian and gull the others into believing that they are great scholars, when Clove proceeds to babble in a vocabulary chosen deliberately from Marston's *Scourge*:

'Now, sir, whereas the ingenuity of the time and the soul's synderisis are but embrions in nature, added to the paunch of Esquiline, and the intervallum of the zodiac, besides the ecliptic line being optic, and not mental, but by the contemplative and theoric part thereof, doth demonstrate to us the vegetable circumference and the ventosity of the tropics, and whereas our intellectual or mincing capreal (according to the metaphysics) as you may read in Plato's *Histriomastix*—You conceive me, sir ? ' [1]

These two worthies are an interpolation. They take no active part in the plot and could be omitted unnoticed. This, with one so careful of his plots as Ben Jonson, is some evidence of later addition.[2]

The Chamberlain's Men were not likely to have sanctioned the publishing of *Every Man out of his Humour* in this form, nor was the manuscript sent to the printer their own copy. It was most carefully prepared for the press by the author. Jonson had thus apparently committed a breach of recognized etiquette, if not of literary honesty, by selling to a printer a play which he had previously sold to the players.

Four months later the Chamberlain's Men sought to prevent the publication of *Every Man in his Humour*. There is a well-known note in the Stationers' Register that *As You Like It, Henry the Fifth, Every Man in his Humour,* and *Much Ado about Nothing* were to be stayed from printing. *As You Like It* was successfully stayed ; *Henry the Fifth* was pirated in a vile bad text ; *Much Ado* was regularly sold to Andrew Wise who had already printed *Richard the Second, Richard the Third,* and both parts of *Henry the Fourth.* But *Every Man in his Humour* was entered by Cuthbert Burby and William Burr on the 14th August. If the question of the literary ownership of the play then arose, as it well might, it would appear that the Stationers' Company decided that the printer could possess separate

[1] Act III, sc. I.
[2] For another instance of such interpolation, see p 262, Demetrius.

ownership. This, however, is a bibliographical problem not immediately concerned with the Stage War.

With *Every Man out of his Humour* Jonson thus directly attacked Marston. The attacks were still without personal malice, but enough to provoke an answer. Marston retorted, albeit very mildly, in *Jack Drum*, wherein Brabant senior has a contempt for poets :

BRABANT JUNIOR. Brother, how like you of our modern wits ? How like you the new Poet Mellidus ?
BRABANT SENIOR. A slight bubbling spirit, a cork, a husk.
PLANET. How like you Musus' fashion in his carriage ?
BRABANT SENIOR. O filthily, he is as blunt as Paul's.
BRABANT JUNIOR. What think you of the lines of Decius ? Writes he not a good cordial sappy style ?
BRABANT SENIOR. A surrein'd jaded wit, but a' rubs on.
PLANET. Brabant, thou art like a pair of balance,
Thou weighest all saving thyself.
BRABANT SENIOR. Good faith, troth is, they are all apes and gulls, Vile imitating spirits, dry heathy turfs.
BRABANT JUNIOR. Nay, brother, now I think your judgment errs.
PLANET. Err, he cannot err, man, for children and fools speak truth always.[1]

Brabant's conceit annoys Planet, who confides in his younger brother, Brabant junior :

> Dear Brabant, I do hate these bombast wits,
> That are puffed up with arrogant conceit
> Of their own worth ; as if Omnipotence
> Had hoised them to such unequal'd height,
> That they survey'd our spirits with an eye
> Only create to censure from above ;
> When good souls they do nothing but reprove.[2]

The answer was very modest, but it annoyed Jonson.

[1] Act IV, l. 37. [2] *Ibid.*, 316.

The next round came with *Cynthia's Revels*. Here Jonson began to attack Marston more fiercely and bitterly. It was a personal assault. Hedon and Anaides, having been circumvented by Criticus, observe him walking ' *in a musing posture at the back of the stage.*' They comment peevishly :

HEDON. 'Sprecious, this afflicts me more than all the rest, that we should so particularly direct our hate and contempt against him and he to carry it thus without wound or passion ! 'Tis insufferable.

ANAIDES. 'Slid, my dear Envy, if thou but say'st the word now, I'll undo him eternally for thee.

HEDON. How, sweet Anaides ?

ANAIDES. Marry, half a score of us get him in, one night, and make him pawn his wit for a supper.

HEDON. Away, thou hast such unseasonable jests ! By this heaven, I wonder at nothing more than our gentlemen ushers, that will suffer a piece of serge or perpetuana [1] to come into the presence : methinks they should, out of their experience, better distinguish the silken disposition of courtiers, than to let such terrible coarse rags mix with us, able to fret any smooth or gentle society to the threads with their rubbing devices.[2]

Anaides a few lines later declares :

... 'Slud, I'll give out all he does is dictated from other men, and swear it too, if thou'lt have me, and that I know the time and place where he stole it, though my soul be guilty of no such thing ; and that I think, out of my heart, he hates such barren shifts : yet to do thee a pleasure, and him a disgrace, I'll damn myself, or do anything.

HEDON. Gramercy, my dear devil ; we'll put it seriously in practice, i'faith.

When these two worthies have gone out, Criticus comes forward and soliloquizes contemptuously :

[1] A kind of serge of which Jonson's only suit was made.
[2] Act II, sc. II.

> ... If good Chrestus,
> Euthus, or Phronimus, had spoke the words,
> They would have moved me, and I should have called
> My thoughts and actions to a strict account
> Upon the hearing: but when I remember,
> 'Tis Hedon and Anaides, alas, then
> I think but what they are, and am not stirred.
> The one a light voluptuous reveller,
> The other, a strange arrogating puff,
> Both impudent, and ignorant enough;
> That talk as they are wont, not as I merit:
> Traduce by custom, as most dogs do bark,
> Do nothing out of judgment, but disease,
> Speak ill, because they never could speak well.
> And who'd be angry with this race of creatures?

Later, in *Satiromastix*, Dekker identified these two with Crispinus and Demetrius, that is, with Marston and himself.

> Nay, I ha' more news [remarks Asinius Bubo]: there's Crispinus and his journeyman poet, Demetrius Fannius, too, they swear they'll bring your life and death upon th' stage like a bricklayer in a play.
>
> HORACE. Bubo, they must press more valiant wits than their own to do it: me a'th' stage? Ha! ha! I'll starve their poor copper-lace workmasters that dare play me. I can bring (and that they quake at) a prepared troop of gallants, who, for my sake, shall distaste every unsalted line in their fly-blown comedies.
>
> ASINIUS. Nay, that's certain; I'll bring a hundred gallants of my rank.
>
> HORACE. That same Crispinus is the silliest dor, and Fannius the slightest cob-web lawn piece of a poet. Oh God!
> Why should I care what every dor doth buzz
> In credulous ears? It is a crown to me,
> That the best judgments can report me wrong'd.
>
> ASINIUS. I am one of them that can report it.

HORACE. I think but what they are, and am not moved:
The one a light voluptuous reveller,
The other a strange arrogating puff,
Both impudent, and arrogant enough.[1]

There was now open war and lofty principles were forgotten. At the time there was an immense volume of excited chatter, gossip, tale-bearing, back-biting, slander, long since silenced: only the plays now remain. Both sides had their champions, and the managers of the Boys' companies profited by the controversy, so that the combatants, and their mouthpieces, the children, were well encouraged.

Marston naturally retaliated. In *What You Will* for the first time he retorted fiercely. He prefaced the play with a full-dress Induction. Hitherto his slight censures of Jonson could be interpreted almost as compliment. Criticism from such as Brabant senior need irritate no one. In this Induction Marston boldly stated his own point of view.

Atticus, Doricus and Philomuse begin by discussing the troubles of authors. Then Philomuse breaks out into abuse in Jonson's manner.

> ... Believe it, Doricus his spirit
> Is higher blooded than to quake and pant
> At the report of Scoff's artillery.
> Shall he be crest-fall'n, if some looser brain,
> In flux of wit uncivilly befilth
> His slight composures? Shall his bosom faint,
> If drunken Censure belch out sour breath
> From Hatred's surfeit on his labour's front?
> Nay, say some half a dozen rancorous breasts
> Should plant themselves on purpose to discharge
> Imposthum'd malice on his latest scene,

[1] Act I, sc. II.

Shall his resolve be struck through with the blirt
Of a goose-breath ? What imperfect-born,
What short-liv'd meteor, what cold-hearted snow
Would melt in dolour, cloud his mudded eyes,
Sink down his jaws, if that some juiceless husk,
Some boundless ignorance, should on sudden shoot
His gross-knobb'd burbolt with—' That's not so good
Mew, blirt, ha, ha, light chaffy stuff ! '
Why, gentle spirits, what loose-waving vane,
What anything, would thus be screw'd about
With each slight touch of odd phantasmatas ?
No, let the feeble palsey'd lamer joints
Lean on opinion's crutches ; let the——

But Doricus interrupts indignantly :

                      Nay, nay, nay.
Heaven's my hope, I cannot smooth this strain ;
Wit's death, I cannot. What a leprous humour
Breaks from rank swelling of these bubbling wits ?
Now out upon't, I wonder what tight brain,
Wrung in this custom to maintain contempt
'Gainst common censure ; to give stiff counter-buffs,
To crack rude scorn even on the very face
Of better audience. Slight, is't not odious ?
Why, hark you, honest, honest Philomuse
(You that endeavour to endear our thoughts
To the composer's spirit), hold this firm :
Music and poetry were first approved
By common sense ; and that which pleased most,
Held most allowed pass : know, rules of art
Were shaped to pleasure, not pleasure to your rules ;
Think you, if that his scenes took stamp in mint
Of three or four deem'd most judicious,
It must enforce the world to current them,
That you must spit defiance on dislike ?
Now, as I love the light were I to pass
Through public verdict, I should fear my form,
Lest ought I offer'd were unsquared or warp'd.

> The more we know, the more we want:
> What Bayard bolder than the ignorant?
> Believe me, Philomuse, i'faith thou must,
> The best, best seal of wit is wit's distrust.

It is the common-sense answer to the spluttering theorist.

Jonson was furious. He now determined to settle this controversy once and for all by making his enemy look so ridiculous that he would be shamed into silence. Plays on worthies of Greek and Roman history had always been reasonably popular, and the classics, especially those dealing with history and politics, were much studied at this time. In the last two years the Chamberlain's Men had produced *Julius Cæsar*, and *Troilus and Cressida*. Henslowe records another version of *Troilus and Cressida*, *Orestes*, *Agamemnon*, *Jugurtha* and *Hannibal and Scipio*.

Ben Jonson, as something of a scholar, was naturally led back to his originals, and he conceived the notion of a play on a Roman theme which should be based, not on English versions of French translations of classical authors, but a play directly translated from the classics themselves. Let a comedy of humours be set in Roman times, and then Horace, Virgil, Ovid and the rest would provide him with some of his incidents and much of his dialogue. The most famous Roman poets were all part of the group round the Emperor Augustus. Added to this, Jonson felt an affinity with Horace; and indeed there are genuine Horatian qualities about Jonson's lyric verse at its best, though when he tried to make his Romans talk they have that stiff pomposity which is usually considered the natural pose of such memorable persons.

So Jonson began work on *Poetaster*, and in fifteen weeks it was ready for the performance by the Children of the Chapel Royal, who produced it at the Blackfriars playhouse, probably in the early autumn of 1601.

There was no pretence of concealing individuals. Horace was Jonson himself, Crispinus was Marston. Nevertheless it is possible that the play was not originally conceived as so bitter a personal attack. Up to the end of the second act there is little hint of anything directly against Marston. Crispinus appears as one of several characters at Chloe's party, but he is not specially picked out, at first, and is rather a nonentity. He suddenly takes on personality in Act III. Jonson was not the man to keep silence about his great revenge. He boasted openly about it, and probably read tit-bits to his tavern cronies. There was a goodly company of tale-bearers to drop hints to his enemies, who soon learned of the grand indictment.

The Chamberlain's Men were now feeling the pinch. Keen competition between the two Boys' companies was doing them great harm, and they had no kindly feelings for Jonson. They had made him when they acted *Every Man in his Humour*, and now he abused them vilely in all companies. The new Fortune also was almost empty. Dekker, who had written so industriously for Henslowe, was out of employment. He agreed to answer Jonson. Jonson heard of this alliance as he was finishing the great work. So he hastily invented Demetrius Fannius (*alias* Dekker) to be a fellow-sufferer with Crispinus-Marston.

In writing his play Jonson dropped the Induction, and instead brought up Envy, rising from beneath to hiss venom at the author. Then, as the monster sinks, the Prologue enters. He hopes that the audience will not accuse the author of arrogance : that would be even worse than base dejection.

> There's a mean 'twixt both,
> Which with a constant firmness he pursues,
> As one that knows the strength of his own muse.

And this he hopes all free souls will allow,
Others, that take it with a rugged brow,
Their moods he rather pities than envies:
His mind it is above their injuries.

The Prologue having withdrawn, Ovid junior is revealed writing verses—a passage from the *Elegies*, for which Jonson provided a translation, not much above Sixth Form standard, in rhymed couplets. He is so employed when Ovid senior bursts in, accompanied by Lupus, the magistrate, and Captain Tucca, who is a mixture of Bobadil, Falstaff and Simon Eyre, a very frankly spoken gentleman who comments without reserve. When Lupus waxes indignant at the wickedness of players who ' rob us magistrates of our respect, bring us upon their stages, and make us ridiculous to the plebians,' Tucca replies:

' Th'art in the right, my venerable crop-shin, they will indeed: the tongue of the oracle never twanged truer. Your courtier cannot kiss his mistress's slippers in quiet for them: nor your white innocent gallant pawn his revelling suit, to make his punk a supper. An honest decayed commander cannot skelder, cheat nor be seen in a bawdy house, but he shall be straight in one of their wormwood comedies. They are grown licentious, the rogues; libertines, flat libertines. They forget they are i' the statute, the rascals, they are blazoned there, there they are tricked, they and their pedigrees; they need no other heralds, I wis.' This was another hit at Shakespeare's coat-of-arms.

' Methinks,' Ovid senior continues, ' if nothing else yet this alone, the very reading of the public edicts [1] should fright thee from commerce with them; and give thee distaste enough of their actions. But this betrays what a student you are: this argues your proficiency in the law.'

[1] i.e. the Statute against Vagabonds renewed in the Parliament of 1597-8.

Ovid junior replies:

> They wrong me, sir, and do abuse you more,
> That blow your ears with these untrue reports.
> I am not known unto the open stage,
> Nor do I traffic in their theatres.
> Indeed, I do acknowledge, at request
> Of some near friends and honourable Romans,
> I have begun a poem of that nature.

This is an illuminating passage, for it explains why the gentlemen authors did not, if they could avoid it, write for the public theatres, and why the private playhouses became popular.

In the second act, Jonson returns to the kind of society which had occupied his attention for the last two years: wealthy citizens and their ambitious wives, silly gallants, young ladies itching for experience, rich churls screwing their way into gentility. Chloe, the wife of Albinus, the merchant, despises her doting husband, for she yearns after more genteel company. They give a party to the wits and fashion of Rome. Their guests arrive: Gallus, Ovid, Tibullus, Propertius, Julia, the Emperor's daughter and Ovid's mistress, and the rest. The scene is an admirable picture of the Elizabethan equivalent of that dreariest form of amusement, a literary cocktail party.

In the third act Jonson gets down to the real business of the play. He introduces Horace, who is avowedly himself. It is a dramatization of the Ninth Satire, of the First Book, in which the real Horace told how he was taking his morning walk along the Sacred Way, when a bore accosted him and almost drove him silly with his chatter. So Jonson-Horace enters meditating an ode to Mæcenas. Crispinus, *alias* Marston, pursues him. He has long wished to become acquainted with the great man. Crispinus chatters in his frothy way about ladies, and gentlemen, and fashions, and his own poetry. Horace becomes more and more agitated ; even Crispinus' flattering enthusiasm annoys him, though it gave Jonson a chance to work in a compliment to himself :

' Troth, Horace,' exclaims Crispinus, ' thou art exceeding happy in thy friends and acquaintance ; they are all most choice spirits, and of the first rank of Romans. I do not know that poet, I protest, has used his fortune more prosperously than thou hast. If thou would'st bring me known to Mæcenas, I should second thy desert well ; thou should'st find a good sure assistant of me ; one that would speak all good of thee in thy absence, and be content with the next place, not envying thy reputation with thy patron.'

Horace is at last saved (as the original Horace was saved in the Satire) by the arrival of a friend and the arrest of Crispinus at the suit of Master Minos for a debt. Horace hastily slips out whilst Crispinus is arguing with his captors. Captain Tucca passes by and goes bail for him. Then an actor enters. Tucca asks who it may be stalking by. When he learns that it is one of the players he commands him to come forward. He will patronize these poor vermin and allow them to make him a supper :

' There are some of you players honest gentleman-like scoundrels and suspected to ha' some wit, as well as your poets ; both at drinking, and breaking of jests : and are companions for gallants. A man may skelder ye, now and then, of half a dozen shillings, or so. Dost thou not know that Caprichio there ? ' He waves a hand at Crispinus lurking modestly in the background.

' No, I assure you, Captain,' answers the player.

' Go and be acquainted with him then,' Tucca cries ; ' he is a gentleman, parcel-poet, you slave : his father was a man of worship, I tell thee. Go, he pens high, lofty, in a new stalking strain ; bigger than half the rhymers in the town, again; he was born to fill thy mouth, Minotaurus, he was: he will teach thee to tear and rand; rascal, to him, cherish his muse, go; thou hast forty, forty shillings I mean, stinkard, give him in earnest, do, he shall write for thee, slave. If he pen for thee once, thou shalt not need to travel, with thy pumps full of gravel, any more, after a blind jade and a hamper: and stalk upon boards and barrel heads, to an old cracked trumpet——'

After further talk Tucca makes his pages show off their skill in acting in parodies of current plays. Then he falls to talking of individual players, and mentions a few who must not be brought to the supper:

... and do not bring your eating player with you there; I cannot away with him. He will eat a leg of mutton while I am in my porridge, the lean Poluphagus, his belly is like Barathrum, he looks like a midwife in man's apparel, the slave. Nor the villainous out-of-tune fiddler Ænobarbus, bring not him. What hast thou there? six and thirty? ha?

HISTRIO. No, here's all I have, Captain, some five and twenty. Pray, sir, will you present, and accommodate it unto the gentleman, for mine own part, I am a mere stranger to his humour; besides, I have some business invites me hence, with Master Asinius Lupus, the tribune.

TUCCA. Well, go thy ways; pursue thy projects, let me alone with this design; my Poetaster shall make thee a play, and thou shalt be a man of good parts in it. But stay, let me see; do not bring your Æsop, your politican, unless you can ram up his mouth with cloves; the slave smells ranker than some sixteen dunghills, and is seventeen times more rotten. Marry, you may bring Frisker, my zany: he's a good skipping swaggerer; and your fat fool there, my Mango, bring him too: but let him not beg rapiers, nor scarves, in his over familiar playing face, nor roar out his barren bold jests, with a tormenting laughter, between drunk and dry. Do you hear, stiff-toe? Give him warning, admonition, to forsake his saucy glavering grace and his goggle eye; it does not become him, sirrah: tell him so. I have stood up and defended you, ay, to gentlemen, when you have been said to prey upon puisnes and honest citizens, for socks or buskins : or when they have called you usurers, or brokers, or said you were able to help to a piece of flesh—I have sworn, I did not think so. Nor that you were the common retreats for punks decayed in their practice. I cannot believe it of you.

Then Tucca notices someone in the background ' with the half-arms there that salutes us out of his cloak like a motion.'

Oh, sir [says the player], his doublet is a little decayed. He is otherwise a very simple honest fellow, sir, one Demetrius [i.e. Dekker], a dresser of plays about the town here ; we have hired him to abuse Horace, and bring him in, in a play, with all his gallants ; as, Tibullus, Mæcenas, Cornelius Gallus, and the rest.

TUCCA. And why so, stinkard ?

HISTRIO. Oh, it will get us a huge deal of money, Captain ; and we have need of it ; for this winter has made us all poorer than so many starved snakes. Nobody comes at us, not a gentleman nor a ———.[1]

In the fourth act Jonson returns to his humorists. Chloe's party assemble ready to go to Julia's scandalous banquet. Crispinus and Demetrius and Tucca naturally belong to them. Not much is said of the poetasters, though Demetrius makes a remark which was a true comment by Jonson on himself.

' Alas, sir, Horace ! He is a mere sponge ; nothing but humours and observation ; he goes up and down sucking from every society, and when he comes home, squeezes himself dry again. I know him, ay.'

When they have gone out the player comes to Lupus and informs him what has happened. Julia's banquet is a

[1] In the version subsequently printed in a folio of Jonson's works, after this scene he here added a new scene, a stiff dialogue of 140 lines which was a free translation of Horace's First Satire of the Second Book.

scandalous affair. Those present pretend to be gods and goddesses and the talk runs faster and faster. Suddenly the Emperor Augustus himself appears, with Mæcenas, Horace, Lupus and the rest. The Emperor vents his high indignation on Ovid and his daughter. The baffled rioters repent and slink away. Ovid, before going off to banishment stands sadly beneath Julia's window and bids her farewell—a passage which would hardly have been written had not Shakespeare composed *Romeo and Juliet* first.

In the fifth act Jonson achieved his revenge. Augustus Cæsar has assembled his Court to do honour to poets in general and to Virgil especially. Horace praises Virgil sincerely (showing thereby that Ben Jonson could appreciate the real thing when he saw it). Then Virgil himself appears and all treat him with veneration.[1]

Virgil reads a portion of the fourth Book of the *Æneid*, and again Jonson translates about forty lines in halting rhymed couplets. The recitation is interrupted by the arrival of Lupus with Tucca, Crispinus, Demetrius, the player and the lictors. Lupus denounces Horace. He has found an emblem in his study. It must be a seditious document. Cæsar is not impressed and asks a few questions.

' Who first informed ? '

' The player,' answers Lupus.

' Ay,' echoes Tucca, ' an honest sycophant-like slave, and a politician besides.'

Cæsar peremptorily orders him to be whipped. Then at the request of his Court, he decrees that those who have calumniated Horace shall forthwith be tried. The reluctant Crispinus and Demetrius are led forward and indicted.

---

[1] The notion expressed by Sidney Lee and others that Virgil is Shakespeare is nonsense. Jonson was attacking the Chamberlain's company, amongst others, and at this time he regarded Shakespeare as a lucky ignoramus.

Tucca takes a leading part in their defence. The charge is that '... you (not having the fear of Phœbus, or his shafts, before your eyes), contrary to the peace of our liege Lord, Augustus Cæsar, his crown and dignity, and against the form of a Statute, in that case made and provided; have most ignorantly, foolishly and (more like yourselves) maliciously, gone about to deprave and calumniate the person and writings of Quintus Horatius Flaccus, here present, poet and priest to the Muses : and to that end have mutually conspired and plotted, at sundry times, as by several means, and in sundry places, for the better accomplishing your base and envious purpose; taxing him, falsely, of self-love, arrogancy, impudence, railing, filching by translation, etc. Of all which calumnies, and every of them, in manner and form aforesaid, what answer you? Are you guilty, or not guilty?'

They plead not guilty, and the written evidence is put in.

The first is a copy of verses, which Crispinus admits to be his own. They are read aloud :

> Ramp up, my genius; be not a retrograde :
> But boldly nominate a spade, a spade.
> What, shall thy lubrical and glibbery Muse
> Live, as she were defunct, like punk in stews?
> Alas! That were no modern consequence,
> To have cothurnal buskins frighted hence.
> No; teach thy incubus to poetize;
> And throw abroad thy spurious snotteries,
> Upon that puffed-up lump of barmy froth,
> Or clumsy chilblain'd judgment; that, with oath,
> Magnificates his merit; and bespawls
> The conscious time, with humorous foam, and brawls,
> As if his organons of sense would crack
> The sinews of my patience. Break his back,
> O Poets all, and some : for now we list
> Of strenuous venge-ance to clutch the fist.

It was a brilliant parody of Marston's style at its worst, carefully picked out from the *Scourge of Villainy*.

Then Demetrius' effort is read :

> Our Muse is in mind for th' untrussing a poet :
> I slip by his name ; for most men do know it :
> A critic, that all the world bescumbers
> With satirical humours and lyrical numbers :
> And for the most part, himself doth advance
> With much self-love and more arrogance :
> And (but that I would not be thought a prater)
> I could tell you, he were a translator.
> I know the authors from whence he has stole,
> And could trace him too, but that I understand 'em not
>   full and whole.
> The best note I can give you to know him by,
> Is that he keeps gallants' company;
> Whom I would wish, in time should him fear,
> Lest after they buy repentance too dear.

Horace breaks out into indignation. Virgil rebukes the pretenders with lofty scorn. Then the Court deliver their verdict. The accused are guilty. Demetrius is dragged forward and asked what cause they had to malign Horace.

'In troth, no great cause, not I, I must confess, but that he kept better company (for the most part) than I ; and that better men loved him than loved me ; and that his writings thrived better than mine and were better liked and graced ; nothing else.'

Crispinus receives more drastic treatment. He is given an emetic which makes him bring up his monstrous and high-sounding words—an episode which Jonson borrowed from one of the anti-Martin plays.[1] One after another they drop into the basin, *retrograde, reciprocal, incubus, glibbery, lubrical* and *defunct, magnificate, spurious, snotteries,*

---

[1] See p. 39, l. 24.

chilblained, clumsy, barmy froth, puffy, inflate, turgidous, ventositous, oblatrant, furibund, fatuate, strenuous, conscious, damp, prorumped, clutched, snarling gusts, quaking custard; and then, with a final heave, *obstupefact*. After this he feels better.

Virgil, still in the lofty strain, lectures him, and sentence is passed, Tibullus acting as clerk to the Court :

' Lay your hands on your hearts. You shall here solemnly attest and swear : That never (after this instant) either at book-sellers' stalls, in taverns, two-penny rooms, 'tiring houses, noblemen's butteries, puisne's chambers (the best and farthest places where you are admitted to come) you shall once offer or dare (thereby to endear yourself the more to any player, ingle, or guilty gull, in your company) to malign, traduce or detract the person or writings of Quintus Horatius Flaccus ; or any other eminent man, transcending you in merit, whom your envy shall find cause to work upon, either for that, or for keeping himself in better acquaintance, or enjoying better friends : Or if (transported by any sudden and desperate resolution) you do, that then you shall not under the bastoun, or in the next presence, being an honourable assembly of his favourers, be brought as voluntary gentleman to undertake the forswearing of it. Neither shall you at any time (ambitiously affecting the title of the untrussers or whippers of the age) suffer the itch of writing to overrun your performance in libel ; upon pain of being taken up for lepers in wit, and (losing both your time and your papers) be irrecoverably forfeited to the hospital of fools. So help you our Roman gods and the Genius of great Cæsar.'

A few lofty words from Cæsar bring the play to a close.

So Dekker set to work to answer Ben Jonson. He lacked Jonson's classical education, but he was far quicker. It was nothing to write a complete play in three weeks, and he had the advantage of recent first-hand study of Ben Jonson and his ways. Only two years since they had written together for Henslowe;[1] and now Dekker used his observation and gave a portrait of Jonson from the life. The new play was called *Satiromastix or the Untrussing of the humorous Poet*, and it was staged both by the Chamberlain's Men and the Children of Paul's. In the circumstances speed was essential. He had almost ready a romantic drama on the subject of Walter Terrill and King William Rufus: into this drama he thrust a subject of Elizabethan domestic intrigue, and a few scenes of Roman Horace.

Satiromastix is thus an extraordinary mixture. It starts with two gentlewomen strewing flowers, and a good deal of bawdy talk, in preparation for the wedding of Celestine and Walter Terrill. The guests arrive, including Crispinus and Demetrius, whom Dekker took over from *Poetaster*, as well as Captain Tucca and Horace. Bride and bridegroom and the whole party move on to church.

The second scene opens with the curtains drawn to disclose '*Horace sitting in a study, a candle by him burning, books lying confusedly.*' He is in the throes of composition, writing a wedding ode in honour of the occasion and finding some difficulty in choosing the right rhymes. His meditations are interrupted by the arrival of Asinius Bubo, his ingle, a big-hearted little man, and a specimen of the young gallants who patronized Ben Jonson. Horace reads some of the better lines of the ode to Bubo, fishing for compliments the while:

'Yet with kisses will they fee thee'
—my Muse has marched, dear rogue, no farther yet; but how is't? How is't? Nay, prithee, good Asinius, deal plainly, do not flatter me, come, how?——
    ASINIUS. If I have any judgment——

[1] See p. 201.

Horace. Nay, look you, sir, and then follow a troop of other rich and laboured conceits. Oh the end shall be admirable! But how is't, sweet Bubo, how, how?

Asinius. If I have any judgment, 'tis the best stuff that ever dropped from thee.

Horace nods agreement.

Crispinus and Demetrius arrive. They have come to make their peace with Horace. Horace offers the usual excuse of a satirist—that his enemies anatomize his lines too closely. It is their fault if they draw the wrong conclusions. 'I wonder then,' retorts Demetrius,

> ... that of five hundred, four
> Should all point with their fingers in one instant
> At one and the same man.

But they make peace and shake hands on it. Then comes in Captain Tucca. He was a gift to Dekker, who needed just such a character to say what he thought of Horace without control. Tucca's epithets and his odd remarks are very much to the point. He wonders why they are wasting their time with that 'whoreson, poor lime and hair rascal.' He rounds on Horace as a 'thin-bearded hermaphrodite,' 'a bench whistler,' 'a brown-bread-mouth stinker,' 'a starved rascal.'

'... You must have three or four suits of names, when like a lousy, pediculous vermin th' ast but one suit to thy back: you must be called Asper, and Criticus, and Horace; thy title's longer a reading than the style a' the big Turk's—Asper, Criticus, Quintus Horatius Flaccus.'

Indeed Tucca knew a good deal of Horace's private life:

'... I ha' seen thy shoulders lapped in a player's old cast cloak, like a sly knave as thou art; and when thou ranst mad for the death of Horatio, thou borrowedst a gown of

Roscius the stager, that honest Nicodemus, and sentst it home lousy, didst not ? *Responde*, didst not ? '

Horace is utterly put out, to the anxiety of Asinius Bubo, who has only seen him dashed worse once, when he went on a rainy day with a speech to the tilt yard and they called him names that a dog would not put up with—an occasion which Jonson did not apparently mention to Drummond. So Tucca marches off with Crispinus and Demetrius, leaving Horace gnashing with fury.

In the second act the play returns to the wedding party with its set of Elizabethan characters, who are humorists also in their own way, but are a section of society with which Dekker was more familiar. Sir Vaughan Ap Rees and Sir Adam Prickshaft, are both wooing the Widow Minever. The wedding party return, and the King appears. He is, incidentally, King William Rufus, but it certainly did not trouble Dekker, any more than it troubled his audience, to see Roman Horace or Elizabethan Captain Tucca in a Norman court. The King has a roving eye. He dares Terrill to send his bride to the Court for that night.

Then Horace comes back. He is very peevish. He has written epigrams on Tucca and Crispinus and Demetrius, which he gives to Bubo to distribute amongst the gallants. He joins the party round Mistress Minever. Demetrius and Crispinus produce Horace's epigrams and Tucca swears vengeance on his abuser. The King takes leave of the bridegroom and Terrill reluctantly sends his bride to Court, very apprehensive of what will happen to her.

In the fourth act Sir Vaughan also gives a party, in honour of Mistress Minever. Since Sir Adam, his rival, is bald, he hires Horace to write a poem against baldness.

Tucca is still angry. He challenges Bubo to a duel for distributing Horace's rhymes. Meantime Sir Adam has brought Crispinus along to praise bald-heads; and the honours are even. Tucca brings in Horace muffled and places him where he may hear what is said. They fall to talking of him.

'That same Horace,' remarks one of the ladies, 'methinks, has the most ungodly face, by my fan; it looks for all the world like a rotten russet apple when 'tis bruised: it's better than a spoonful of cinnamon water next my heart, for me to hear him speak, he sounds it so i' th' nose, and talks and rants for all the world like the poor fellow under Ludgate; oh fie upon him!'

'By my troth,' adds Mistress Minever, 'sweet ladies, it is cake and pudding to me to see his face make faces when he reads his songs and sonnets.'

This was an unkind cut, for Jonson fancied himself a reader.

Tucca becomes so angry that he stabs at Horace, but with a blunt dagger. Then they fall on him, toss him in a blanket and run him to Court.

In the fifth act Celestine drinks the poison which her father has prepared that she may avoid the worse fate. She is carried into the King's presence in a chair, but when he looks at her she is dead. Terrill denounces him as a lustful tyrant. He repents suitably, and then the bride wakes, for it was but a sleeping-draught after all.

The story is interrupted by a hue and cry. Sir Vaughan is searching for Horace. Horace and Bubo are caught. Horns are thrust on their heads and they are dragged in, bound. Tucca crowns Horace with nettles and denounces him to the King; 'You nasty tortoise,' he cries, 'you and your itchy poetry break out like Christmas, but once a year, and then you keep a-revelling and arraigning and a-scratching of men's faces as though you were Tiber, the long-tailed Prince of Rats, do you?'

They accuse him of usurping the name of Horace.

'... Thou hast no part of Horace in thee but's name and his damnable vices : thou hast such a terrible mouth that thy beard's afraid to peep out : but, look here, you staring Leviathan, here's the sweet visage of Horace ; look, parboiled face, look : Horace had a trim long-beard, and a reasonable good face for a poet (as faces go nowadays). Horace did not screw and wriggle himself into great men's familiarity (impudently) as thou dost, nor wear the badge of gentlemen's company, as thou dost thy taffeta sleeves, tacked to only with some points of profit ; no, Horace had not his face punched full of eyelet holes, like the cover of a warming-pan. Horace loved poets well, and gave coxcombs to none but fools ; but thou lovest none, neither wise men nor fools, but thyself. Horace was a goodly corpulent gentleman, and not so lean a hollow-cheeked scrag as thou art ; no, here's the copy of thy countenance, by this will I learn to make a number of villainous faces more, and to look scurvily upon the world as thou dost.'

So Sir Vaughan and Tucca continue to abuse him antiphonally.

SIR VAUGHAN. You shall swear not to bombast out a new play with the old linings of jests, stolen from the Temple's Revels.

TUCCA. To him, old tango.

SIR VAUGHAN. Moreover, you shall not sit in a gallery when your comedies and interludes have entered their actions, and there make vile and bad faces at every line, to make gentlemen have an eye to you, and to make players afraid to take your part.

TUCCA. Thou shalt be my ningle for this.

SIR VAUGHAN. Besides, you must forswear to venture on the stage, when your play is ended, and to exchange courtesies and compliments with gallants in the lords' rooms, to make all the house rise up in arms, and to cry ' that's Horace, that's he, that's he, that's he, that pens and purges humours and diseases ? '

Thirdly [Sir Vaughan continues], 'and last of all, saving one, when your plays are misliked at Court, you shall not cry mew like a puss cat, and say you are glad you write out the courtier's element.'

TUCCA. Let the element alone, 'tis out a' thy reach.

SIR VAUGHAN. In briefliness, when you sup in taverns amongst your betters, you shall swear not to dip your manners in too much sauce, not at table to fling epigrams, emblems or play speeches about you (like hail-stones) to keep you out of the terrible danger of the shot, upon pain to sit at the upper end of the table, a' the left hand of Carlo Buffon. Swear all this, by Apollo and the eight or nine muses.

Horace puts up no fight, and swears acquiescence at once; Tucca wins Mistress Minever; and the play ends with a dance.

As a comedy *Satiromastix* was poor stuff; as an immediate counter-blast, devastating. Jonson had had enough. Dekker challenged an answer, but Jonson had little spirit left. He wrote an apologetic dialogue which was once spoken on the stage, but then forbidden by authority. In this little piece, Nasutus and Polyposus come to visit the Author, who professes himself unhurt.

Polyposus is not so sure.

Ay, but the multitude, they think not so, sir,
They think you hit and hurt, and dare give out
Your silence argues it in not rejoining
To this or that late libel.

Nasutus, who has not seen the play, asks why it should offend so deeply:

AUTHOR. Shall I tell you?
NASUTUS. Yes, and ingenuously.

AUTHOR.   Then, by the hope,
Which I prefer unto all other objects,
I can profess, I never writ that piece
More innocent or empty of offence.
Some salt it had, but neither tooth nor gall,
Nor was there in it any circumstance,
Which, in the setting down, I could suspect
Might be perverted by an enemy's tongue.
Only, it had the fault to be call'd mine.
That was the crime.

   POLYPOSUS. No? why they say you taxed
The Law, and lawyers, captains, and the players
By their particular names.

   AUTHOR.   It is not so.
I us'd no name. My books have still been taught
To spare the persons and to speak the vices.
These are mere slanders, and enforced by such
As have no safer ways to men's disgraces,
But their own lies, and loss of honesty.

The Author cannot understand it at all. This much he will concede:

                                      ... But sure I am, three years
They did provoke me with their petulant styles
On every stage. And I at last, unwilling,
But weary, I confess, of so much trouble,
Thought I would try, if shame could win upon 'em.
And therefore chose Augustus Cæsar's times,
When wit and arts were at their height in Rome,
To show that Virgil, Horace and the rest
Of those great master-spirits did not want
Detractors then, or practisers against them :
And by this line (although no parallel)
I hoped at last they would sit down and blush.

Then he tries to justify himself. As for his alleged attacks on the law, why, they were all to be found in Ovid.

For the players, it is true he taxed them, and yet but some, and those but sparingly.

The rest had not the wit to keep quiet. He is not angry with them;

> If it gave them meat,
> Or got 'em clothes; 'tis well, that was their end.
> Only amongst them, I am sorry for
> Some better natures, by the rest so drawn,
> To run in that vile tone.

Contrariwise, if he seriously meant to attack anyone—

> They know, I dare
> To spurn or baffle 'em; or squirt their eyes
> With ink, or urine: or I could do worse,
> Armed with Archilochus' fury, write iambics
> Should make the desperate lashers hang themselves.
> Rhyme 'em to death, as they do Irish rats
> In drumming tunes. Or, living, I could stamp
> Their foreheads with those deep and public brands
> That the whole Company of Barber-Surgeons
> Should not take off, with all their art and plasters.
> And these my prints should last, still to be read
> In their pale fronts, when, what they write 'gainst me,
> Shall like a figure drawn in water, fleet,
> And the poor wretched papers be employed
> To cloth tobacco, or some cheaper drug.
> This I could do, and make them infamous.
> But, to what end? When their own deeds have marked 'em,
> And that I know within his guilty breast
> Each slanderer bears a whip that shall torment him
> Worse than a million of these temporal plagues:
> Which to pursue were but a feminine humour,
> And far beneath the dignity of a man.

He will make no further answer. Meanwhile, since the comic muse has proved so ominous, he will try if Tragedy have a more kind aspect. His countenance changes; the gusts of inspiration begin to play. Nasutus reverently tiptoes away.

Such was the outline of the famous Stage War. There were certain side issues, most of which cannot now be traced. Other dramatists took a hand, amongst them Shakespeare. At Christmas time the young gentlemen of St. John's College in Cambridge acted the *Second Part of the Return from Parnassus* which mirrors general opinion exactly. They discuss contemporary writers. Ben Jonson, says Judicio, is ' the wittiest fellow of a bricklayer in England.'

But Ingenioso retorts :

' A mere empyric, one that gets what he hath by observation, and makes only nature privy to what he indites. So slow an inventor that he were better betake himself to his old trade of bricklaying, a bold whoreson as confident now in making a book as he was in times past in laying of a brick.' [1]

Later on in the play, Burbage and Kemp are introduced as characters. They talk about student dramatists and players :

' Few of the university,' says Kemp, ' pen plays well, they smell too much of that writer Ovid and that writer Metamorphosis, and talk too much of Proserpina and Jupiter. Why here's our fellow Shakespeare puts them all down, ay, and Ben Jonson too. O, that Ben Jonson is a pestilent fellow, he brought up Horace giving the poets a pill, but our fellow Shakespeare hath given him a purge that made him bewray his credit.' [2]

This remark, as might be expected, has set many ingenious minds working. Some suggest that Shakespeare's contribution was in *Troilus and Cressida,* and that Thersites or Ajax was intended for Jonson ; others that at some time *Hamlet* included a passage which has now disappeared. The simplest of explanations is to take words literally. If so, Shakespeare

[1] Act I, sc. II.   [2] *Ibid.,* IV, sc. III.

THE STAGE WAR

in some play which has not survived took a hint that Jonson himself had given in the Induction to *Every Man out of his Humour*,[1] which started the whole business. Maybe he also produced a Horace and gave him a pill to purge and make him fit for fair society—a scene which, though not appropriate for the School Certificate, would have been effective.

After *Satiromastix* the Stage War, except for occasional rumblings, was ended. There is no need to take it too seriously. Both Jonson and Marston were much hurt and embittered at the time, but the wounds soon healed, and in 1604, Marston dedicated his best play, *The Malcontent* :

BENIAMINO IONSONIO

POETAE

ELEGANTISSIMO

GRAVISSIMO

AMICO

SVO CANDIDO ET CORDATO

IOHANNES MARSTON

MVSARUM ALUMNUS

ASPERAM HANC THALIAM

D D

---

[1] See page 200, l. 3

Chapter XVI

THE END OF AN ERA

MEANWHILE, in the public theatres, matters improved after the disastrous spring and summer of 1601. At the Fortune more new plays were being commissioned. Henslowe now had a strong team of playwrights. Chapman had left him some months before to write for the Paul's Boys, but after *Satiromastix*, Dekker came back. Chettle had been constantly employed; Munday and Drayton still came in occasionally. Even Jonson made one brief return. On the 22nd June 1602 he drew £10 from Henslowe in earnest of a play called *Richard Crookback*, and for new additions to the old *Spanish Tragedy* of all plays! *Crookback* (if it was ever completed) was not one of those plays which Jonson collected for the folio edition of his own works. But this was Jonson's last appearance for some time. On the 12th February 1603 Manningham noted in his Diary: 'Ben Jonson the poet now lives upon one Townsend and scorns the world.'

There were also newcomers. John Day had been writing for a couple of years, but as yet had not produced any piece which survives. In May 1602 a new name appeared— John Webster, but in spite of his two masterpieces, *The White Devil* and *The Duchess of Malfi*, hardly anything else is known of him.

The new plays during these months were: *The Six Clothiers, Too Good to be True, The Spanish Fig, Malcolm*

King of Scots, Love parts Friendship, The Bristow Tragedy, Jephthah, Tobias, Cæsar's Fall or The Two Shapes, Richard Crookback, The Danish Tragedy, The Widow's Charm, A Medicine for a Cursed Wife, Samson, Philip of Spain, William Cartwright, Felmelanco, Mortimer, The Earl of Hertford, Joshua, Randal Earl of Chester, Merry as May Be, The Set at Tennis, The London Florentine, Hoffman, Singer's Voluntary, The Four Sons of Aymon, The Boss of Billingsgate, and *The Siege of Dunkirk with Alleyn the Pirate.* None survive.

All these new plays were acted at the Fortune. The Rose meanwhile had been empty except for a couple of days in October 1600 when some of Pembroke's Men who had been travelling as a provincial company attempted to make a fresh start in London. Henslowe opened a new account with the usual formula ' My Lord of Pembroke's Men began to play at the Rose the 28 of October 1600 as followeth.' The experiment was a failure. Henslowe drew 11s. 6d. on the 28th, and 5s. on the 29th, after which the entries ceased. From August 1602, however, the Rose was continually occupied by the players of the Earl of Worcester, who now began to make regular appearances in London.

There had been a Worcester's company in the early 1580's, patronized by the third Earl of Worcester, which has left its mark in the city records of Norwich and Leicester, where they made themselves a nuisance. In those early days Edward Alleyn himself was one of the junior members. This company had probably disbanded before the death of their patron in 1589. The new Earl, who was now Master of the Horse to Queen Elizabeth, gave his patronage to a company of players whose names appear in various country records between 1589 and 1602.

Worcester's Company acted for the first time at Court on the 3rd January 1602. They included some competent actors and playwrights, for Thomas Heywood joined them, and above all, Will Kemp, who had not been welcomed back to the Chamberlain's on his return from the unlucky expedition to Rome. When Worcester's Men came to play at the Rose in August 1602, Henslowe acted as their agent in the same way as he acted for the Chamberlain's Men at the Fortune. Between August and the following March they produced fifteen or sixteen new plays : *Four Prentices of London*, *Albere Galles*, *Marshal Osric*, *Cutting Dick*, *Biron*, *The Two (Three) Brothers*, *Lady Jane or The Overthrow of Rebels*, *Christmas comes but Once a Year*, *The Black Dog of Newgate*, in two parts, *The Blind eats many a Fly*, *The Unfortunate General*, *A Woman Killed with Kindness*, *The Italian Tragedy* and *Shore*.[1]

Of these plays one at least was a piece of quick theatrical journalism. The play, which Henslowe called *Burone*, or *Berowne* concerned Charles, Duke of Biron, and followed hard after events. Biron had occupied in France a position similar to that of Essex in England. At the end of August 1601 he paid a state visit to Queen Elizabeth, with a following of three hundred persons, which attracted much notice. On arrival in London Sir Walter Ralegh had been appointed to conduct the party to see the sights, and afterwards Biron followed the Queen to Basing, where she was then making a progress. The French noblemen, to the astonishment of the English Court, all wore plain black, which caused Ralegh to ride by night to London to provide himself with a plain black taffeta suit and a black saddle. The Queen received Biron very affably and conversed with him most frankly. Amongst other things, she discussed Essex and his rebellion.

Biron's departure from England was equally ceremonious.

[1] It is not always possible to tell from Henslowe's payments whether a play is new or revised or was ever acted.

Ten months later he was arrested by the orders of the French King and tried for high treason. The affair caused much excitement in England, especially as it came so quickly after the visit and similar troubles at home. On the 19th July Biron was beheaded in the Bastille, where his behaviour on the scaffold was furious and reluctant. Henslowe did not record any payment for the author of the play, but on the 25th September he lent John Duke £5 ' to bye a blacke sewt of satten for the playe of burone '; and early in October he laid out 13*s*. ' to macke a scafowld and bare for the playe of berowne.'[1]

A very remarkable play of Worcester's Men was Thomas Heywood's *Woman Killed with Kindness*, which has been much praised by critics. There was a kind of double dramatic morality in plays of this time. If a play was labelled comedy, then it was considered good sport to cuckold a husband, and no particular blame attached to the wife; if a tragedy, then the wife's lapse was to be visited with dreadful doom on all who were intimately or remotely concerned. There was no intermediate way.

In *A Woman Killed with Kindness* Heywood produced an interesting contrast to the usual pattern of domestic tragedy. It begins with the wedding of the Frankfords; the husband and wife as devoted as can be, and everything in the match to guarantee that they shall live happy ever afterwards. Into this Eden enters Master Wendoll, who, in spite of the squirming worm of conscience, falls utterly and passionately in love with Mrs. Frankford, to whom he reveals his feelings. She, after rebuking him hotly in one speech, falters in the next, and falls in the third. But Wendoll is a clumsy seducer, for he fails to notice that his lovemaking is overheard by Nicholas, Master Frankford's faithful servant. When Master Frankford learns of his wife's faithlessness, he

[1] Henslowe's *Diary*, i, 181-2. III *Elizabethan Journal*, pp. 199-202.

plans elaborately to surprise her. He pretends that he must make a long journey. But at midnight he comes back and finds Wendoll and his wife in bed together. He chases Wendoll out of the house in his night-shirt—a moment which might easily become comic—and then confronts his wife and all the servants who have been aroused and stand around in their bed-gear, wringing their hands. Frankford addresses his erring wife and passes sentence. He is magnanimity incarnate . . .

> . . . I'll not martyr thee,
> Nor mark thee for a strumpet; but with usage
> Of more humility torment thy soul,
> And kill thee even with kindness.

So he sends her away to one of his manors with everything that may remind him of her, except the children, who have been born inconspicuously between the second and fourth acts. Mrs. Frankford goes off into exile, but the thought of her husband's overwhelming generosity is too much for her; she dies brokenhearted and penitent. To squeeze the last drop of pathos in the final scene, her husband, realizing that he has indeed succeeded in killing her with his kindness and that her last moments have come, forgives and takes her in his arms as she passes away.

To contrast with this story, Heywood provided another problem in domestic morality in the story of Sir Charles Mountford, his sister Susan, and Sir Francis Acton, who, for the convenience of the plot, is made Mrs. Frankford's brother. Sir Charles and Sir Francis quarrel over a wager, and in the fight that follows, Sir Charles kills two of Sir Francis's servants. He is acquitted of the murder, but his enemy pursues him so relentlessly that at last he finds himself penniless and in prison. Sir Francis falls in love with Susan, discharges Sir Charles's debts, but expects Susan to pay his price. Sir Charles leads her to his enemy as a willing sacrifice, and bids him do his will. Sir Francis is so overwhelmed by this exhibition of brotherly and sisterly affection that he accepts Susan from his hands, not as mistress but as wife. At this generosity Susan can only exclaim in wonder:

> You still exceed us: I will yield to fate,
> And learn to love, where I till now did hate.

Some of the situations in the tragedy are very effectively staged, but unless one happens to accept the implied moral values, the emphasis is wrongly placed and the justice very dubious. The real villain of the piece is the seducer Wendoll, but he is allowed simply to fade out with a couple of soliloquies in which he first bemoans his everlasting remorse, and then reflects that he will go abroad, learn the useful tongues, and when he comes back . . .

> My worth and parts being by some great man praised,
> At my return I may in court be raised.

The bourgeois morality of this piece was well suited to its audience, for the Rose attracted citizens rather than gallants. As might be expected, Sir Adolphus Ward nodded maudlin approval over *A Woman Killed with Kindness*:

'This exquisitely pathetic conception is carried out with dramatic force, and with a manly simplicity of tone showing true delicacy of feeling. We pity the weakness of the unhappy wife even in her fall, and feel that the punishment inflicted upon her is true justice. If in the scene where, after having become aware of her infidelity, the husband watches her demeanour and that of her paramour we are to some degree distracted by the cleverness of the way in which the situation is managed, the subsequent scene of the actual discovery is thrilling in its power. The terrible suspense of the situation when the husband accompanied by a faithful servant returns to his polluted home to surprise his guilty wife has few parallels in the Elizabethan drama—it might almost be termed a " prose " reproduction of the terrors of *Macbeth* itself. Doubly effective is the gentle softness of the close of the play, which seems to solve in a harmony of forgiveness the awful problem of the consequence of sin.' [1]

Both the Rose and the Fortune were thus in use in 1602. The Swan also had survived the order for its demolition in 1600, though it does not seem to have been used again for plays; but from time to time there were entertainments which were sometimes sensational. On the 6th November an impudent gentleman named Richard Venner played a prank on the public. He issued a play-bill [2] which announced:

THE PLOT OF THE PLAY CALLED
ENGLAND'S JOY

To be played at the Swan this 6 of November, 1602.

First, there is induct by show and in action, the civil wars of England from Edward the Third to the end of Queen Mary's reign, with the overthrow of usurpation.

2. Secondly then the entrance of England's Joy by the Coronation of our Sovereign Lady Elizabeth; her Throne attended with Peace, Plenty and Civil Policy: a sacred prelate standing at her right hand, betokening the serenity of the Gospel; at her left hand Justice; and at her feet War, with a scarlet robe of peace upon his armour; a wreath of bays about his temples, and a branch of palm in his hand.

---

[1] *A History of English Dramatic Literature*, ii, 114. This was first published in 1875: other times, other morals.

[2] This is the only surviving Elizabethan play-bill, and the sole copy is in the collection of the Royal Society of Antiquaries. A type facsimile is reproduced in Dr. W. W. Greg's *Elizabethan Dramatic Documents*. Play-bills of a similar kind were normally distributed before the first performance of new plays.

3. Thirdly is dragged in three Furies, presenting Dissension, Famine, and Bloodshed, which are thrown into hell.

4. Fourthly is expressed under the person of a Tyrant, the envy of Spain, who to show his cruelty, causeth his soldiers drag in a beautiful Lady, whom they mangle and wound, tearing her garments and jewels from off her; and so leave her bloody, with her hair about her shoulders, lying upon the ground. To her come certain gentlemen, who seeing her piteous despoilment, turn to the Throne of England, from whence one descendeth, taketh up the Lady, wipeth her eyes, bindeth up her wounds, giveth her treasure, and bringeth forth a band of soldiers, who attend her forth. This Lady presenteth Belgia.

5. Fifthly, the Tyrant more enraged, taketh counsel, sends forth letters, privy spies and secret underminers, taking their oaths and giving them bags of treasure. These signify Lopus, and certain Jesuits, who afterward, when the Tyrant looks for an answer from them, are showed to him in a glass with halters about their necks, which makes him mad with fury.

6. Sixthly, the Tyrant, seeing all secret means to fail him, intendeth upon violence and invasion by the hand of War, whereupon is set forth the battle at Sea in '88, with England's victory.

7. Seventhly, he complotteth with the Irish rebels, wherein is laid open the base ingratitude of Tyrone, the landing there of Don John de Aguila, and their dissipation by the wisdom and valour of the Lord Mountjoy.

8. Eighthly, a great triumph is made with fighting of twelve gentlemen at Barriers, and sundry rewards sent from the Throne of England, to all sorts of well deservers.

9. Lastly, the Nine Worthies, with several coronets, present themselves before the Throne, which are put back by certain in the habit of angels, who set upon the Lady's head which represents her Majesty, an Imperial Crown, garnished with the sun, moon and stars. And so with music both with voice and instruments she is taken up into Heaven, when presently appears a Throne of blessed

souls, and beneath under the stage set forth with strange fireworks, divers black and damned souls, wonderfully described in their several torments.[1]

The public were attracted. A few days later John Chamberlain wrote a gossipy letter to his friend, Dudley Carleton, and noted in the course of it:

'... And, now we are in mirth, I must not forget to tell you of a cozening prank of one Venner, of Lincoln's Inn, that gave out bills of a famous play on Saturday was sevennight on the Bankside, to be acted only by certain gentlemen and gentlewomen of account. The price at coming in was two shillings or eighteen pence at least; and, when he had gotten most part of the money into his hands, he would have showed them a fair pair of heels, but he was not so nimble to get up on horseback, but that he was fain to forsake that course, and betake himself to the water, where he was pursued and taken, and brought before the Lord Chief Justice, who would make nothing of it but a jest and a merriment, and bound him over in five pound to appear at the sessions. In the mean time the common people, when they saw themselves deluded, revenged themselves upon the hangings, curtains, chairs, stools, walls and whatsoever came in their way, very outrageously, and made great spoil; there was great store of good company and many noblemen.'[2]

There was another sensation on the 7th February following, when two well-known fencers, Turner and Dunne, played at the Swan for prizes, and Dunne was fatally wounded by a thrust in the eye.

Of the activities of the Chamberlain's Men little is known.

---

[1] For Lopus (or Dr Lopez) see I *Elizabethan Journal*, and for Tyrone, Don John de Aguila, and Lord Mountjoy, see III *Elizabethan Journal*.
[2] *Letters written by John Chamberlain during the Reign of Queen Elizabeth*, edited by Sarah Williams, p. 163.

They acted at Court three times during the Christmas holidays of 1601–2, at Shrovetide in 1601, once in the Christmas following, and again at Shrovetide 1602. *Othello* may have first been produced in this year, and perhaps *All's Well that Ends Well*. *Twelfth Night* was acted in the hall of the Middle Temple on the 2nd February. John Manningham, who was present, noted in his diary :

'At our feast we had a play called '*Twelfth Night or What you Will*,' much like the *Comedy of Errors* or Menechmi in Plautus, but most like and near to that in Italian called *Inganni*. A good practice in it to make the Steward believe his Lady widow was in love with him, by counterfeiting a letter as from his Lady in general terms, telling him what she liked best in him, and prescribing his gesture in smiling, his apparel, etc., and then when he came to practise making him believe they took him to be mad.'[1]

At the Blackfriars there was some reorganization in the management, for Evans was called before the Star Chamber for his high-handed actions with Master Clifton's son, (see page 236). Their Lordships took a serious view of the matter. They censured him severely and decreed that all agreements made with him should be cancelled.

Nothing of the plays acted by the Children of the Chapel is known, but on the 18th September a distinguished foreigner, the young Duke of Stettin-Pomerania, was taken with his followers to see a performance. They were told, according to the journal kept by one of the party, that the Children were required to act a play once a week that they might learn courteous manners. They observed that in spite of the high cost of admission, there was a good audience, many of them reputable women, because useful precepts and good doctrine were displayed there ! Plays, it was noted, were acted by the light of candles and for an hour before

[1] *Diary of John Manningham*, edited by J. Bruce, p. 18.

the play started there was a concert of music. The journal is not necessarily accurate, for the Duke was a booby and the legs of his party may have been pulled.[1]

If the boys did indeed only act once a week, then the number of new plays produced at the private houses must have been small. This would have meant that a popular play such as *Poetaster* would have had a long run.

By this time the Paul's Boys had a number of competent authors writing for them. As well as Marston, Middleton and Chapman were producing plays for them. During the year they acted Middleton's *Blurt, Master Constable,* and early in 1603 they produced *The Old Joiner of Aldgate,* written by Chapman and unheard of till Professor Sisson disinterred its unseemly remains from the Public Record Office.[2]

The case is an important footnote to stage history. It confirms the impression that there was far more personality behind Elizabethan comedy, and especially comedy written for the boy players, than has always been realized. *The Old Joiner of Aldgate* was in fact a direct dramatization of a current scandal in which one of the parties concerned supplied Chapman with the plot in order to make his opponents look foolish.

The affair started in September 1600, when a certain Mrs. Sharles, a childless widow, who owned a glass-shop and other properties worth in all between £2,000 and £3,000, died, leaving her money to her niece, Agnes Howe, the daughter of John Howe, a barber-surgeon of no standing, and Agnes his wife. This was too great a temptation for the barber-surgeon, who immediately looked round to see how

---

[1] *Diary of the Duke of Stettin's Journey,* Transactions of the Royal Historical Society, New Series, vol. vi, 1892.

[2] *Lost plays of Shakespeare's Age,* by C. J. Sisson, chap. 2, where the whole story should be read.

part of the legacy might be diverted to his own use. The most obvious method was to find the girl on appropriate terms a suitable husband. Various members of the family were also interested in the same quest, and there was such enthusiasm amongst prospective bridegrooms that at least six approached Howe with various offers. By February 1601 no fewer than three claimed to have won Agnes's consent, and, which was more important, to have been formally pledged before witnesses. Pre-contract was a serious matter and legally binding. If one of the parties could succeed in proving, to the satisfaction of the Courts, that the girl had formally declared her intention of taking him as her husband, he could claim fulfilment of the pledge and prevent any other marriage. The three claimants went to law. They were: John Flaskett, a stationer, Thomas Field, a gentleman, and Henry Jones, also a gentleman.

The barber-surgeon was in great perplexity. Flaskett's claims were strongest, he favoured Field himself, but Jones had some strong evidence. With three law-suits depending, Howe, in his difficulties, decided to consult the Reverend Dr. John Milward, preacher at Christchurch. Dr. Milward solved the problem for him. He eloped with Agnes and married her secretly, but with such irregularity that his disappointed enemies were able to have him arrested and imprisoned in the Clink. Then followed a long war of legal battles, the chief combatants being now Flaskett and the Doctor. The Doctor won the first round; lost the second, when his marriage was proclaimed null and void; but he won the final battle in the Star Chamber, when the marriage, after four years' litigation, was finally declared valid on the 12th November 1604; and what remained of Mrs. Sharles's legacy passed into his keeping. At no time did the Law consider it relevant to inquire into Agnes Howe's feelings in the matter.

Chapman came into the business at Christmas-time 1602. Flaskett wished to stir up feeling against his rivals. He persuaded Chapman to write a play which would annoy them, and particularly Dr. Milward. Flaskett provided the plot and the details of the story, from which Chapman wrote the play, calling it *The Old Joiner of Aldgate*. He sold it to the Paul's Boys for £13 6s. 8d. This was a handsome sum for a play, the standard rate at the time offered by Henslowe being about £6. The Paul's Boys acted it with great success which was due not a little to the notoriety of the case. Chapman, of course, declared that he was quite innocent of any libellous intention, but as his chief characters were named Snipper-Snapper (the barber), an aunt called Mrs. Glasbie, Tresacres (otherwise Field), Touchbox (otherwise Flaskett), Umphrevile, (otherwise Humphrey Roger, the fourth suitor), he was obviously lying. The Rev. Dr. John Milward appeared conspicuously, but in the guise of a French doctor.

But the activities of the Paul's Boys, as of all other companies, were soon brought to an end. In the theatres, and in public life, these months were a time of waiting for the inevitable change. The Queen had survived the great shock of Essex's rebellion apparently uninjured, but to those in closest contact it was clear that she could not live much longer. On all sides men were looking to the future, and Sir Robert Cecil, her Secretary, among the first. There was a very general dread that on her death the succession would be disputed and that anarchy was inevitable. The most hopeful solution was that King James of Scotland might succeed unopposed. Travellers on the Great North Road became more numerous. Amongst those who visited Scotland during the last years of the reign was a company of English players led by one Laurence Fletcher, which toured in Scotland in 1595, 1599, 1601. King James was delighted

THE END OF AN ERA

with them and rewarded them handsomely, but in 1599 they were the cause of great disturbance between the King and the Kirk of Edinburgh.[1]

The trouble subsided, and in October 1601 Fletcher was granted the freedom of Edinburgh. Some have supposed that Shakespeare was amongst those whom Fletcher took with him, but of this there is no direct evidence.

The Christmas festivities at the Court were gay, but early in March the Queen was seen to be failing. She became very melancholy and sleepless. For a while she seemed to be recovering, but on the 17th the Council were already beginning to take emergency measures. On the 19th the order went round to the Lord Mayor and the Justices of Middlesex and Surrey that they should restrain stage plays until further notice. In the early hours of the 24th March the Queen died, and by midday King James had been peacefully proclaimed as her successor.

It was indeed the end of the Elizabethan Age of the English Theatre in more ways than one. Hitherto the players had existed precariously, and in theory at least, they were only tolerated in order that they might keep in training to amuse the Queen. One of the first acts of the new King was to appoint the Chamberlain's Men as his own players. A licence was issued on the 19th May 1603 to Laurence Fletcher, William Shakespeare, Richard Burbage, Augustine Phillips, John Hemmings, Henry Condell, William Sly, Robert Armin, Richard Cowley and the rest of their associates. At the same time the Admiral's Men found a new patron in Prince Henry, the King's eldest son. The Children of the Chapel became the Children of the Queen's Revels.

The change was not merely nominal. Henceforward the players were no longer to be regarded as vagabonds at the

[1] For details see *Elizabethan Stage*, ii, 265.

mercy of any officious magistrate, but favoured royal servants. The number of performances which they gave at Court greatly increased. Between Christmas 1598 and March 1603, the Chamberlain's men had played fourteen times at Court, and the Admiral's twelve. In the first four years of the new reign, the King's Men performed forty-one times, and Prince Henry's twenty-five.

These changes were reflected also in drama itself. The players more and more ceased to care for the groundlings and the common spectators and to turn their attention to gentlemen and courtiers. The change was immediately more paying, but it was not to the advantage of drama; for drama, or any form of art, to endure, needs some leavening of common coarseness. In the next few months English drama indeed reached the peak of its achievement in the greatest of Shakespeare's tragedies, *Macbeth*, *King Lear*, *Antony and Cleopatra*, but thereafter it declined to a level of competent craftsmanship. The most astonishing fact about the Elizabethan drama is the speed of its growth. Less than twenty years had separated *Tamburlaine* and *King Lear*; but *King Lear* belongs to Jacobean drama, which is another story.

INDEX

Adams, Prof. J. Q., 23 n., 25 n.
Admiral's Men, The, 137, 169, 172, 184, 225, 228; plays performed by, 93, 139–44, 154, 168, 173, 201, 202–3, 230, 245–6, 282–3; members of, 137–8, 166–7, 170; at Newington Butts, 137; at Court, 148, 150, 230, 296; at Fortune Theatre, 245, 282–3; become Prince Henry's Men, 295
Agamemnon, 261
Albere Galles, 284
Alexander and Lodovick, 143
All Fools, 201
All is not Gold that Glisters, 245
All's Well that Ends Well, 291
Alleyn, Edward, 46, 62, 69, 116, 137, 166, 167, 169, 172, 189–90; biographical details of, 46, 94; his reputation, 46–7, 138; parts played by, 47–8, 72, 90 and n.; on tour 130–2; his style of acting, 47–8, 173; letters of, 131–2; and Fortune Theatre, 221–2, 228
Alleyn, Giles, 21, 43, 150, 191–3
Alleyn, Joan, 94, 131–2; letters of, 133–6
Alphonsus, King of Aragon, 82–6, 140, 173
Anderson, Chief Justice, 43
Andronicus, 137
Antonio and Mellida, 208–13
Antonio's Revenge, 214–21
Antony and Valia, 141
Apology for Poetry, 11–13, 26
Appleby, Mistress, 106

Arcadia, 26
Armin, Robert, 295
As plain as plain can be, 10
As You Like It, 193–4, 255

Bacon, Sir Francis, 48, 239
Baheire, Robert, 152
Baines, Richard, his accusations against Marlowe, 119–21, 127
Ball, Cutting, 61
Bancroft, Dr. Richard, 38
Barnado and Fiammetta, 142
Barrow, Henry, 117
Bartholomew Fair, 62 n.
Bathurst, Dr. Ralph, 176
Battle of Alcazar, The, 245
Beane, John, 194
Bear Garden, The, 190
Beard, Thomas, 125
Bee, William, 225
Beeston, Christopher, 188
Bel Savage Inn, The, 11, 42
Bellendon, 137
Bentley, John, 46, 47
Bird, Christopher, 105
Bird (or Borne), William, 161, 167, 169, 170
Biron, 284
Biron, Charles, Duke of, 284–5
Bispham, William, 152
Black Dog of Newgate, The, 284
Blackfriars Theatre, The, 25–6, 30, 240, 261, 291; taken over by Burbage, 150–1; petition against, 151–2; plays at, 29, 30, 201; rented by Evans, 233. *See also* Chapel Royal, Children of the

297

INDEX

Blacksmith's Daughter, The 11
Blank verse, 72, 73
Blind Beggar of Alexandria, The, 142, 154, 156–7, 173
Blind eats many a Fly, The, 284
Blount, Sir Charles, 186
Blunt, Edward, 26
Boas, Dr. F. S., 114 n.
Boice, Henry, 152
Bonnetti, Rocco, 150
Borne, William. *See* Bird.
Boss of Billingsgate, The, 283
Bowes, Henry, 152
Boy players. *See* Chapel Royal, Children of the; Paul's, Children of; Windsor Chapel, Children of
Bradley, William, 78
Brayne, John, 13, 22, 42, 43
Brazen Age, The, 141
Breton, Nicholas, 253
Brian, George, 130
Bridges, Dr. John, 36
Bristow Tragedy, The, 283
Broome, the widow, 145
Brown, Ned, 98
Browne, Capt. George, 194
Browne, Sir Thomas, 56
Browne, Thomas, 152
Brownists, 118
Buckholt, Harman, 152
Bull Inn, The, 11, 42
Burbage, Cuthbert, 21, 153, 191, 192
Burbage, James, 13, 18, 138, 150; builds the Theatre, 21–2; his quarrel with Brayne, 42–3; and Blackfriars Theatre, 150–3, 233
Burbage, Richard, 21, 139, 148, 153, 188, 192, 233, 280, 295; his reputation, 138; as Richard III, 146
Burby, Cuthbert, 109, 255
Burghley, William Cecil, Lord, 43, 52, 122, 124
Burr, William, 255

Cæsar and Pompey, Part I, 140; Part II, 141
Cæsar's Fall or The Two Shapes, 283
Cambises, 5–9, 13
Camden, William, 174, 176, 179, 181, 182
Campaspe, 26, 29, 145
Cardinal Wolsey, 246
Carleton, Dudley, 158, 185, 290
Catiline's Conspiracies, 11
Cecil, Sir Robert, 122, 124, 224, 294
Chamberlain, John, 55, 158, 290
Chamberlain's Men, The, 188, 194, 201, 202, 225, 227, 228, 246, 284; members of, 138–9, 188, 295; plays performed by, 145–6, 148–50, 170, 184, 194, 197–8, 272; at Newington Butts, 137; build the Globe, 191–3; and Essex rebellion, 238–40; and Stage War, 262, 272; at Court, 148, 240, 291, 296; become the King's Men, 295
Chambers, Sir E. K., 23, 148 n.
Chapel Royal, Children of the, 24, 25, 233, 236, 291–2, 295; plays performed by, 29, 201, 233, 247, 261
Chapman, George, 75, 182, 184, 294; his *Blind Beggar of Alexandria*, 142, 154, 156–7, 173; his *Humorous Day's Mirth*, 143, 154, 158–60, 168, 185, 231; other plays of, 201, 249, 292, 294; writes for Paul's Boys, 282, 292, 294
Chettle, Henry, 61, 109, 110, 173, 230, 245, 282
Chinon of England, 142
Chloris and Orgasto, 95
Chomeley, Richard, 121–4
Christmas comes but once a Year, 284
Clarke, Francis, 122

298

INDEX

Clarke, John, 152
Clifton, Thomas, 236, 291
Clowns, Sidney on, 13
Cobham, Lord, 171
Coke, Sir Edward, 238–9
Collier, Jeremy, 39
Comedy of Errors, 146, 148
Comedy of Humours, The, see *Humorous Day's Mirth, An.*
Condell, Henry, 139, 188, 295
Conquest of Spain by John of Gaunt, The, 245
Conquest of the West Indies, The, 245
Contemporary figures on stage, 185, 197, 200–1, 201–2, 241, 245, 284, 292, 294. *See also* Stage War, The
Cooper, Dr. Thomas, 37, 38
Court, plays at, 10, 24, 29, 30, 35, 148, 150, 230, 240, 283, 291, 296
Cowley, Richard, 132, 295
Crack Me this Nut, 141
Crooke, John, 152
Cross Keys Inn, The, 42
Curtain, The, 22–3, 24, 42, 163, 176, 188, 191, 215, 228, 240–1; plays at, 193, 196
Cutlack, 137
Cutting Dick, 284
Cynthia's Revels, 233–6, 257–8

Danish Tragedy, The, 283
Day, John, 282
Dekker, Thomas, 53–4, 215 n.; writes for Admiral's Men, 142, 173, 201, 282; his *Satiromastix*, 184, 250, 258, 272–7; other plays of, 142, 201, 230, 245, 249; writes for Chamberlain's Men, 262, 271–2
Delawarr, Sir William West, Lord, 26, 28
Deloney, Thomas, 201
Derby, dowager Countess of, 137
Derby, fourth Earl of, 136
Derby, Ferdinando Stanley, fifth Earl of, 136, 137
Derby, William Stanley, sixth Earl of, 137, 205
Derby's Men, 136
Dioclesian, 140
Disguises, The, 142
Doctor Faustus, 47, 74, 114–16, 140, 168
Dollin, John, 152
Donne, John, 214
Downton, Thomas, 161, 167, 169, 202
Drake, Sir Francis, 122
Drayton, Michael, 173, 202, 282
Drummond of Hawthornden, William, his conversations with Jonson, 180–4
Drury, Anne, 194
Duchess of Malfi, The, 282
Duke, John, 188, 285
Dunne, —, 290
Dunstan, James, 138
Dutton, Thomas, 138, 170

Earl of Gloucester, The Honourable Life of the Humorous, 246
Earl of Hertford, The, 283
East, Gilbert, 225
Eastward Ho!, 182
Edward the Second, 78–9, 114, 149
Edwards, John, 152
Egerton, Stephen, 152
Elementary, The, 63–4
Elizabeth, Queen, 75, 123, 200–1, 284, 294; grants patent to Leicester's Men, 18, 19; and Tarlton, 44, 45; and Essex, 237–8, 294; death of, 295
Endimion, 30, 32–3, 145
England's Joy, 288–90
Essex, Robert Devereux, Earl of, 75, 186, 193; his rebellion, 237–40, 294
Esther and Ahazuerus, 137
Euphues, 26, 27–8, 60, 155, 173
Euphues and his England, 28, 109
Evans, Henry, 25, 26, 232–3, 236, 291

INDEX

Every Man in his Humour, 184–8, 253, 255, 262
Every Man out of his Humour, 194, 198–201, 207, 252, 253, 254–5, 256

Farrant, Mistress, 25
Farrant, Richard, 24, 25, 150
Fastolfe, Sir John, 171–2
Feild, Richard, 152
Felmelanco, 283
Field, Nathan, 233
Field, Thomas, 293, 294
Five plays in one, 143
Flaskett, John, 293, 294
Fletcher, Dr., 165
Fletcher, Laurence, 294–5
Fortescue, Sir John, 236
Fortunatus, 142
Fortune Theatre, The, 221–5, 227–8, 232, 284, 288; plays at, 245, 282–3
Fortune's Tennis, 245
Fount of New Fashions, The, 173
Four Letters, 57, 60–1, 105–7, 161
Four Letters Confuted, 61–2
Four Prentices of London, 284
Fowler, Thomas, 165
Frederick and Basilia, 144
French Comedy, The, 141, 143
French Doctor, The, 140
Friar Bacon and Friar Bungay, 91–3, 95
Friar Rush and the Proud Woman of Antwerp, 246
Frizer, Ingram, 124, 125
Fuller, Bishop, extracts from his *Worthies*, 44–5, 171–2, 174–5

Galathea, 30, 31, 145
Galiaso, 140
Gascoigne, Mr., 106
Gerileon, 111
Gilbert, Thomas, 227
Giles, Nathaniel, 30, 233, 236
Glanfield, Eulalia, 202–3
Globe Theatre, The, 193 and n., 194, 202, 221, 227, 228, 238; plays at, 202, 238
Godfrey of Bulloigne, 140
Gosson, Stephen, 10, 11
Gray's Inn Revels, 146–8
Grecian Comedy, The, 140
Greene, Robert, 57, 70 n., 102, 110–11, 129, 138; biographical details of, 57–61, 80–2; his *Repentance*, 58–60, 104–5, 109–10; his *Groatsworth of Wit*, 80–2, 107–9, 138; his *Alphonsus*, 82–6, 140, 173; his *Looking Glass for London*, 86–90; his *Friar Bacon and Friar Bungay*, 91–3, 95; his novels, 60, 79–80; his conny-catching pamphlets, 95–8; his quarrel with Harvey, 103–7; death of, 104–5; and players, 107–9
Greene's Vision, 110
Greenwood, John, 117
Groatsworth of Wit, 80–2, 107–9, 138
Guido, 143

Hall, Joseph, 158, 162
Hamlet (pre-Shakespearian), 137
Hamlet, 69, 239–40, 246
Hannibal and Scipio, 245, 261
Harriott, Thomas, 75, 119, 127
Harry of Cornwall, 95, 132
Harvey, Dr. Gabriel, 52, 57; his quarrel with Greene, 60–1, 103–7; his quarrel with Nashe, 157, 161; his *Four Letters*, 57, 60–1, 105–7, 161
Harvey, Richard, 103
Hathway, Richard, 202
Haughton, William, 230, 245
Have with you to Saffron Walden, 161
Hayward, Dr. John, 237–8
Helmes, Henry, 147
Hemmings, John, 130, 139, 188, 295
Hengist, 144

INDEX

Henry, Prince, 295
Henry the First, The Life and Death of, 144
Henry the Fourth, Part I, 170, 172
Henry the Fourth, Part II, 172–3, 193
Henry IV, Hayward's history of, 237–8.
Henry the Fifth (Shakespeare's), 193, 255
Henry the Fifth, 142
Henry the Fifth, The famous Victories of, 5, 142, 170
Henry the Sixth, 95, 138, 145
Henslowe, Philip, 94, 113, 166, 189, 202, 282, 284, 294; his *Diary,* 94–5, 137, 140–4, 166, 168–9, 184, 202–3, 225, 230, 232, 283, 285; letters of, 133–6, 189–90; builds Fortune Theatre, 221–5
Hercules, I and II, 141
Heywood, Thomas, 141, 285–7
Hinson, Francis, 152
Histriomastix, 207
Hoffman, 283
Holmes, —, 17
Homes, Thomas, 152
Hot Anger soon Cold, 173
Howard, Lord Charles, Lord Admiral, 113, 122, 124, 130, 222, 224
Howard, Lord Thomas, 128
Howe, Agnes, 292, 293
Howe, John, 292, 293
Humorous Day's Mirth, An, 143, 154, 158–60, 168, 185, 231
Humours, theory of, 154–6, 198–9
Hunnis, William, 24, 25, 233
Hunsdon, George Carey, Lord, 151, 152, 153, 224
Hunsdon, Henry Carey, Lord, 122, 124, 138, 151

Isle of Dogs, The, 161, 165–6, 184, 188
Italian Tragedy, The, 284

Jack and Jill, 10
Jack Drum's Entertainment, 206, 231–2, 256
James, King, 99, 127, 178–9, 235, 294–5
Jealous Comedy, The, 130
Jeffes, Anthony, 169, 170
Jeffes, Humphrey, 169, 170
Jephthah, 283
Jeronimo, 143
Jew, The, 11
Jew of Malta, The, 47, 73–4, 95, 114, 115, 137, 146
John a Kent and John a Cumber, 141
Johnson, William, 18
Jones, Henry, 293
Jones, Richard, 137, 161, 166, 167, 169, 170
Jonson, Ben, 62 n., 165, 168, 169, 201, 207, 282, 283; joins Admiral's Men, 166; writes for Admiral's Men, 173, 282; biographical details of, 173–84; his conversations with Drummond, 180–4; his theory of comedy, 184; his theory of humours, 198–9; his *Every Man in his Humour,* 184–8, 253, 255, 262; his *Every Man out of his Humour,* 194, 198–201, 207, 252, 253, 254–5, 256; kills Gabriel Spencer, 188–9; writes for Chamberlain's Men, 189; his quarrel with Marston, 198, 199, 232, 247, 250–81; returns to Admiral's Men, 201; writes for Children of the Chapel Royal, 233, 247; his *Cynthia's Revels,* 233–6, 257–8; his *Poetaster,* 182, 247, 250, 261–71, 292
Juby, Edward, 137, 169, 170
Jugurtha, 261
Julian the Apostata, 142
Julius Cæsar, 196, 261

Keep the Widow Waking, 249

INDEX

Kemp, William, 130, 138, 148, 188, 227, 246–7, 280; dances to Norwich, 225–7, 231 n.
Kemp's Nine Days' Wonder, 227
Kindheart's Dream, 61, 110–11
King John, 149
Knack to Know an Honest Man, A, 140
Knell, —, 46, 47
Kyd, Thomas, 64, 72; biographical details of, 62; his *Spanish Tragedy*, 48, 62 and n., 64–8, 69, 72, 95, 143, 168, 186, 195, 282; his dramatic technique, 68, 128–9; suspected of atheism, 118, 126–8

Lady Jane or The Overthrow of Rebels, 284
Langley, Francis, 161
Lanham, John, 18
Lanman, Henry, 22
Lanthorne and Candlelight, 53–4
Lavine, William de, 152
Lee, Richard, 152
Lee, Sir Sidney, 268 n.
Leicester, Earl of, 13, 18, 25, 44, 52
Leicester, Earl of, his Company, 10, 15, 18, 21
Le Mere, John, 152
Lent, playing restricted in, 141, 142, 143, 225, 229
Leven, Sir Melchior, 186
Ley, Edward, 152
Life and Death of Ned Brown, The, 98
Lochard, Owen, 152
Lodge, Thomas, 86, 108, 158
London, Aldermen of, 14, 15, 17, 43
London, Lord Mayor of, 20, 24, 112, 118, 152; his complaints about playing, 14, 15, 17–18, 162–4
London Florentine, The, 283
Long Meg of Westminster, 141
Longshanks, 141

Looking Glass for London, A, 86–90
Lord Strange's Men, 94, 111, 112–13, 138; plays performed by, 95, 130; on tour, 130–36; become Derby's Men, 136, 137; become Admiral's Men, 137
Love of an English Lady, The, 140
Love parts Friendship, 283
Love's Labour's Lost, 14, 145
Lyly, John, 60, 109, 232; biographical details of, 26, 60; plays of, 29–35, 145; influence of, 41, 145, 233; his *Euphues*, 26, 27–8, 60, 155, 173; and Marprelate controversy, 35, 38, 39
Lyons, Andrew, 152

Machiavel, 95
Mack, The, 141
Mahomet, 140
Major, Ezechiell, 152
Malcolm King of Scots, 282–3
Malcontent, The, 281
Mamillia, 60
Manningham, John, 55, 282, 291
Marlowe, Christopher, 90, 93, 108, 110, 146; biographical details of, 69–71; his dramatic technique, 72, 73, 74, 115, 129, 208; his *Tamburlaine*, 47, 69, 71–3, 74, 79, 83, 90, 114 n., 140, 141, 146, 173; his *Jew of Malta*, 47, 73–4, 95, 114, 115, 137, 146; his *Edward the Second*, 78–9, 114, 149; his *Dr. Faustus*, 47, 74, 114–16, 140, 168; his *Massacre at Paris*, 130, 140; suspected of atheism, 75, 118–21, 122, 123; imprisoned, 78; his death, 124–6, 178 n.; and Kyd, 126–7
Marprelate controversy, 35–40, 103, 117, 125, 157
Marshal Osric, 284
Marston, John, 55, 182; his satires, 160, 199, 205; his

INDEX

quarrel with Jonson, 198, 199, 232, 247, 250–81 ; biographical details of, 205–6 ; writes for Paul's Boys, 205, 208, 214, 231, 241 ; his stage directions, 206, 210, 211, 244 ; revises *Histriomastix*, 207 ; his *Antonio and Mellida*, 208–13 ; not appreciated by Victorian critics, 213 ; his *Antonio's Revenge*, 214–21 ; his *Jack Drum's Entertainment*, 206, 231–2, 256 ; his *What You Will*, 241–5, 259–61 ; his *Malcontent* dedicated to Jonson, 281
Martin Smart, 144
Massacre at Paris, The, 130, 140
Matthew, Toby, 184–5
Maunder, Henry, 118
Medicine for a Cursed Wife, A, 283
Melancholic Humours, 253
Menaphon, 38, 80
Merchant of Emden, The, 140
Merchant of Venice, The, 149
Meredith, William, 152
Meres, Francis, 173
Merry as May Be, 283
Meyricke, Sir Gilly, 238–9
Midas, 30, 33–4, 145
Middleton, John, 167
Middleton, Thomas, 292
Midsummer Night's Dream, A, 148
Milward, Dr. John, 293, 294
Monox, Will, 104
More, Sir William, 25, 26, 30
Mortimer, 283
Mother Bomby, 34–5
Mourton, —, 98
Much Ado About Nothing, 255
Mulcaster, Richard, 62–4, 233
Muly Mulocco, 95
Munday, Anthony, 141, 202, 203, 282

Nabuchodonozor, 143
Nashe, Thomas, 70 n., 80, 108 ; and Marprelate controversy, 38–9 ; his *Piers Penniless*, 76–7,
98–102, 110 ; and Greene, 61–2, 98, 104, 108 ; his *Isle of Dogs*, 161, 162, 165–6, 184, 188 ; defends plays, 100–2 ; his quarrel with Harvey, 157, 161
Nayle, Thomas, 152
New Letter of Notable Contents, A, 161
New World's Tragedy, The, 142
Newington Butts Theatre, 113, 137, 143
Newman, John, 25
North, —, 27
Northumberland, Henry Percy, Earl of, 75
Norwich, 10, 57, 58, 59, 283 ; Kemp dances to, 225–7

Old Fortunatus, 230
Old Joiner of Aldgate, The, 249, 292, 294
Oldcastle, Sir John, 170–1
Orestes, 10, 261
Orlando Furioso, 95
Osric, 143
Othello, 291
Oxford, Edward de Vere, Earl of, 17, 26, 28

Paddy, William, 152
Page, —, 202
Page of Plymouth, 201
Painful Pilgrimage, The, 10
Palamon and Arcyte, 140
Palladis Tamia, 173
Parliament, 15, 117
Paradox, The, 143
Parry, William, 123
Parsons, Father Robert, 76
Pascal, Mr., 190
Patient Grissel, 230
Patronage, 52, 53–4
Paul's, Children of, 24, 41, 205 *et seq.*, 232 ; plays performed by, 29, 30, 32, 33, 34, 35, 208, 214, 231, 241, 249, 272, 292, 294 ; and Marprelate controversy, 35,

303

INDEX

39 ; Lyly writes for, 29–35 ; Marston writes for, 205, 208, 214, 231, 241 ; Chapman writes for, 282, 292, 294
Pavy, Salathiel, 233
Peckham, Edmund, 42
Pembroke, Countess of, 52
Pembroke, Earl of, his players, 136, 160–1, 166, 168, 188, 283
Penry, John, 125
Perimedes the Blacksmith, 79
Perkin, John, 18
Philip of Spain, 283
Philipo and Hippolito, 140
Phillips, Augustine, 130, 139, 188, 239, 295
Philopater, D. Andreas, 76
Phocas, 142
Pierce's Supererogation, 161
Piers Penniless, 76, 99–102, 110
Pilgrimage to Parnassus, The, 49. See also, *Return*
Plague, 14, 90, 131, 133, 135, 137 ; stops playing, 19, 114, 117, 128, 130, 143
Platter, Thomas, 196–7
Playbill, Elizabethan, 288–90
Players, early attempts to control, 14, 15, 16, 17, 18, 19, 20
Playing, restriction of. See Lent, playing restricted in ; London, Lord Mayor of ; Essex, Earl of, his rebellion ; plague, stops playing ; Privy Council
Poetaster, The, 182, 247, 250, 261–71, 292
Poley, Robert, 120, 124
Pope Joan, 95
Pope, Thomas, 130, 132, 188
Porter, Henry, 173, 201
Privy Council, 14, 43, 118, 121, 123, 183, 236 ; allows plays, 15, 114, 168 ; and Lord Mayor, 162 ; requests supervision of plays, 39–41, 241 ; and Marlowe, 71, 118–19 ; petitions to, 112–14, 151–3, 223, 224 ; prohibits plays, 117, 153, 164 ; licenses Lord Strange's Men, 130–1 ; and Nashe, 165–6 ; and Fortune Theatre, 223, 224 ; regulates plays, 228–30 ; and Chamberlain's Men and Essex rebellion, 238–40 ; and Curtain, 241
Prodigality, 10
Ptolemy, 11
Puckering, Sir John, 118, 119, 121, 123, 126, 127
Puritan Widow, The, 53
Purpool, Prince of, 146
Pythagoras, 142

Queen's Men, The, 43, 46, 91, 93
Quip for an Upstart Courtier, A, 102–4

Ralegh, Sir Walter, 75–7, 118, 119, 122, 127–8, 179, 182, 284
Rangers' Comedy, The, 140
Rape of Lucrece, The, 138
Renialmire, Ascanio de, 152
Repentance of Robert Greene, The, 58–60, 104–5, 109–10
Responsio ad Elizabethae Edictum, 76–7
Return from Parnassus, Part I, 50–1 ; Part II, 51, 280
Rich, Sir Edwin, 226
Richard the Second, 149, 170, 237, 239, 255
Richard the Third, 146, 255
Richard Crookback, 282, 283
Robbinson, John, 152
Robin Hood's Pen'orths, 245
Robinson, James, 236
Romeo and Juliet, 148–9, 268
Rose Theatre, The, 42, 94, 138, 166, 167, 172, 173, 192, 215, 221, 288 ; plays at, 93, 111–12, 130, 137, 139–44, 154, 156–7, 168, 173, 201–4, 230, 284, 285 ; Pembroke's Men at, 283 ; Worcester's Men at, 283–4

INDEX

Roydon, Matthew, 75, 127
Russell, Lady Elizabeth, dowager, 152, 153

Samson, 283
Sanders, George, 194
Sapho and Phao, 29, 30, 145
Satire, 157-8, 160, 162
Satiromastix, 184, 250, 258, 272-7
School of Abuse, The, 10, 11
Scogan and Skelton, 245
Scourge of Villainy, The, 55, 160, 199
Sebastian, King of Portugal, 245-6
Sejanus, 183
Selio and Olimpo, 141
Set at Maw, The, 141
Set at Tennis, The, 283
Seven Days of the Week, The, Part I, 141; Part II, 142
Shaa, Robert. *See* Shaw
Shakespeare, William, 14, 69, 95 and n., 128, 138, 145, 148, 188, 268 and n., 280, 295; mentioned by Greene, 57, 109, 110; his plays mentioned by Meres, 173; and Chamberlain's Men, 138, 139, 145, 148, 188, 295; his coat of arms, 254, 263; his *Love's Labour's Lost*, 14, 145; his *Hamlet*, 69, 129, 239-40, 246; his *Henry the Sixth*, 95, 138, 145; his *Midsummer Night's Dream*, 148; his *Romeo and Juliet*, 148-9, 268; his *Richard the Second*, 149, 170, 237, 238, 239, 255; his *Merchant of Venice*, 149; his *Henry the Fourth*, 170, 172-3, 193; his *As You Like It*, 193-4, 255; his *Julius Cæsar*, 196, 261; his *Henry the Fifth*, 193, 255; his *Much Ado Much Nothing*, 255; his *Troilus and Cressida*, 261, 280; his *Comedy of Errors*, 146, 148; his *Twelfth Night*, 32, 246, 291; his *Titus Andronicus*, 145
Sharles, Mrs., 292, 293

Shaw (or Shaa), Robert, 161, 165, 167, 168, 169, 170
Sheres, Nicholas, 124
Shoemaker's Holiday, The, 201
Shore, 284
Sidney, Sir Philip, 11-13, 26, 46, 52, 99, 197
Sidney, Sir Robert, 196
Siege of Dunkirk, The, 283
Siege of London, The, 141
Silver Age, The, 141
Singer, John, 137, 166, 169, 170
Singer's Voluntary, 283
Sir John Mandeville, 95
Sir John Oldcastle, 202-3, 230
Sisson, Prof. C. J., 249, 292
Six Clothiers, The, 282
Six Fools, 10
Six Yeomen of the West, The, 246
Skevington, Richard, 165
Slaughter, Martin, 137
Sly, Thomas, 225
Sly, Will, 188, 295
Smith, —, 152
Smith, Richard, 246
Smith, William, 192
Soliloquies, 66, 73-4, 116, 146, 149, 208, 210, 257-8
Southwark, rioting in, 111-12, 141
Spanish Fig, The, 282
Spanish Tragedy, The, 48, 62 and n., 64-8, 69, 95, 143, 168, 186, 195, 282
Spencer, Gabriel, 161, 165, 168, 169, 170, 178 n.; killed by Jonson, 188-9, 190
Spenser, Edmund, 27, 52, 64, 70 n.
Spratt, George, 225, 227
Stage War, The, 248 *et seq.*; chronological table of, 251-2
Stettin-Pomerania, Duke of, 291-2
Stockwood, John, 23
Strange News, 161
Strange's Men. *See* Lord Strange's Men
Strangest Adventure, The, 246
Strangwidge, George, 202

305

INDEX

Street, Peter, 192, 221, 223, 225
Stukeley, 143, 245
Stukeley, Capt. Thomas, 245
Swan Theatre, The, 161, 288, 290

Tamar Cam, 142
Tamburlaine, 47, 69, 71–3, 74, 79, 83, 90, 114 n., 141, 146, 173
Taming of the Shrew, The, 137, 145
Tarlton, Richard, 44–6, 47
Temple, The, 147–8
That will be shall be, 143
Theatre, The, 22, 23, 24, 42–3, 138, 139, 153, 163; and authorities, 43; lease of, 21–2, 150, 191; rebuilt as Globe, 191–3
Theatre of God's Judgment, The, 125–6
Thomas Merry, or Beech's Tragedy, 230
Time's Triumph, 143
Tinker of Totnes, The, 143
Titus Andronicus, 145
Tobias, 283
Tom Dough, 246
Too Good to be True, 282
Topcliffe, Richard, 122, 165
Towne, Thomas, 137, 169, 170
Townsend, —, 282
Toy to please Chaste Ladies, A, 142
Tragedy, Sidney on, 12
Tragedy of the Guise, The, 130, 140
Tragedy of the King of Scots, The, 10
Troilus and Cressida, 261, 280
Troilus and Cressida (non-Shakespearian), 261
Troy, 143
Turner, —, 290
Turnholt, battle of, 196
Twelfth Night, 32, 246, 291
Two Angry Women of Abingdon, The, 201
Two (Three) Brothers, The, 284

Unfortunate General, The, 284
Uther Pendragon, 143

Venetian Comedy, The, 140
Venner, Richard, 288, 290
Venus and Adonis, 138
Vere, Sir Francis, 197
Virgidemiarum, 158, 162
Volteger, 143, 144

Walsingham, Thomas, 118
Ward, Sir Adolphus, 213 n., 287–8
Warlamchester, 140
Warner, —, 127
Warning for Fair Women, A, 194–6
Watermen, Thames, 112, 113
Watson, Thomas, 78
Watts, William, 152
Webster, John, 282
Welshman, The, 142
Wharton, John, 152
What You Will, 206, 241–5, 259–61
White Devil, The, 282
Whitgift, John, Archbishop of Canterbury, 36, 38
Widow's Charm, The, 283
Wilbraham, Mr., 165
William Cartwright, 283
Willoughby, Lord, 223, 224
Wilson, Mr., 202
Wilson, Robert, 18, 47
Windsor Chapel, Children of, 24, 25
Wise, Andrew, 170, 255
Wise Man of West Chester, The, 141
Wit and Will, 10
Witch of Islington, The, 144
Wolfe, John, 238
Woman Hard to Please, 143
Woman in the Moon, The, 35
Woman Killed with Kindness, A, 284
Wonder of a Woman, The, 142
Woodward, Joan, 94
Woodward, Master, 94
Worcester, Earl of, his Company, 46; second company, 283–4, 285; plays performed by, 284
Wright, William, 109, 110

Young, Justice, 122

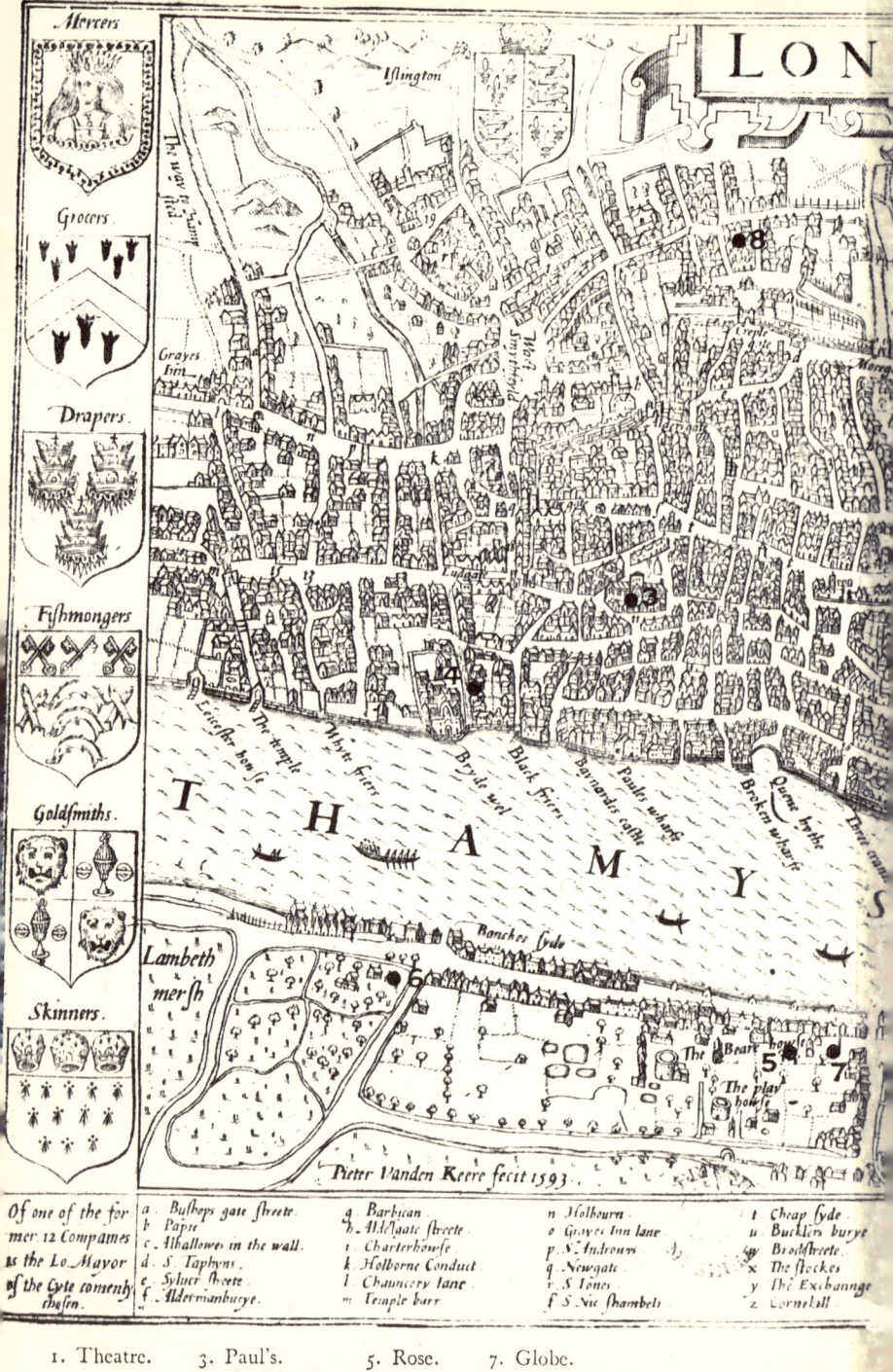

Of one of the for- mer 12 Compames as the Lo. Mayor of the Cyte comenly chosen.	a. Bishops gate streete. b. Papie c. Alhallowes in the wall. d. S. Taphyns. e. Sylver streete. f. Aldermanburye.	g. Barbican h. Aldegate streete. i. Charterhowse k. Holborne Conduct l. Chauncery lane m. Temple barr	n. Holbourn o. Grayes Inn lane p. S. Androws q. Newgate r. S. Iones f. S. Nic Shambels	t. Cheap syde u. Bucklers burye w. Brodstreete x. The Stockes y. The Exchannge z. Cornehill

1. Theatre.   3. Paul's.   5. Rose.   7. Globe.
2. Curtain.   4. Blackfriars.   6. Swan.   8. Fortune.

1 Colmanstreete	8 Fanchurche	14 Fetter lane	20 Winchester house
3 Basting hall	9 Marke lane	15 S. Dunstons	21 Battle bridge
4 Hounsditche	10 Minchyn lane	16 Thames streete	22 Bermodsey streete
5 Leaden hall	11 Paules	17 Lodon stone	
6 Grahous streete	12 East cheape	18 Olde Baylye	Ioannes Norden Anglus
7 Heneage house	13 Fletstreete	19 Clerkenwell	descripsit anno 1593

LONDON AND ITS PLAYHOUSES

ANN ARBOR BOOKS

*a new series of paperbound editions—
reissues of works of enduring merit*

AA 1

The Writer and His Craft
Twenty Lectures to the Young Writer
edited by Roy W. Cowden

AA 2

Elizabethan Plays and Players
by G. B. Harrison

AA 3

The Intellectual Milieu of John Dryden
by Louis I. Bredvold

AA 4

The Southern Frontier, 1670–1732
by Verner W. Crane

The University of Michigan Press